Victorian & Edwardian Architecture

Endpapers: *the main entrance to the Natural History Museum, London, 1873–80, by Alfred Waterhouse. This variegated terracotta façade displays a characteristically Victorian determination to provide an appropriate exhibition space for the wonders of nature*

Facing page: *the New Palace of
Westminster (Houses of
Parliament), London, 1837–67,
by Sir Charles Barry and
A W N Pugin*

Overleaf: *the drawing room and
music room from* A House for
an Art Lover, *1902, a drawing
by Charles Rennie Mackintosh*

Victorian & Edwardian Architecture

CHAUCER PRESS
LONDON

First published in Great Britain by
Chaucer Press
an imprint of the
Caxton Publishing Group
20 Bloomsbury Street
London WC1B 3JH

ISBN 1 904449 02 6

Designed and produced by Superlaunch Ltd
P.O. Box 207, Abingdon, Oxfordshire
OX13 6TA, England
Imagesetting and colour reproduction by
International Graphic Services, Bath
Printed and bound in China by
Sun Fung Offset Binding Company Limited

Contents

Chapter One

A Prelude to the Period

ARCHITECTURAL DEVELOPMENT during the nineteenth century was extremely complex. The extensive Georgian period had culminated in the transitional Regency style of 1811–20, named for the flamboyant regency of the Prince of Wales, who reigned as George IV between 1820–30. In turn this gave way to the revival architecture of the Victorian period and the burgeoning multi-faceted industrial architecture which included such diverse engineering achievements as the Crystal Palace, the great bridges of Telford and Brunel and the notoriously dark satanic mills.

Facing page: *the* art nouveau *doorway to 29 Avenue Rapp, Paris, 1901, by Jules Lavirotte for the ceramicist Alexandro Bigot*

Below: *the Crystal Palace, as depicted on the front of some sheet music in the 1850s*

Right: *an engraving by Gustave Doré depicting the crowded slums of the inner city*

Below: *a popular William Morris wallpaper of the 1880s; known as* Iris and Bird, *it has stood the test of time and is still available today*

It was in these centres of industry, and in the poor quarters of the towns, that the social evils resulting from the exponential increase in population and commerce were becoming all too evident. At that early stage of industrialisation machine-made articles were patently inferior to those made by hand. Grace, tranquillity and dignity seemed no longer to exist in a world of ugliness, meanness and squalor. Thousands of new dwellings were built in the towns, although frequently the town boundaries could not be expanded outwards owing to the system of land tenure still in existence. The resulting ill-built and insanitary slums constituted an environment as horrible as any yet devised.

This state of affairs was felt keenly by such men of sensibility as Philip Webb, William Morris and Edward Burne-Jones. They believed idealistically that it was possible to return to what they saw as the more natural ways of the pre-machine age. In so doing, they would make for themselves a comfortable and harmonious environment. This would more closely reflect the glories of nature while using the materials it produced, and incidentally offer a better quality of life for the makers. The handcraft movement started by John Ruskin and William Morris became a powerful influence.

However, although architects were not attempting to recreate a medieval environment, they admired the methods and principles of medieval styles and forms and used them in buildings otherwise suited to contemporary needs. This search for a fresh approach is a recurrent theme throughout the nineteenth century, typified by the Pre-Raphaelite movement, the Aesthetic movement and the widespread manifestations of *art nouveau*. All brought into question the rigidity of established rules such as those of classical architecture.

At the same time much domestic building, particularly the large estates in the fashionable suburbs, continued to be built in the classical manner, faced with painted stucco. Many commercial, civic and public buildings such as offices, town halls, libraries, and museums were erected in the classical style. The details became coarser and more heavy-handed as the century progressed. The so-called 'battle of the styles' was conducted on the broad basis of classical *versus* medieval, but was as much about opposed philosophies, as an argument about building styles as such.

For the first time in history the architect was exercising his skill in two separate ways: firstly in designing buildings to express their purpose in an appropriately functional way (practical hospital plans, noble law courts) and secondly, seemingly quite separately, in deciding the style in which they should be built. From this unique approach to architectural practice, which lasted for just over a century, arose the common misperception of the role of the architect as that of 'beautifying' buildings by applying style, rather than that of enabling society to function harmoniously by providing an efficiently functioning built environment. The number of styles available for choice appeared almost unlimited by the latter half of the nineteenth century, running the gamut of European cultures down the ages from romanesque through Venetian Gothic to Tudor, Italian, French and Dutch renaissance and many others besides.

A turn towards simplicity gave rise to the Aesthetic movement of the 1870s. In architectural form this was manifested as a liking for red brick, red roof tiles, painted woodwork and simpler interiors favouring dark oak and blue Delft china. The simplified Queen Anne style of Bedford Park, London, and the Dutch gables of Kensington and Chelsea epitomise the movement.

The *art nouveau* movement, with its well-known decorative motifs based on organic plant forms and the sinuous lines of Oriental art, in British architecture tended towards a sophisticated and elegant simplicity. The restrained and disciplined work of Charles Rennie Mackintosh and his colleagues, widely regarded

The Arts and Crafts Movement

This English social and aesthetic phenomenon was born out of a reaction against the quality and design of mass-manufactured artifacts, in particular those that became widely available after the Great Exhibition of 1851, which was a great showcase for contemporary British industry.

The movement's fundamental admiration for the dignity of labour invested in traditional decorative arts and crafts was combined with a romantic longing to recapture the supposed ethos of the medieval craft guilds. The key figure most closely associated with the movement was William Morris, but his ideals can be traced back, via the polemics of Ruskin and the writings of Pugin, to the theories promoted by Jean-Jacques Rousseau (1712–78).

Philip Webb built the Red House for Morris in 1859–60, and Morris then designed the furnishings and decorations specifically for it. He founded the firm of Morris, Marshall and Faulkner in 1861 to produce wallpapers, printed patterned fabrics, and ornamental parts for stained glass windows, in an attempt to recreate a handcraft-based industry in an increasingly mechanised age.

The movement, which influenced young architects and designers, crusaded for aesthetics rather than expedience in building, argued for the preservation and protection of old buildings and engendered the Society for the Protection of Ancient Buildings.

The movement is closely associated with the domestic revival or old English style, based on the picturesque, with elements from the English vernacular such as tall chimneys, gables, tile hanging and leaded lights.

Left: *an 1881 prospectus for Bedford Park, 1875–81, by Norman Shaw, which advertised 'About 500 Houses on the Estate, all in the picturesque Queen Anne style of Architecture', with 'A garden and a Bath Room with Hot and Cold water to every house, whatever its size'*

Above: *'a dining room for a connoisseur' by C R Mackintosh, published in 1901*

as typical, contrasts vividly with the elaborate *fin de siècle* (even decadent) elaboration of the style elsewhere in Europe.

These two movements were philosophically and aesthetically based, and so since the early nineteenth century the supposed incompatibility of industry and aesthetics had meant that much construction for industry and transport was designed by engineers. Thus they came into prominence as a group distinct from architects, yet their works are among the greatest of Victorian architecture.

Such engineers particularly welcomed the new materials that science made available. Sheet glass and cast iron were the two most important of those that had arrived in quantity by the middle of the century, followed by steel. Huge greenhouses such as Decimus Burton's Palm House at Kew inspired and to an extent were the prototypes of Joseph Paxton's Crystal Palace. This vast building was made of standard prefabricated sheets of glass and girders of iron.

The railway companies quickly saw the possibilities of such structures for railway terminus buildings, into which whole trains could steam because the roofs were so high up that they were hardly affected by the smoke from the engines. Enormous volumes of space were enclosed in these shells of iron and glass, creating single-cell buildings far larger than anything ever built before.

Market halls were built also with iron and glass roofs. In many of these iron buildings the decorative possibilities of cast iron were not ignored, and they have beautifully enriched structural members which recall medieval structural embellishment.

Canal and railway bridges of great size were constructed of iron and steel. The Forth Bridge, completed in 1890, takes its place as one of the really great bridges of the world. It is over 2.46km (1.5 miles) long and a single span reaches 521m (1,710ft).

Continuing growth of population and wealth together with further advances in technology, such as reinforced concrete and the introduction of electricity, fuelled demand for larger and more elaborate buildings. Large spans and slender supports had given a freedom in planning hitherto unknown. Fast passenger lifts and safe artificial lighting enabled buildings to be far taller and deeper in plan than had been possible before. Close collaboration between architect and engineer became necessary for successful design and the ever-quickening pace of social change engendered massive housing programmes and slum clearance. The building industry came to rely increasingly on factory-made materials, as craftsmen's time began to cost more and machines became more efficient daily.

The mills and warehouses erected during the later part of the century are admirable not only as part of our industrial heritage, but for their inherent architectural qualities. They were nearly always built as purely functional buildings of brick or stone, without any decoration except perhaps for a louvred bell-cupola on the roof or a pedimented entrance doorway. Yet their solid construction, generous proportions, noble size and evident fitness for their purpose are appealing. In this lies the germ of the functionalist ideal that was to have such a far-reaching influence on the modern movement: successful choice of materials, proportions and forms raises constructions from efficient engineering to good architecture.

The urge towards simplicity in Britain showed itself mainly in domestic architecture, exemplified by the work of Charles Voysey in the 1890s, following the early work of Norman Shaw. Still within a traditional framework, he eliminated almost all period flavour and invented what amounted to a new aesthetic of quasi-rural

Above: *the Palm House in the Royal Botanic Gardens, Kew, Surrey, 1844–48, by Decimus Burton with the help of the civil engineer, Richard Turner; it is 110 metres (360ft) long*

Facing page, below: *Hotel van Eetvelde, 4 Avenue Palmerston, Brussels, 1895–97, by Victor Horta*

Below: *the train shed, Paddington Station, London, 1852–54, by I K Brunel with M D Wyatt*

Above: *houses in Hampstead Garden Suburb, London, 1906*

Port Sunlight

This model village was created in 1888 by W H Lever (1851–1925) for workers at the Lever Brothers (now Unilever) soap factory at Birkenhead, on the Wirral peninsula. It was designed for a population of 3,000 and has nearly 900 houses set in gardens, with extensive open spaces, an art gallery, a church, a library and a social hall.

domesticity, featuring horizontally-arranged rows of windows, white walls and huge chimneys. He, and later Sir Edwin Lutyens, demonstrated for the first time that houses for the comparatively wealthy need be neither elaborate nor pompous. Traditional materials were used in a traditional way for simple buildings suited to their purpose. The new materials and techniques already being used for industrial buildings were not used, probably because houses, by their scale and nature, require for their construction no more demanding techniques than those commonly used for centuries.

Towards the end of the century some wealthy and enlightened employers conceived the garden city and variants on it, laying out housing estates for their workers with gardens for the houses, space for allotments and planted or grassed verges to the roads. Port Sunlight and Bournville were the products of the 1880s and 1890s and were followed by Letchworth, Welwyn and Hampstead.

Letchworth was the first of the British garden cities, founded in 1903 as the result of Ebenezer Howard's visionary essay *Tomorrow: A Peaceful Path to Real Reform* (1898), in which he projected a vision of total environment and a new urban society. Howard saw the city in social, economic and political terms, with the city population limited to 32,000 and built on a 2,430ha (6,000 acre) site. The residential area was to occupy 405ha (1,000 acres) at the centre, and the rest of the land given over to industry and agriculture.

These developments in English domestic architecture had some effect in both Europe and America. By the time that Queen Victoria died in 1901 and her son the Prince of Wales was crowned Edward VII, communications between all parts of the world had become so rapid that national differences in aesthetic and technique had almost ceased to exist, except insofar as these are conditioned

Right: *the style employed at Welwyn Garden City, 1920, by Louis de Soissons, was almost exclusively neo-Georgian*

Left: *grouped cottages for businesswomen, with a communal dining room, at Meadow Way, Letchworth, 1916, by the Howard Cottage Society Ltd. The dominent professional figures in the Garden City Movement were Barry Parker (1867–1947) and Raymond Unwin (1863–1940), who were in partnership between 1896 and 1914, and it was their scheme for Letchworth that was adopted*

by different climates. As the individualism, romanticism, traditional preoccupation with styles and ability to utilise superbly designed and crafted fittings and furnishings of the most skilled Victorian architects became as irrelevant as a leaning towards the picturesque had been in the nineteenth century, an international style became inevitable. This reappraisal of architecture in the 1900s, known as the modern movement, was rooted in the nineteenth-century technological developments and their influence on building techniques.

National temperament still governed the speed with which new ideas were accepted, however, so it was that in Holland, Germany and France more rapid change was possible than in conservative Britain. It is in these countries, more particularly in Germany, that the modern movement developed.

Left: *the street front of the House of Lilly and Hugo Steiner, Vienna, 1910, by Adolf Loos, who ingeniously arched a metal roof from the three-storey back of the house down over the front to the top of the first storey, in order to comply with planning regulations*

Chapter Two

Towns: Buildings and Town Planning

THE TERRACED AND SEMI-DETACHED HOUSES that determined the character of the Victorian cities formed by far the largest group of early Victorian buildings. Fortunately they remain in such sufficient numbers that even today they represent a significant element in our urban environment.

At the beginning of the Victorian period the provision of housing was regarded as the responsibility of capitalist enterprise, a remnant of the speculative practices that had become rife in Georgian England. As time progressed, the philanthropic organisations and more enlightened employers increasingly assumed responsibility for development before local authorities also began to become involved in the provision of housing at the end of the century, although this was primarily for working people.

The majority of properties were still constructed by the speculative builders, with letting continuing to form a large section of their business activities. The range of houses so built ranged from the single-room tenements of Glasgow to the mansions of Belgravia, with each builder free to determine the need and viability of his own ventures.

Then, as recently, there appears to have been an alternating cycle of boom and bust conditions. Demand for homes in a boom period was met, but the building process continued, being incapable of being quickly stopped. This produced first a surfeit, then a glut and eventually bankruptcies for the developers until demand began to increase once more as the surplus properties were let or sold. Victoria's succession to the throne followed a house building slump of the early 1830s, and although production was on the increase, by the end of the 1840s there was widespread unemployment and depression. House building enjoyed a revival with the advent of the Great Exhibition of 1851, that was cut short by the lack of capital that had been diverted to fund the Crimean War. Thereafter

Facing page: 37 Harley Street, London, 1899, by Arthur Beresford Pite

Below: 30 Wimpole Street, London, 1890s, by Sir Banister Flight Fletcher

Belgrave Square, London, laid out originally in 1826 but still under construction in 1844 to designs by George Basevi for the builder Thomas Cubitt. It was built in the Georgian tradition with uniform classical terraces around a large communal garden. The terraces were built of local brick and faced with stucco. They were composed as a single unit with central and flanking features. Detached houses were sited at the corners of the square, each of a different design, thus contriving to break the formal appearance of the square

Grey Street (east side), Newcastle-upon-Tyne, 1837, by John Dobson for the developer Richard Grainger; a more monumental type of grand terrace but still in the Georgian tradition

Lewes Crescent, Brighton, (*below*) was planned by Thomas Read Kemp in 1823 but was completed by Thomas Cubitt in the early Victorian period after Kemp became over-extended. The Cubitt houses echo the style of his Belgravia work.

College Cross Street, Barnsbury Estate, London, 1836–43, by Thomas Cubitt; less expensive houses, each of which is two bays wide and two storeys high above a basement, with additional accommodation provided for in the roof area. Each is faced on the ground floor with rusticated stucco, which contains a door with a lunette over it and an arched window. The first floor is brick-faced with a pair of rectangular windows, above which there is a stucco cornice and parapet

Clifton Way, Camberwell, London 1846–47; a terrace of small houses with stuccoed ground floor and exposed brickwork above. The two upper-floor windows of each house are united by an enclosed arched surround. A continuous cornice is crowned by low pediments.

the booms of the late 1860s and 1870s were followed by depressions in the early 1870s and 1890s, then another boom in the late 1890s.

The prevailing conditions of growing population, expanding towns, the relatively quick and easy travel and transportation of goods afforded by the tentacles of the sprawling railway networks and money that was widely available on generous credit provided ample opportunity for the speculative builder, be he an individual building a single house or a company developing an estate.

Nor did the speculative builder usually encounter difficulty in obtaining land, as even then building land commanded a higher price than agricultural land, so there was no shortage of willing sellers. When the construction of a large estate was involved the ground landlord most often formulated an extensive plan, showing not only the roads but also the size, type and in some instances the design of the houses to be built there.

It appears that the only concern of the developer when considering the development of estates of houses for the less affluent was to cover the area with as many buildings as possible, and in doing so invariably they adopted lower standards of layout and construction. Public Health Acts were introduced from 1848 onwards and did rectify the lack of proper sanitation, an expense that the unscrupulous developer had all too often not incurred.

The planning of Victorian developments shows a gradual shift towards a more picturesque layout, with the introduction of curving roads in place of squares and crescents. By 1875, with the design of Bedford Park, the curving tree-lined street was established as the pattern for spacious suburban developments for the remainder of the Victorian period.

The actual construction of the majority of houses was very little changed from Georgian times; external walls and party walls were brick or masonry-built with local materials much in evidence, though Welsh slates gained tremendously in popularity for roofing, especially in the major cities. Internally, the roof and floor joists, floorboards and stairs were of timber and internal walls most often consisted of timber studs covered with lathes and then plastered.

Sash windows were the norm, which in the early Victorian period had glazing bars that made way for plate glass in the middle of the period especially for the more expensive houses, or for casement windows with leaded lights as vernacular revivals became popular.

The semi-detached suburban house with its single shared party wall was made popular by the publication of *The Suburban Gardener and Villa Companion* by J C Loudon in 1838. In this book Loudon depicted his own semi-detached house at 3 Porchester Terrace, London, 1823, which was then newly built. By the mid-century the semi-detached house was a common feature of speculative developments.

Meanwhile the apartment block, which was already popular both in Scotland and in Europe, never gained popularity in England during the Victorian period. There were some early examples, such as those at Victoria Street, London, 1853, designed by Henry Ashton for the speculator Mackenzie, and Queen Anne's Mansions, London. This fourteen-storey block by E R Robson was constructed unattractively in yellow brick; it was demolished in 1971.

A far more pleasing design appeared later at Albert Hall Mansions, London, 1879–86, by Richard Norman Shaw, where red brick was used in a Queen Anne style. It also had sash windows and balconies which acted to unite the entire composition into a gratifying whole. Whitehall Court, 1884, by Thomas Archer and Arthur Green, which overlooks the River Thames on the Victoria Embankment, is a massive block of flats designed in the style of a French château.

During the middle to late Victorian period in London, stucco remained popular for the more conservatively-designed houses, being used to cover the entire façade yet not their sides or backs. By the late 1860s, however, stucco did begin to lose favour with many builders, especially at the higher end of the market. At this point the Gothic style, inspired by the works of Ruskin and the high Victorian Gothic architects, was growing in popularity, with its polychrome decoration in the form of contrasting coloured brick or stone bands becoming widespread. Roofs also appeared with slates in differing colours.

By the late Victorian period the most common house type

Above: *Albert Hall Mansions*
Below and below left: *two London buildings by Charles H Worley;* below, *Wimpole House, 28 and 29 Wimpole Street, 1893; and* below left, *42 Harley Street, 1892*

Below: *44 (right) and 46 Harley Street, London; No 46 was built in the 1890s and was the work of Sir Banister Flight Fletcher*

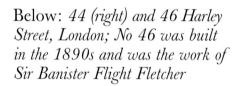

Typical mid and late Victorian town houses

Holland Park Estate, London, 1860–79, by William and Francis Radford; 77 detached houses of three storeys and an attic in the roof, double-fronted with a central door and short flight of steps
Cedars Estate, Clapham, London, 1860, by Sir James Knowles; two blocks of houses of five storeys plus attics in high French roofs, faced with pale brick
Grosvenor Place, Grosvenor Estate, London, begun in 1868 by Thomas Cundy III; stone-faced terraces grouped as pavilions under separate mansard roofs

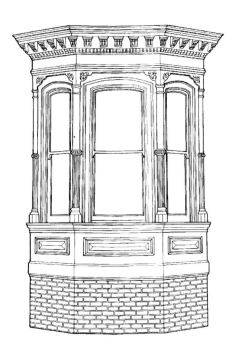

Above: *bays with paned sash windows were the most popular type in the second half of the nineteenth century, with Italianate bays like that above being favoured in America. In England this most characteristic of Victorian features most commonly had deeper bracketed sills and larger sheets of plate glass, especially when the improved glassmaking techniques that made the glass stronger and less expensive were coupled with the abolition of window tax in 1851. The windows also required fewer glazing bars. Thus, as the Victorian sash windows became plainer, so their openings made increasing use of decorative brickwork, stucco and prefabricated terracotta*

in London took the form of a three-storeyed building, but no longer having a basement. Its entrance was still located on the ground floor and protected by a small porch, to the side of which was a two-storeyed bay window with sash opening and plate glass. The bay was detailed with piers and capitals supporting thin lintels of stone. A parapet crowned the top bay, above which on the third storey there was usually a double window divided by a single column. The façade was completed by a single window on each of the two upper storeys above the door.

The arrangement of space inside was a front parlour with the bay window at the front. Behind the parlour, and generally separated from it by folding doors, was a dining room of roughly the same size. Above both rooms on the first floor would be a bedroom, with further bedrooms similarly positioned on the second floor. To the back of the house, on the ground floor, would be the kitchen, bathroom and perhaps a water closet, although this was more often externally sited.

Towards the end of Queen Victoria's reign, this style of house gave way to a smaller two-storeyed house, still with bay windows, but now topped by a polygonal hipped roof, and the bathroom and the water closet were elevated to the first floor above the kitchen from the ground floor. At the turn of the century, such a house in the London suburbs would be sold leasehold for about £300.00. Similar houses were common throughout the provinces, although most dispensed with the entrance hall, which meant that visitors walked straight into the parlour.

Other popular styles of urban accommodation included the two-storeyed buildings, now known as maisonnettes, that were divided horizontally to form a pair of flats, each with its own entrance, and the back-to-back terrace houses. These were a feature found more in the industrial areas of the north of England, especially in Leeds. There two rows of terrace houses are built literally back to back, so that each house is built with party walls to the sides and back, except that the two end houses which each have one outside side wall.

There was also a further style of Victorian speculatively-built house, derived from the Queen Anne revival. This style had been used for individual town houses from the 1860s onwards, using a combination of red brick, sash windows, rubbed brickwork, bay windows and gables. The Red House, now demolished, at 140 Bayswater Road (formerly 3 Bayswater Hill), London, 1871, by John James Stevenson was one of the prime examples. The style became very popular in London, especially in the Kensington and Chelsea areas, before watered-down variants of the style for larger town houses spread all over the country. Smaller houses in the suburbs also began to appear, with features that imitated those Chelsea properties that had become popular with the artist and designer protagonists of the Aesthetic movement.

Queen Anne revival

2 Palace Green, Kensington, London, 1860–62, by Frederick Hering for William Makepeace Thackeray
1 Palace Green, Kensington, London, 1868–73, by Philip Webb for the Hon George Howard

Red House, 140 Bayswater Road, London, 1871, by John James Stevenson (demolished). A three-storey house built in red brick with tall sash windows and glazing bars that had a porch set to one side, and on the other a bay window extended

to the full three-storey height. Two gabled dormers projected from the attic and tall chimney-stacks stood above the roof
Lowther Lodge, 1 Kensington Gore, London, 1873–75, by Richard Norman Shaw (now the Royal Geographical Society); also with an off-centre porch but with gables of differing shapes
Old Swan House, 17 Chelsea Embankment, London, 1875–77, by Richard Norman Shaw; one of a group in red brick. This has a varied window treatment, including three large oriels to the first floor. Here again, gabled dormers are set in the roof

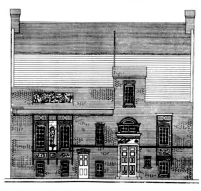

White House, Tite Street, London, 1877–79, by E W Godwin for painter James McNeill Whistler (demolished). Finished in whitewashed brick
39 Harrington Gardens, Kensington, London, 1882, by Sir Ernest George with Harold Peto. They used lavish

Far left top: *1 Palace Green*
Far left bottom: *Red House*
Top left: *White House*
Below and bottom right: *39 Harrington Gardens; the lower drawing also shows (right) number 41*

brick and stone decoration for the house, built for W S Gilbert. It has mullioned windows with leaded lights and magnificent brick gables. An exceptional property for its time, it had a bathroom on every floor, extensive central heating and telephones

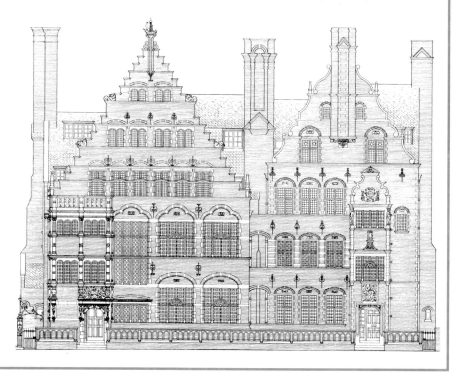

One of the more adventurous and influential schemes to favour the Queen Anne style was that of the Bedford Park Estate, Chiswick, London, begun in 1875 by E W Godwin. He was replaced by Richard Norman Shaw, assisted by Maurice B Adame and E J May until 1880, when May replaced Shaw. Almost 500 houses were constructed on the estate, the vast majority being built in red brick and comprising two storeys plus attic. The mix of terraced, semi-detached and detached properties each had its own garden. Here the speculative developer was a cloth merchant, Jonathan Carr (1845–1915), for whom Shaw built a large house on the estate which was decorated with wallpapers designed by William Morris.

Right: *an advertisement depicting various properties that were available on the Bedford Park development; and* above, *an example of the revived Queen Anne style at Bedford Park*

The last remaining major form of Victorian town housing is the important category of shelter that was provided by an employer or by a charitable individual. By the end of the nineteenth century this had developed into the larger and much-needed social responsibility of local authorities' housing provided for poorer working people as tenants.

The origins of this housing sector date back to the Duke of Devonshire, who moved the village of Edensor out of sight from his Chatsworth residence in 1838. The re-formed village, designed primarily to provide housing for his estate workers, was laid out by his then gardener, Joseph Paxton who, along with John Robertson of Derby, also designed most of the new houses. Each of these new Edensor houses was different from its neighbours, with a mix of cottages and villas clustered informally around the church. This layout influenced future simple estates which were based on the cottage style, with its gabled and half-hipped roofs.

William Butterfield built the estate at Baldersley St James, Yorkshire, where he included small and simple cottage-style housing built in brick and stone, together with a church, a vicarage and a school, in the mid-1850s.

In the following decades Eden Nesfield built estate cottages of a more picturesque nature at Crewe Hall Estate, Cheshire, where each cottage has a projecting gable and a tile-hung upper floor, on an estate that also included farms and a smithy.

In parallel to the villages created by the large country-house estates were those developed by the industrial manufacturers for their workers. An early example of these estates is Saltaire, near Bradford, Yorkshire. Here, Sir Titus Salt with the architects H F Lockwood and R Mawson developed mainly stone-built terraces with Italianate detailing, laid out to a rigid plan that saw the initial 150 houses that were constructed by 1854 rise to 820 by 1872.

Left: *frontage of a house at Saltaire, West Yorkshire*

Far left: *half-timbered cottages in a Tudor style at Port Sunlight, Birkenhead*

City Flats

Peabody Estate, Greenman Street, London, 1865, by Henry A Darbishire
Hyde Park Court, Hyde Park, London, completed in 1890 by the firm of Archer and Green.
Boundary Estate, Shoreditch, London, 1893, for London County Council (*below* and *bottom left*)
Millbank Estate, London, 1897, for London County Council; a red brick block in simplified Arts and Crafts style

Later there were industrial estates at Bournville, Birmingham, which was begun in 1879 by the Cadbury family's company for the workers in their cocoa factories; and at Port Sunlight, Cheshire, begun in 1888 by the soap manufacturer Lever Brothers.

There was a genuine attempt, promoted by the charitable thoughts of some of the more fortunate members of Victorian society, to improve the housing conditions of working people. They wanted to abolish the slums then mostly caused by the deterioration of earlier Georgian properties, and to avert the outbreak of diseases such as the cholera outbreak of the 1840s. They formed a number of associations including the Society for Improving the Conditions of the Labouring Classes, which was founded in 1844, and championed stricter bylaws governing the quality and density of housing, while they strove to erect dwellings for poorer families.

This Society erected a block of 'model houses' at Streatham Street, London, 1849–50, by Henry Roberts who was the Society's architect. These proved to be very influential on the future design of such dwellings, for although very plain the block was solidly constructed in brick with stucco, four storeys high, and consisted of self-contained flats that were arranged around three sides of a courtyard.

A major feature of these model houses was their open brick galleries with iron balconies that led to individual front doors, an arrangement that was to remain a feature for well over the next 100 years for the building of such blocks.

Other schemes were the result of the activity of single individuals, including Miss Angela (later Baroness) Burdett-Coutts, who financed the flats at Columbia Square, Bethnal Green, London, 1857–60, by Henry A Darbishire. The American banker, George Peabody, set up a trust in 1862, and employed Darbishire as the Trust's architect to design a block of flats in Commercial Street,

Spitalfields, London. With Darbishire's help, Peabody established a standard design that he then used for future blocks of flats, which were all built in yellow brick to a height of five storeys and characterised by their small deep-set windows.

Eventually, towards the end of the Victorian period, local authorities began slowly to provide flats. Liverpool and London pioneered this movement, when London County Council embarked on a slum clearance programme coupled with the construction of replacement blocks of flats. Within London, however, they were still limited in their designs by the 1874 London Building Act, which restricted new building to a height of 24.4m (80ft) with additional storeys permitted in a roof pitched no steeper than 75 degrees. London County Council set up its Housing of the Working Class Branch in 1893, and the best remaining example of this work is the Boundary Street Estate which housed more than 5,500 people.

From the beginning of the twentieth century tall buildings in multiple occupation and, primarily, those that demanded a higher rent, began to take on a new appearance both externally and internally. The Arts and Crafts and *art nouveau* elements began to be replaced by more conservative period styles; for example, both Coleherne Court, Redcliffe Gardens, London, and Old Brompton Road, 1901–03, by Walter Cave, were already in the later English Renaissance style with restrained carved swags on shallow bay windows.

The new century witnessed the return to simplicity but also a disregard of scale. What F S Chesterton and J D Coleridge had done to achieve a more intimate scale in Hornton Street, Kensington, was ignored when the same architects came to design Hornton Court, Kensington High Street, London. Frank Verity, on the other hand, maintained a just sense of scale and introduced the straight lines of the new classicism derived from his Paris training, in so individual a way at Cleveland Row, Berkeley Square, Bayswater Road and later Marble Arch, that his buildings are immediately recognisable.

These mansion flats were just one aspect of the changing face of London in the early twentieth century. As leases fell in on the houses of the ducal estates of Mayfair, Marylebone, Kensington and Chelsea the opportunity to rebuild the front, or even to rebuild entirely, was eagerly seized. On the Cadogan estate when Cadogan Square and Pont Street were developed, the face of the area turned to terracotta and carved red brick at the hands of architects such as Ernest George and Harold Peto. In the first decade of the new century in the area of the Grosvenor estate, between New Bond Street and Park Lane, which had undergone its first metamorphosis between 1885 and 1899, individual commissions were awarded to a variety of architects. Here they were able to illustrate their ample skills in town house planning and façade building.

Facing page, bottom right: *Peabody Buildings, Wild Street, Westminster, London. George Peabody donated £500,000 to establish a charitable trust which pioneered the provision of 'cheap, cleanly, well-drained and healthy dwellings for the poor'. By 1890, the Trust had provided more than 5,000 dwellings for the poor of London*

Above: *nos 6 and 7 Collingham Gardens, Kensington, London, a composition that reflects nineteenth-century Gothic. They were designed by Ernest George with Harold Peto in the 1880s; No 7 was fronted entirely in terracotta. Harold Peto had lived at number 9, also designed and built by the firm of Ernest George and Peto, before moving into no 7, living there between 1889 and 1892*

Letchworth and Hampstead

The Garden City concept is based on the principle of having a community that enjoys the right balance of agricultural land, factory and residential areas, public and educational buildings and parks, and where all are held in trust for the lessees who then share in the appreciation of land values. These ideals were promoted by Sir Ebenezer Howard in his book *To-morrow, a Perfect Path to Real Reform*, 1898, and the revised version, brought out later in the same year under the title of *Garden Cities of To-morrow*.

The Garden City Association was formed in 1899 to promote the ideas of Howard. It selected a site at Letchworth, Hertfordshire, and the First Garden City Limited was formed in 1903. Its first directors included the cocoa refiners Joseph Rowntree and Edward Cadbury, and W H Lever, the founder of the model village of Port Sunlight, Cheshire.

The architects selected to design the garden city were Richard Barry Parker and his brother-in-law and partner Raymond Unwin. Their design was carried out almost exactly as originally planned. The Cheap Cottages Exhibition was held in 1905, for which 120 cottages were built, and the Great Northern Railway erected a temporary station and sold excursion tickets in order to attract potential householders. A second such event was organised in 1907, known as the Urban Cottages Exhibition. Both events were reasonably successful, although manufacturers were slower to occupy the factory sites.

In the same year, Unwin left the project in order to plan the Hampstead Garden Suburb. This residential estate, built on the London periphery, was unique in offering its new occupants a wide range of houses that were intended to reflect a wide span of occupations and incomes. The idea was that of Henrietta Octavia Barnett (1851–1936). She and her husband, the Rev Samuel Barnett, spent her weekends at Heath End House, Hampstead Heath. He was the vicar of St Jude's, Whitechapel, and they renamed the house St Jude's Cottage. There, from their windows, they could see the untouched fields of Middlesex.

On being appointed an honorary secretary to the Hampstead Heath Extensions Council Mrs Barnett instigated the acquisition of 32.4ha (80 acres) as an extension to the Heath. Later, she is reported to have written some 12,000 letters to influential people and organisations, both seeking assistance in the conservation of the Heath against the encroaching urbanisation of north London and at the same time outlining alternative proposals to accommodate the ever-growing need for housing. The result of her efforts was the foundation of the Hampstead Garden Suburb Trust, which was able to purchase 98.4ha (243) acres from Eton College in 1907.

Raymond Unwin was then pursuaded to move from Letchworth to plan the new Garden Suburb, following the ideals outlined by Mrs Barnett. These allowed for groups of cottages, a village green complete with clubhouse, an institute, two churches of which one would be Anglican, tea-houses, shops, homes for the elderly, playgrounds, allotment gardens, and schools. Larger homes would also be included, with the intention of attracting lawyers and bankers who were to reside in close proximity to brewers, millers and their tenants.

Unwin began work on the northern end of the site, while Sir Edwin Lutyens, who had been engaged as a consultant, had asked for and was granted the planning of the central area with its institute and churches. The building line was varied by Unwin, which enabled the clever and ecconomical planning of closes and cul-de-sacs with some houses sited on the frontage line while others were set well back behind it. He also contrived to provide views from the house that could be enjoyed looking either to the back or to the front. His undoubted ability was clearly demonstrated in the creation of an estate that came together as a single work of art during a seven-year period, a planning and planting of 98.4ha (243 acres) that has never been equalled as a suburban estate.

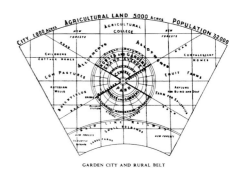

Above: *the garden city and its rural belt as conceived by Howard*

Left: *houses at Hampstead Garden Suburb, the first to embody Howard's garden city concept, which was put into practice by Sir Raymond Unwin*

Banks

The Joint Stock Bank legislation of 1826 and 1833 permitted banks to be formed as joint stock companies, although the Bank of England retained the sole right to print money. The first London bank that was formed in this way was the London and Westminster Bank, in 1833. It built the company's new building in Lothbury, London, in 1837, designed by C R Cockerell but now demolished. It was a neoclassical design with the first two storeys rusticated and lines of simple rectangular window openings below the main cornice. There was a smaller third storey, set back above the cornice, and the main banking hall had a small glazed dome.

Cockerell also built the Sun Fire and Life Assurance building, Threadneedle Street, London, 1839–42, also now demolished. This was followed by branch offices for the Bank of England at Bristol (demolished), Liverpool and Manchester between 1844 and 1846. In Manchester he ingeniously combined his liking for classical splendour with the practical requirements of a functioning bank by separating the pediment from the cornices so that a third storey could be squeezed in between.

In 1848 J E Gregan built Heywood's Bank (later renamed by its successive owners), St Ann's Square, Manchester, with a rusticated ground floor pierced by large Venetian windows. To the right of the façade is an arch which links the bank to the manager's house, thereby creating a sort of simple palazzo façade. This is idea had been seen earlier in the century at the Reform Club and it was to became popular, particularly in the larger cities for commercial building, though generally not until the 1850s. The formula was carried on into the 1880s, especially with branches of the National Westminster Bank which were built by John Gibson, and which often featured a top-lit grand banking hall. However by then Gibson's banks were already beginning to look too restrained in comparison with their competitors' more picturesque buildings.

Banks with palazzo façades had appeared earlier in Scotland, for example the British Linen Bank at the junction of Queen Street and Ingram Street, Glasgow. Built in 1840 by David and James Hamilton, it displayed a variety of classical features. The British Linen Bank, St Andrews Square, Edinburgh, 1846–51, by David Bryce was also effected in an ornate palazzo style.

James Hamilton continued the ornate style in Ireland, with an arcaded elevation that had a flat-topped two-storey portico on the Ulster Bank, Waring Street, Belfast, 1858–60.

The building styles of banks became confused in the later Victorian and Edwardian decades, with none being dominant. Possibly this may have reflected the banking profession's eagerness to express outwardly an enduring stability, but it resulted in the buildings appearing unimaginative, with a predominance of classical features.

Below: *the former West of England and South Wales Bank, Corn Street, Bristol, 1854–56, by W B Gingell and T R Lysaght; a high-renaissance style based on the Library of St Mark, Venice*

Office buildings

By the mid-nineteenth century, office and professional chambers existed primarily in the cities, where a speculator had bought up a row of old houses and then converted them into suites of rooms that could be rented out.

After a few years the building would be replaced by a larger structure, so that by the end of the century, this gradual extension meant that there were very few people living in the City of London, where the office building clearly predominated.

The façades of these offices were almost invariably classical, and thus they fitted into the townscape, on the exterior looking not too different from the neighbouring palatial homes and clubs. More storeys were added as demand for space grew, and when rebuilding took place, it was now possible to include much larger windows and thus provide improved lighting.

The practical requirements of those warehouses that were located within city centres were different, in that more storeys were required, commonly five or six. They also needed large windows for maximum daylight. The Brunswick Buildings in Liverpool, 1841, by A and G Williams, now demolished, was a huge three-storey building with large windows and a rusticated ground floor. Richmond Buildings, 26 Chapel Street, Liverpool, 1857, by J A Picton, also of three storeys and now demolished, had rounded-arched openings forming arcades which afforded even more light.

Meanwhile in Manchester, the J Brown and Son Warehouse, 1851, now demolished, by Edward Walters was another of the early impressive palazzo-formula buildings. It had six storeys, with one storey and a mezzanine behind the ground floor elevation while the sixth storey was hidden behind the very large balustrade. The whole composition was held together visually by heavily rusticated corner piers. In 1853 Walters used the palazzo effect for the first time for a public building, the Free Trade Hall, in Manchester.

Slightly earlier in London, Edward I'Anson had built the Royal Exchange Buildings, Freeman's Place, 1842–44, now demolished, as an arcade of shops with three floors of chambers above although the third did not extend to the full depth of the block.

By the late 1850s the Italian renaissance was not being promoted so much, the classical style was confused with French renaissance motifs, and the Gothic designers appeared reluctant to associate their style too closely with office architecture, so there was no dominant style. The three-bay wide Crown Life Office, New Bridge Street, London, 1858, now demolished, by Benjamin Woodward with its Georgian proportions had wide semi-circular arches with huge piers between the windows, the whole set off by a rich sculptured decoration. The high Victorian style had definitively arrived.

Below: *the Free Trade Hall, Manchester, 1853, by Edward Walters, is in the neo-Renaissance style. The work included rich arcading and decoration, all framed by a massive cornice*

Right: *the General Credit and Discount Company building, Lothbury, London, 1866, by George Somers Leigh Clarke*

Below: *Oriel Chambers, Liverpool, 1864–65, by Peter Ellis, was considered to be very much ahead of its time, having delicate ironwork in the plate-glass oriel windows and curtain walling, at the back of which the retracted vertical supports were visible from the outside*

A little later there were a few all-iron façades; Liverpool was home to two of the more impressive of these, Oriel Chambers, Water Street, 1864, and two years later 16 Cook Street, both by Peter Ellis. He used a thin iron framework with stone in the façade; in the former building the iron framed vertical rows of oriel windows.

By the late Victorian period the wide range of styles applied to office buildings ran from Queen Anne and the vernacular revival via a châteauesque baroque to the new grand manner. The first major commercial building in this style, though not strictly an office, was the Institute of Chartered Accountants building, London, 1888–93, by John Belcher.

At the end of the century, buildings such as that of the Royal Society of Medicine, Henrietta Street, London, by the firm of Belcher and Joass displayed both *beaux-arts* and mannerist tendencies, while other, more mammoth, prestige office buildings sprouted cupolas reminiscent of those of Greenwich Hospital. The first of these in the twentieth century was the overdone Electra House (now City of London College), Moorgate, London, 1902, also by Belcher. This building was to epitomise the era which included Belfast City Hall, 1898–1906, by Sir Brumwell Thomas, which probably can

Above: *the Institute of Chartered Accountants office building, Great Swan Alley, London, 1890s, by John Belcher*

Left: *the Public Record Office, Chancery Lane, London, 1850–51, by Sir James Pennethorne*

Below: *the Royal Liver building in Liverpool was constructed with reinforced concrete*

lay claim to having the largest cupola of the period, while the offices of the Mersey Docks and Harbour Board, Pier Head, Liverpool by Briggs, Wolstenhome and Thornley boasts a quincuncial arrangement of domes. However, the style was soon to be overshadowed in England by the introduction of reinforced concrete frame construction, one such early example of which was the very large Royal Liver Building, also in Pier Head, Liverpool, 1908–11, by Walter Aubrey Thomas.

Chapter Three

Rural Buildings

FOLLOWING THEIR SUCCESSFUL INVESTMENTS under the lengthy reign of the Georgian succession, members of the early Victorian landed aristocracy still retained their pre-eminent position. They paraded this in the most visible and tangible way they knew, in the form of country houses.

The house also represented a symbol for the *nouveau riche*, a step towards the higher echelons of social standing. The country house represented more than a mere dwelling; its size defined and determined social position and ambition, and the layout of the house plan was shifting to give emphasis to more functional considerations.

The country house was thus evolving into a multifunctional unit combining a home, business premises and guest house. In order to fulfill these functions it was necessary for the household to employ a large number of servants, all of whom knew their clearly defined places within the hierarchy and their functions within the running of the house.

Facing page: *the drawing room ceiling at Castell Coch, Glamorganshire 1872–79 by William Burges*

Left: *Eaton Hall was remodelled by Waterhouse for the first Duke of Westminster, but, with the exception of the chapel, clock tower and stable court, it was demolished in 1961*

It is recorded that at Eaton Hall, Cheshire, 1870–82, by Alfred Waterhouse, the Duke of Westminster employed some 50 full-time indoor servants. As elsewhere, guests were expected to arrive with their own entourages of personal attendants.

The various activities within the house were separately organised and expected to run to regular schedules. The family and guests met only at set times in formal reception rooms, otherwise they went about their business independently, with both kept well away from those who visited the owner on business.

Typically the ground-floor house plan would comprise a drawing room, dining room, library, morning room, breakfast room, smoking room and chapel for the family and guests.

The first floor was comprised basically of bedrooms for the family and their guests, who reached it via a grand staircase. It was divided into areas by marital status, with the bachelors' quarters located in a different area of the floor to those of the unmarried females of the household and guests.

The indoor servants, segregated into upper and lower stairs, had their own quarters which revolved around the servants hall. Their exclusive work areas included the kitchen, scullery, larder, pantry, cold store and bakehouse. They reached their own sleeping quarters via a back stair and, as with the family and guests, such was Victorian etiquette that the male servants were segregated from the maids.

While these very proper Victorian attitudes were being enforced, there was also an ever-growing improvement in the comfort that the household enjoyed. Plumbing advances enabled water to be piped throughout the house. With a growing frequency this included hot water, which was heated by open coal fires with back boilers. Open fires were themselves beginning to make way for central heating systems that produced either hot air or hot water, though this was limited to just the principal rooms.

Gas lighting, which had been developed by the end of the eighteenth century, was becoming widely used although oil lamps and candles remained common, especially in the bedrooms.

The indoor water closet was another new feature that became instantly popular, although the bathroom took a lot longer to gain wide acceptance. Many households continued to wash in basins filled by hand from ewers and hot-water cans, and to bathe in hip-baths that were brought into the bedrooms and filled from buckets.

Funding for this newly opulent life style was supplied by tenant farmers, who paid rents to the landowner when the house was the centre of a large estate. In return, some of the more enlightened landowners provided cottages for tenants and also for the other workers on their estates, for example at Peckforton Castle where Lord Tollemache provided each labourer with a cottage and a three-acre strip of land for his own cultivation. Furthermore, a

Below: when the Scottish baronial style came south of the border it took on its most splendid expression in the form of Highclere Castle (photograph by kind permission of the Earl of Carnarvon)

great pride was taken in the running of the home farm, promoting it as a model of good practice for the tenants to follow.

Whereas the plan of the early Victorian country house had become slowly less classical, the layout of the gardens took on a more regimented and orderly display. This necessitated a large gardening staff in addition to the house servants, to keep hedges neatly clipped, lawns cut and the flower beds with as much bloom as possible. The gardeners were kept working during the winter in the vast conservatories for the cultivation of exotic and tender plants. The era witnessed a marked interest in botany and expansion in horticulture, and the development of the garden progressed from an organised uniformity to the more 'natural' or woodland type designed by Gertrude Jekyll in the later Victorian period.

The variety of architectural styles available to the housebuilder for his country house was now very diverse, and the style of the moment was more fluid than in the previous Georgian period. Thus we find all styles of architecture, ranging from the Greek and Roman classical modes that had fallen out of fashion with the crowning of Victoria, to the Italian renaissance. This remained popular, though not as fashionable as the 'English' styles; of these, English Gothic was probably just slightly more popular than the Elizabethan style. The latter was particularly exploited by the Victorians, who liked to combine a picturesque exterior with sumptuous surface decoration.

There were also the romantic medieval castle style and its closely related cousin, the Scottish baronial style, so named because it was popular north of the border. When Pugin remodelled Scarisbrick Hall he re-established the great medieval hall. Though even by then it was somewhat impractical, it was to become a feature of many later Victorian houses, including Peckforton Castle. Peckforton was extremely well arranged, with the accommodation designed around a large courtyard.

Below: *the entrance front of Scarisbrick Hall, where A W Pugin began work to remodel and alter the existing house in 1837. The end result was somewhat different from Pugin's original sketch. On the right of the photograph is the drawing room; in the centre, to the left of the entrance, is the great hall and on the right (west) is the (now demolished) clock tower. Scarisbrick Hall was sold in 1963 for conversion into a school*

Right: *Peckforton Castle, where Salvin created a functional Victorian home in the style of a twelfth-century castle, which was constructed in stone brought from a quarry 1.6km (one mile) away (photograph by kind permission of the owner of Peckforton Castle)*

As new wealth derived from burgeoning industrial exploitation was added to the earlier agricultural wealth accumulated in the third quarter of the century, the Victorian country house came into its epoch. Whatever the style followed, newly-built houses then were invariably impracticably oversized, and many an existing Georgian structure was modified and extended in pursuit of gigantism.

This was the high Victorian period, and its richly ornamented style of Gothic can be seen in houses such as Milton Ernest Hall, Bedfordshire, 1853–56, where William Butterfield used red brick to enrich the stone walls and complemented them with high-pitched roofs and tall chimneys. The front of the house has a three-storey bay window. Although this example was not large by

Below right: *the entrance front of Milton Ernest Hall, and a few of its tall chimneys*

Far right: *Sir George Gilbert Scott was known for his Gothic churches, but he also advocated the Gothic for public buildings and houses. The rebuilding of Kelham Hall, which had been gutted by fire in 1857, provided him with an exceptional opportunity. He produced a spacious, well-lit house that was, in hindsight, not a successful domestic building but one that was huge and heavy in appearance*

contemporary standards, Kelham Hall, Nottinghamshire, 1858–61 by Sir George Gilbert Scott was. This red brick house with stone banding and a myriad disparate Gothic features pales into insignificance, however, when compared to the vast Gothic palace which was Eaton Hall. Here Alfred Waterhouse rebuilt a house that had already been rebuilt and enlarged twice previously, making it look like a French château with an abundance of towers, turrets and high-pitched roofs. Sadly, the house was almost entirely demolished in 1961–62.

The variety of earlier Victorian styles now began to give way to the emerging interest in the French Gothic, Italian Gothic and French renaissance modes. The *nouveaux riches*, especially from the banking and finance fraternity, tended to plump for the latter style. Wykehurst Park, Sussex, 1871–74, by Edward Middleton Barry, was built for a banker for example, and created an impression not only externally. The house, which had cavity walls, also featured hot-air central heating and a bathroom to each bedroom suite.

Not to be outdone, the Rothschilds employed the French architect Gabriel-Hippolyte Destailleur to build Waddesdon Manor, Buckinghamshire, 1874–89, a château that could have been transported directly from the Loire Valley, and then decked it out with Louis XV furniture, Savonnerie carpets and Sèvres porcelain.

By now the fashion for the castle style was beginning to wane, but Cardiff Castle, 1868–81, by William Burges, is a lasting epitaph to the unchastened Gothic revival architecture of the period. Solid at its base, it blossoms in an array of turrets, spires, pyramidal roofs and finials. Internally the decoration was concentrated on coloured carvings and painted ceilings.

The great age of the Victorian country house really came to an end in the late 1870s, but not before one last flourish of fantasy. Castell Coch, Glamorgan, 1875–81, also built by William Burges, is set on a wooded hillside. Its many features include stout cylindrical towers capped by conical roofs, but this austere exterior only emphasises the flamboyant colours and elaborate decoration of the interior. Although country house building did not cease after that grace note, the buildings did tend to become smaller, and their function appears to have shifted to that of being retreats from urban life rather than the centres of great estates.

The Victorian age became increasingly the age of the middle-classes, and the most characteristic expression of their aspirations was the detached house, whether in the country or a suburb.

The small suburban detached house with its own garden is a peculiarly English ideal. When it first became popular it was most readily expressed in the form of the picturesque Italian villa or cottage styles. Both had been popularised by John Nash, and it is characteristic of much of this type of housing that it follows the high fashion of a previous generation. Stucco-covered villas were built alike in the Italian style, the cottage style, and even the Gothick

Above: *Wykehurst Park, built for Henry Hugh, was the grandest and most impressive of the French renaissance country houses*

Below: *the flavour of Waddesdon was overwhelmingly French; the main rooms were lined with French wood panelling, exclusively French furniture and* objects d'art *were scattered throughout the house, and the gardens were by the French landscape gardener Lainé*

Three views of Cardiff Castle: top left, *the octagon staircase;* top right, *the Arab room ceiling, which is on the first floor of the Herbert Tower, and was the last room that Burges worked on at Cardiff. He died in 1881, with the decoration of Cardiff Castle still incomplete.* Below, left, *is the library door*

Far right: *another landmark by Burges, Castell Coch, as rebuilt by him. The southern portion of the castle is built directly onto an outcrop of rock, with massive stone abutments to hold up the towers. The lower parts of the abutments are of red stone, above which Burges used grey limestone*

style as late as the 1850s and even beyond. Many followed plans that had been published in *Rural Residences* by J B Papworth in 1818 and *Villa Rustica*, 1832, by Charles Parker.

In the middle-Victorian period of 1855–75, however, such small houses and parsonages came under the influence of Pugin, and his style of Gothic that had first been seen in his own house, St Marie's Grange, Alderbury near Salisbury, Wiltshire, 1835–36. It was constructed in red brick with Gothic details, stone dressings and a slate roof. This influence manifested itself through such architects as William Butterfield, William White and George Edmund Street, who built their houses from readily available local stone or red brick, with the evolved Gothic detailing tempered to suit the needs of nineteenth-century living.

Butterfield expressed the style admirably in the vicarage that he built at Cowick, Yorkshire, in 1853. This red brick building has wooden window frames and a steep roof with simple gables.

This style was developed by both White and Street, and

can be seen in one small house, White's Penmellyn, St Columb Major, Cornwall, *c.* 1855. This is constructed in stone with slate hanging used at the tops of the gables and in the spandrels of the wooden-framed windows. The chimney-stacks project from the wall, and to the side of the house is a small oriel, triangular in shape and supported on a wooden bracket.

Penmellyn is not too dissimilar from Street's style of that time, although his vicarages did become more austere later in the decade. By the time of the one that he built at New Bradwell, Buckinghamshire, 1857–60, he had abandoned polychromy and eliminated buttresses from what were now plain red brick walls with simple wooden sash windows.

This later style of Street's was echoed by Philip Webb in the famous Red House, Bexleyheath, Kent, 1859–60, which was built for William Morris. Although not a large house, it gives every appearance of solidity and permanance, without being at all pretentious.

Internally, however, the Red House was much more lavish, embellished with Burne-Jones's stained glass, Morris's own coloured wallpapers in highly-wrought designs, and some heavy furniture. The drawing-room featured a built-in settle at one end, which is crowned by a miniature minstrels' gallery.

In the later Victorian period architects began to discard the styles promoted by the pattern books, and to seek out the easier, simpler, and less formal attributes of vernacular buildings for their inspiration.

This direction was encouraged by the high church Anglican architects in mid-century and ably executed by such practitioners as George Devey, Eden Nesfield and Richard Norman Shaw, the latter two having shared an office in their early careers.

Above: *the Red House, Bexleyheath, Kent, 1859–60, by Philip Webb for William Morris. Morris, though not an architect, commissioned Webb to build a house that, while retaining many features of the Gothic revival, showed a distinct move towards the Arts and Crafts movement style of homespun intimacy*

Below: *Betteshanger House, near Deal, Kent, is a rambling mishmash of a country house, the design for which was worked out over a period of 26 years*

Devey was one of the most prolific of the Victorian country house architects, his reputation having been established out of recommendations from satisfied clients. His homes invariably utilised local materials, as can be seen at the rambling Betteshanger House, Kent, 1856–82. Here he used a variety of local materials, including stone, flint, both red and yellow bricks, and tiles which, combined with the abundance of chimney-stacks, mullioned bay-windows and Dutch gables, unite to create a truly amazing house built in an undeniably picturesque style.

This picturesque vernacular or 'Old English' style was popularised by Nesfield and Shaw. Shaw built many houses in the Sussex Weald which had tall brick chimneys, mullioned windows and tile-hanging. Typical of these was Leyswood, near Withyham, Sussex, 1866, where the accommodation was arranged around three sides of a courtyard. Unfortunately the main part of the house has been demolished, leaving only the gate tower and the courtyard.

Above, *Cragside, as seen through the gardens from the valley;* right, *an engraving by Shaw of the exterior of Leyswood, and* below: *the central pavilion of Kinmel Park*

Facing page: *two of Lutyens' great Romantic houses;* above, *Munstead Wood, and* below, *Deanery Gardens, designed in 1901 for the (then) publisher of* Country Life *magazine, Edward Hudson*

Whereas Devey shunned publicity, Shaw embraced it and this enabled him to build houses of similar character throughout the country, including Cragside, Rothbury, Northumberland, 1870–*c.*85. The house, which is situated in a wooded estate and is hidden from view until the final stretch of a long approach drive, rises high above in a melée of timber-framed gables and tall chimney-stacks surmounted by a crenellated tower.

Meanwhile, Nesfield was creating one of the earliest and largest manifestations of country-house architecture in the Queen Anne style at Kinmel Park, near Abergele, Denbighshire, in 1868. His house plan is irregular, including a courtyard around which are the service quarters at one end and, at the other, the reception rooms. The symmetry is further broken by chimney-stacks and dormers which, combined with the high mansard roofs, create an impression more of a French château than of the relative severity of the greater Gothic English country house.

The vernacular revival was continued through the work of Charles F Annesley Voysey, who had been employed by Devey at one time. Voysey concentrated on smaller buildings and used white roughcast walls to good effect, in low buildings combining them with wide eaves, mullioned windows and hipped slate roofs. Good examples may be seen at The Cottage, Bishops Itchington, Warwickshire, of 1888 and Broadleys, Lake Windermere, Lancashire, of 1898, which established a style that would be replicated throughout Britain for the next forty years.

Some of the most remarkable houses in the vernacular revival style were those designed by Edwin Lutyens, that appeared at the end of the Victorian period. His early career was influenced by Gertrude Jekyll, for whom he built Munstead Wood, near Goldalming, Surrey, 1896, though Tigbourne Court, Surrey, 1899, which is built of local stone with seventeenth-century vernacular detailing, is more exciting.

Gertrude Jekyll 1843–1932

From 1861, Gertrude Jekyll studied at the South Kensington Schools and on leaving in 1867, she attended Fiori's drawing classes in London before going to Gigi's Academy on the via Margutta, Rome, in 1868.

She met William Robinson in January 1875, when she called on him at the offices of *The Garden*, the paper which Robinson had founded in 1872 and which he used as a means of spreading his ideas concerning natural gardening and the attractions of the 'wild garden'.

The following year, 1876, her father died and she moved with her mother to Munstead Heath, Surrey. Here they had a house built, that was designed by John James Stevenson. It was here, too, that she developed her first garden, which Robinson regarded very highly.

Miss Jekyll began the first of her new homes, The Hut, which was built on land adjoining her mother's home, in 1894. This was her first collaboration also with Edwin Lutyens, who was then 25 years old and lived at nearby Thursley.

Her mother died in 1895, after which Gertrude Jekyll and Edwin Lutyens embarked on the building of Munstead Wood, a house which was eventually to become the model for the many later Surrey farmhouses, although lacking a farm. Here Miss Jekyll cultivated her ground and refined the furnishings of her house until the garden came to represent the 'Surrey School' of gardening, and equally the house became the pattern for other Surrey and Sussex houses where the internal decorations are carefully matched with the studied simplicity of their designs and their settings.

Miss Jekyll moved into Munstead Wood in 1897, and continued to play a part in Lutyens' success as an architect of country houses, teaching him the best use of natural stone, brick and timber, and how to plan house and garden together as a single harmonious work. Munstead Wood brought her a long succession of commissions, running to three hundred or more, of which more than forty were with Sir Edwin Lutyens. Others she did in collaboration with many of the other leading architects of the day.

Miss Jekyll was also concerned with the introduction of new plants and new varieties and her theories and practice were recorded in her many writings which included *Wood and Garden* (published in London, 1898), *Wall and Water Gardens* with Lawrence Weaver, *Garden Ornament* with Christopher Hussey and *Gardens and Small Country Houses*, also with Weaver.

Right: *Tigbourne Court, Surrey, 1899, by Sir Edwin Lutyens*

Below: *elevation of Tower House, Bognor, Sussex, and* right, *The Orchard, Chorley Wood, Buckinghamshire, 1900, both by Charles Voysey*

Right: *Hill House, Helensburgh, Scotland, 1902–06, by Charles Rennie Mackintosh*

George Devey had done much to free domestic architecture from the discipline of the drawing board, while Richard Norman Shaw, Eden Nesfield and Philip Webb developed their own styles based on stone, timbered and plastered houses of the sixteenth and seventeenth century, in a vernacular revival that eclipsed Gothic.

Webb established his style based on first principles, a line that was followed by others such as the Arts and Crafts architects Charles Voysey, Edgar Wood, Baillie Scott, Edward Schroeder Prior, William Richard Lethaby, Charles Robert Ashbee, Arthur Heygate Mackmurdo, James MacLaren and Charles Rennie Mackintosh in Scotland. Of these, Voysey was the most successful while the Scottish houses of Mackintosh showed a new simplicity.

Above: *the frontispiece of Mackmurdo's* Wren's City Churches, *1883*

Left: *Peter Behrens' manifesto for* Deutsche Kunst und Dekoration, c. *1900; and* far left, *Behrens' drawing of the front elevation of his own house, Darmstadt, Germany, 1901*

In addition to their building prowess, these architects also displayed a great deal of creative imagination and inventiveness with the design of their interiors and furniture, with Voysey's style becoming the stock-in-trade of the house furnishers of the early twentieth century. Through the pages of magazines such as *Deutsche Kunst und Dekoration* this new force in the English style was propagated abroad, to the extent that Mackintosh had a greater influence in Vienna, Munich and Turin than in Britain; so much so that he was invited to join the ranks of the Vienna Secession. Such was the growing influence of the burgeoning creativity of English architecture that in 1896 Hermann Muthesius, an attaché to the Imperial Prussian Board of Trade, was despatched to England to study and record domestic architecture in Britain from 1880. His study continued until 1904, when he returned to home. His findings were published in two volumes; *Englische Baukunst der Gegenwart*, 1900, that concerned town houses, and *Das Englische Haus*, 1904, which described country houses.

Chapter Four

Churches

THE CLAPHAM SECT had been actively campaigning for the abolition of slavery in England since about 1790, and slowly it had gained influence. The group was based at the church of John Venn (1759–1813) rector of Clapham from 1792 until his death. It included William Wilberforce, Henry Thornton, James Stephen and Lord Macaulay. Many of these Anglican philanthropists were members of Parliament who worked additionally for prison reform, and who zealously endeavoured to bring the Bible, decency and morality into every house by campaigning against drunkenness and vice. In short, they were the guiding conscience of the Victorian age, practising philanthropic benevolence and preaching literacy, hygiene and sobriety to the swelling urban population. They called for efforts to ensure the triumph of decent family living, a crusade undertaken at a time when the social influence of the established church was in decline.

It is thus a remarkable achievement that this civilizing influence on the urban masses and the stabilisation of society is mostly attributable to the church through the heroic efforts of both clergymen and the laity. Extraordinary advances in adult literacy, conditions of housing and general cleanliness were made during the Victorian era, and there is a visible memorial to the men and women who achieved this amazing transformation in the vast number of surviving Victorian churches and chapels.

Since the Great Fire of London in 1666, notable Acts of Parliament to establish new church buildings came about in 1711, with the 'fifty new churches' act, and in 1818. Then, £1m was donated for the building of additional churches in populous parishes, known as the commissioners' churches. By 1828 that later Act had reached its fruition in the construction of 214 new churches. Most of these, indeed over 170, were in a pointed Gothic style. This uniformity provided an economy of scale made necessary by the limited funds available. Nevertheless, a considerable range of

Facing page: the entrance to All Saints, Margaret Street, London, 1849–59, by William Butterfield

Right: *a plate from Pugin's* Contrasts in Architecture, *1836. At the top of the composition is the National Gallery above details from two blocks (by Shaw and Abraham) in Regent Street. The remainder of the plate is enclosed within a frame caricaturing Dance's Ammonite order, as used in the Shakespeare Gallery, 52 Pall Mall, London. In the frieze are, left to right, All Souls, Langham Place; St Philip's, Regent Street; Westminster Hospital; The Holme, Regent's Park; and St Mary Haggerston. In the space between the columns, arches in the style of Soane, pendentives, and acroters provide a setting for the Carlton Club and the Inner Temple Library, while (left to right) are the steeples of St Peter's, Regent Square, and St John's, Waterloo Road*

Below: *Pugin's Roman Catholic Cathedral of St Mary, Newcastle, 1844, was built as a parish church. The 67m (220ft) spire was added in the 1860s by Joseph Aloysius Hansom*

religious buildings were erected in the Victorian age, for a wide variety of religious groups.

During the 1820s and 1830s there was an easing of the social and political restrictions on members of the Roman Catholic faith, which led to a gradual revival in Catholicism. The full church hierarchy was re-established by the middle of the century, and as it progressed, so the larger towns were more able to provide a sufficiently extensive congregation to warrant a Catholic church.

The Catholic cause received a considerable boost from the writings of Augustus Welby Northmore Pugin, who converted to Catholicism in 1834 and published his *Contrasts in Architecture* in 1836. This was a damning polemic in which he claimed that Gothic architecture had a wonderful superiority over the buildings of the

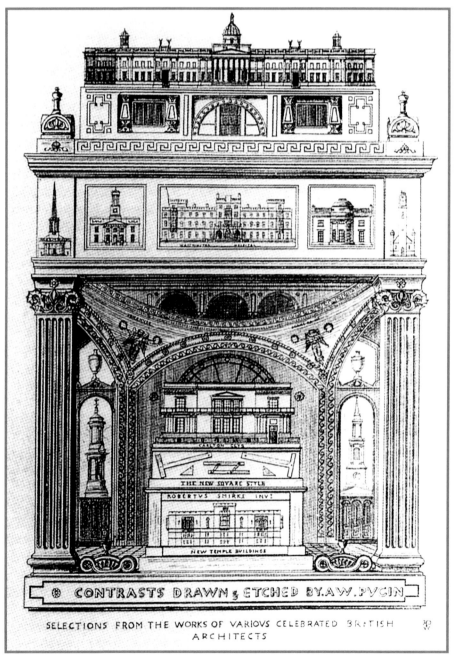

renaissance and classical revivals and that in it alone the Christian faith was embodied and made manifest for all to see. He described classical architecture as pagan, and regarded it as a monster, as he did Protestantism. He blamed the latter for the destruction of 'pointed' (Gothic) architecture which had been designed by Catholics for those of the Catholic faith.

He argued further that art is immediately connected with the state of the society that produces it, declared that the Middle Ages offered the only example for the good life, and maintained that only when the piety and communal spirit of the medieval period had been re-established could a true and noble Christian architecture be reborn.

Catholicism was strongest in the rural communities and among the aristocracy in the early nineteenth-century. At the time, new Catholic churches tended to be derived from the Anglican model which traditionally had segregated seating arrangements, where private family pews were leased out for fees and remained in the same family from generation to generation.

The Catholic church interiors tended to be spartan, lacking statues and decoration, and their altars were basic. By the middle of the century there had been an increase in the number of services, and the churches became more lavishly furnished. However, for the most part, the churches then being built were still dull, although there were a few notable exceptions such as the Cathedral of Salford, 1844–55, by John Grey Weightman and Matthew Edison Hadfield, and St Walburga's church, Preston, Lancashire, 1850, by Joseph Aloysius Hansom, with its very high and beautifully pointed spire.

This impressive spire had been borrowed from the French early second pointed style of about 1300, and as such was seen as being free from Anglican adulteration. This European reference was continued after Pugin's death in 1852, by his son Edward Welby Pugin, most notably in his St Francis' church, Gorton, Manchester, 1864–72, which is a showpiece of continental revival Gothic. Its west front has a tall striped bell turret set over a crucifixus, rising from a large central buttress that is set between two large traceried windows.

Many architects had produced building designs for the Catholic Church since the 1820s, and thus there were many able contestants for the design of a new church for the London Oratory of St Philip Neri and the Church of the Immaculate Heart of Mary at Brompton when it was announced in 1878. The design chosen for what was to become the most prominent Catholic church to date, by Herbert Augustus Keate Gribble, was to be Italian renaissance. Gothic had remained the popular style throughout the Victorian period; Gribble's Roman baroque was quite unfamiliar in England, and very different to the eventual Byzantine style of Westminster Cathedral, 1895–1903.

The Cathedral, by John Francis Bentley, is a vast brick

Right: *the fine Roman baroque exterior of the London Oratory of St Philip Neri and the Church of the Immaculate Heart of Mary at Brompton, Kensington, London, 1878, by Herbert Augustus Keate Gribble*

Right: *the sumptuous interior of the Brompton Oratory echoes the baroque of the exterior, with massive piers separating the side chapels*

construction with stone dressings. The original proposal was that the building should be based on the Basilica of St Peter, Rome. This original preference was amended when a new Cardinal took office and insisted on applying a 'modern' Byzantine revival style to the basilican concept, which had been intended to reflect the unity of the Catholic community and its newly-restored heirarchy with the great tradition dating from the time of St Peter the Apostle. The church has a nave flanked by outer chapels, a domed crossing, and transepts that do not project beyond the walls and chancel. The walls are generally flat outside, because all of the supports are on the inside. The red brick is relieved towards the top with stripes of white Portland stone. Most of the major flanking turrets and the tall tower terminate in small domes.

The new acceptability of the Catholic church was most manifest in its energetic building effort, and it prompted the

DOMINE·JESU·REX·ET·REDEMPTOR
PER·SANGUINEM·TUUM·SALVA·NOS

Above: *the Catholic Cathedral of Westminster, London, 1894, by John Francis Bentley. Built in the Byzantine revival style based on studies Bentley made in Italy, it combines a nave with outer chapels, a domed crossing, transepts that do not project beyond the walls, and a chancel, all of which are transformed into a longitudinal domed building in the Gesù scheme, i.e. that which was evolved for the mother church of the Society of Jesus in Rome, Il Gesù, 1568–73, by Giacomo Barozzi da Vignola and Giacomo della Porta*

Left: *the west front portal of Westminster Cathedral*

Anglicans to action in their turn. The University Societies at Oxford and Cambridge encouraged the study of church architecture and promoted the cause of Gothic art and architecture, seeing it as a means through which to revive the Anglican church.

At the time following the Great Reform Bill of 1832, the Anglican church thought it was under threat, not only from the polemics of Pugin, but also from the evangelical movement and its buildings which were free from any semblance of religious imagery. The result was that the embattled group of Anglicans, who published the *Ecclesiologist* magazine, adopted Pugin's architectural ideals. Adapting them to their own uses, they began building new churches in the middle pointed Gothic revival style. They also imposed their new-found zeal upon existing buildings, that thus lost their original Early English or Perpendicular fabric.

About 1,500 new churches were built in England between

The pointed Gothic styles

There were three principal types of pointed Gothic during the Victorian revival of the style. The many variations within each were largely dependent upon the building materials which were available locally. They imitated the original styles, as follows; the original name is shown on the left, the Victorian equivalent on the right:

Early English = first pointed
Decorated = middle pointed
Perpendicular = third pointed

1830 and 1861, and building continued at the rate of about 100 new churches each year until the end of the century. It was a remarkable period of church building which also included the restoration of one third of all parish churches by 1873 and of virtually all of them by the end of the century. The power wielded by the *Ecclesiologist* was immense, affecting both the architects who were employed and the dictates that were imposed upon them. If anything, there was an over-provision of churches, and thus not only were far too many under-endowed, but also the districts in which they stood were far too small to support them.

The initial surge of church building, between 1820 and 1845, had been dominated by the third pointed style, although the first pointed Early-English style was also prominent. When the Ecclesiological Society became a national body in 1845, it coincided with a time when the Anglican Church was in turmoil, and in seeking solutions to its many problems, decided to build in the second or middle-pointed Gothic style. The reasoning was that this style had originated in the early fourteenth century Decorated style, which incorporated the best elements of Gothic and was regarded as the common architectural language of the cultured European nations. It was, therefore, thought to be the one which would act as a catalyst for bringing unity to the church.

The Ecclesiologists, however, saw the style purely as a stepping-stone to a more refined type of Gothic that they considered appropriate to their time, which we call the high Victorian period. Colour was prominent in high Victorian church design, which at its most developed can be seen in the remodelling of the Albert

All Saints Church, Margaret Street, London

This was the model church of the Ecclesiological Society, and was built between 1849 and 1859 by William Butterfield on a site that had had on it just a few small houses and shops in 1848.

The plan was for a clergy-house and a choir school to share the cramped site with the church itself. The former was planned to accommodate several priests living communally on the site, in order to maintain the daily requirements of Tractarian observance.

It was one of the first major Victorian buildings in which constructional colour was used, and it marks the beginning of the high Victorian phase of the Gothic revival. It signifies the start of Butterfield's polychrome style, with its skin of brick and tile. Red brick was used with bands, voussoirs, and diaper-work of black brick and Bath stone dressings on the exterior. Lead

and slate were used for the broach spire and the roof.

The church occupies the northern part of the site, the choir school is to the southwest corner and the clergy-house to the southeast.

The arched gateway from the street leads into a courtyard, from which the powerful design of the buildings can be fully appreciated.

The buildings truly represented the Church's desire for a style that encompassed European culture. Its structural polychromy was derived from Germany, and its interiors from Italy. Middle-pointed Gothic work can be seen in the tracery of the church windows, while the diaper patterns in the brickwork are associated with Perpendicular. It is therefore not surprising that at a very early stage in its construction All Saints was regarded as a building of exceptional originality and significance and its influence was to become considerable.

Memorial chapel, Windsor, Berkshire. The interior work was carried out during the 1860s in an amazingly rich style, with strong French and German influences evident in this powerful continental Gothic piece. Soon, however, the clustered piers were to give way to the oversized cylinders typical of the early Burgundian Gothic of the thirteenth century, and gradually the lively polychrome fell from grace.

In its place came the muscular churches such as St Andrew's, Plaistow, Essex, 1867–70, by James Brooks, and a return to a more primitive French first pointed Gothic. Brooks' style encompassed wide, high naves, narrow aisles, lofty clerestories and Burgundian-type wide, short lancets complete with plate tracery. All of these can be best appreciated at his church of St John the Baptist, Holland Park, London, 1872–1911, where he mixed this Burgundian Gothic with thirteenth-century English Cistercian.

As vivid polychromy fell from fashion, imposing geometric shapes emerged, together with symbolic decoration and prominent, powerful sculpture. This style was promulgated by William Burges and may be seen in his Yorkshire churches of St Mary, Strudley Royal, 1870–78, and Christ the Consoler, Skelton-on-Ure, 1870–76.

Yet arguably the greatest churches of the 1870s were those of John Loughborough Pearson, which ranged from the small church of St Mary the Virgin, Freeland, Oxfordshire, 1868–73, to that of St Augustine with St John, Kilburn Park Road, London, 1871–98. This magnificent red-brick building with its vaulted interior

Above: *the Church of St Mary, Studley Royal, Yorkshire, 1870–78, by William Burges*

Left: *one of Pearson's wonderful rural churches, St Mary the Virgin, Freeland, Oxfordshire, 1868–73*

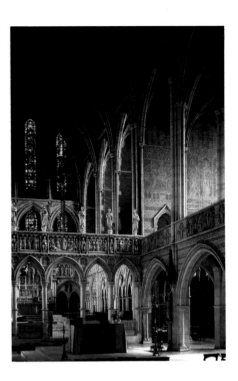

High Victorian churches

All Souls, Haley Hill, Halifax,
Yorkshire, 1855–59, by Sir George
Gilbert Scott; his best work, a mixture
of first and second pointed with nave
piers and early French Gothic capitals

St Michael, Lyndhurst, Hampshire,
1858–70, by William White; a big red
and yellow brick first pointed building
with stained glass by William Morris

St Michael, Leafield, Oxfordshire,
consecrated 1860 but completed 1874
by Sir George Gilbert Scott; early
thirteenth-century style with lancets,
quarterfoils and a high crossing tower
with spire

St Andrew, Jarrom Street, Leicester,
1860–62, by Sir George Gilbert Scott;
in the first pointed style of continental
Gothic red brick with blue/black
bricks and stone dressings

St Leonard, Newland, Worcestershire,
1862–64, by Philip Charles Hardwick;
paired marble columns in an early
French Gothic style

St Peter's, Vauxhall, London, 1863–65,
by John Loughborough Pearson; early
French first pointed, with a tall clerestoried
brick nave continuing into an apsidal
chancel, both having ribbed vaulting

St Saviour's, Aberdeen Park, London,
1865, by William White; an example
of polychrome Gothic, with a fine
brick interior embellished with
stencilled patterns (no longer used for
worship)

St Mary Magdalene, Woodchester
Square, Paddington, London, 1867–78,
by George Edward Street; first
pointed style for the first centre for
High Anglicanism in Paddington

is one of the largest Victorian churches in London. St Mary's has plate-tracery to the aisleless nave windows, a sumptuous vaulted chancel and an apse pierced by lancets. In addition, the chancel is roofed with a rib-vault of pinkish grey stone, carried on red wall shafts. The whole is described by Nikolaus Pevsner as demonstrating the Ecclesiologists' theories of the beauty of holiness. St Augustine displays a tower and spire derived from the Abbaye-aux-Hommes, Caen, France and its very deep internal buttresses are derived from the cathedral at Albi, France. Pearson continued to build in the French Gothic style, with his Truro Cathedral, Cornwall, 1880–1910, where he combined French and English first pointed.

During the last decades of Victoria's reign, the experiments with muscular continental Gothic began to pall and a new delicacy emerged, with the revival of English late Gothic styles. The shift away from the high Victorian and into the late Victorian Gothic was encapsulated in the Church of the Holy Angels, Hoar Cross, Staffordshire, 1872–76, by George Frederick Bodley and Thomas Garner. Here there is an astonishingly beautiful aisleless clerestoried chancel with a ceiling of tierceron vaults, and both the transepts and the nave have timber wagon-roofs. The building style is late Decorated, with a tower that introduces an element of Perpendicular themes.

The late style of Bodley attracted many followers, but the younger English architects began to turn away towards a Perpendicular (third pointed) style.

Thus, in little more than half a century, the wheel had turned full circle from the early churches of Augustus Welby Northmore Pugin such as St Mary's, Derby, 1837–39, and St Alban's, Macclesfield, 1838–41, both in the Perpendicular style with small chancels and windows with typical third-pointed tracery, to the church of St George, Buxton Road, Stockport, Cheshire, 1893–97, by Edward Graham Paley and Hubert James Austin, also in a Perpendicular style although a more powerful, assured and spectacular Perpendicular than that of Pugin.

The Gothic revival had undergone three distinct phases, but by 1901, all of its greatest practioners were dead apart from Bodley and John Francis Bentley. Thus there was a new generation of architects designing churches, but with few exceptions they continued the traditions revived by their masters.

Some of these notable exceptions were inspired and supported by the Art Workers' Guild and the Arts and Crafts movement. Holy Trinity church, Sloane Street, Chelsea, was completed by Henry Wilson with the support of fellow Art Workers and Craftsmen. All Saints, Brockhampton-by-Ross, Hertfordshire, 1902, was concrete-vaulted, by William Richard Lethaby and St Andrew, Roker Park, Sunderland, 1906–07, by Edward Schroeder Prior was perhaps the best of the churches inspired by the Arts and Crafts movement.

The Mount Vernon Hospital chapel, Northwood, Middlesex, by Frederick Wheeler is almost *art nouveau* in style, while Art Deco, the next movement to emerge in the visual arts, was anticipated by Charles Harrison Townsend in the church of St Mary the Virgin, Great Warley, Essex, 1902–04, with its vault decorated in aluminium leaf to a pattern of roses.

By the end of the nineteenth century there was also a revival of interest in Byzantium and its early Christian churches, which led to some striking departures from the Gothic tradition. Examples of this trend include the church of St Sophia, Lower Kingswood, Surrey, by Sidney Barnsley, and perhaps most remarkable of all the Catholic Metropolitan Cathedral of Westminster (*see page 47*).

Facing page, left: *Albi's fortress-like buttresses on the external south-west corner of the cathedral;* centre, *the west front of Truro Cathedral, seen illuminated at night; and* right, *interior of the church of St Augustine with St John, Kilburn Park Road, London. The bridges over the transepts owe their origins to those of St Mark's in Venice*

This page, above: *the interior of the church of St George, Stockport, Cheshire;* far left, *St George, Osborne Road, Jesmond, Newcastle-upon-Tyne, 1888–89, by T R Spence, who followed the precepts of the Arts and Crafts movement and integrated the decoration with the structure. It was well executed and very progressive in style for its date;* left, *St Jude's, Hampstead Garden Suburb, London, 1909–13, by Sir Edwin Lutyens was one of two churches to be built by him in the centre of the Garden Suburb*

Chapter Five

Market and Industrial Buildings

Bridges

The first twenty years of Victoria's reign saw the increasing application of iron and its use on neoclassical industrial buildings, especially city warehouses, railway stations and, even more significantly, rail and road bridges. There were substantial advances in both foundry and engineering knowledge, opening up enormous possibilities for structural innovation, and none more so than the development of the single span.

Iron Bridge, Coalbrookdale, 1777–81, had been composed of five cast-iron ribs linked at the apex to span the River Severn; however the relative brittleness of cast iron and the cost of making the stronger wrought iron meant that their uses had been restricted in the intervening years. The Menai Straits Bridge, 1826, by Thomas Telford, a suspension bridge, was designed to carry the main road from London to the Irish ferry at Holyhead and did

Facing page: the former Wait and James Granary, Welsh Back, Bristol, 1869, by Archibald Ponton and W V Gough

Left: *the Iron Bridge, Coalbrookdale, 1777–81, by Abraham Darby, used 378.5 tons of iron and was the first cast-iron arch span, bridging a distance of 30.5 metres (100ft)*

Above left: *the 521-metre (1,710 ft) Menai Straits Bridge, which is both an architectural and an engineering masterpiece; and* right, *the Royal Border Bridge, which spans the River Tweed at Berwick, has 28 semi-circular arches. It was constructed of masonry and brick with rubble infill. The bridge was opened by Queen Victoria in 1850*

Facing page, top: *the Garabit Viaduct, which carried a single-track railway, was the climax of Gustave Eiffel's bridge-building career; and* centre, *the Forth Rail Bridge was constructed between 1882 and 1889, using a total of 58,000 tons of steel*

Other important bridges

Water Street Bridge, 1829, by George Stephenson; the first bridge to use Eaton Hodgkinson's flanged beams Tower Bridge, London, 1886–94, by Sir John Wolfe-Barry; one of London's most famous monuments, it is built with a steel frame covered by stone. It was embellished in all its elaborate Gothic detail by Sir Horace Jones Glenfinnan Viaduct, 1897–1901, erected by McAlpines for the West Highland Extension Railway; Britain's first reinforced concrete bridge of any substance. It consists of 21 arches of 15.2m (50ft)

indicate the possibilities that lay ahead when it was erected successfully without causing any disruption to shipping. Another bridge over the Menai Straits, the famous box-girder Britannia Bridge, 1845–50, was built by Robert Stephenson. He used rectangular-section tubes constructed of riveted plates of wrought-iron, with rows of rectangular tubes or cells for the floor and roof respectively. The bridge consists of two of these enormous hollow beams laid side by side, one for the 'up' and the other for the 'down' traffic of the railway, and each of about 400m (0.25 mile).

Perhaps surprisingly, Stephenson was simultaneously building bridges in stone such as the Royal Border Bridge, which was built to carry the main east-coast railway line across the River Tweed at Berwick. Meanwhile his contemporary Isambard Kingdom Brunel was responsible for much more originality in his bridges, such as his suspension bridge at Clifton built between 1836 and 1859, the Chepstow Bridge, 1852, over the River Wye, and the Royal Albert Bridge, 1859, over the River Tamar at Saltash.

In the 1870s and 1880s advances in the manufacture of steel resulted in cheaper prices. This material had the advantages over iron of being both stronger and less brittle. One of the first steel bridges was at St Louis, Missouri, USA 1874 by James B Eads, but

steel was not immediately accepted universally as a replacement for iron. For instance, the 135m (443ft) high Garabit Viaduct over the River Truyère in the Massif Central, France, 1879, by Alexandre Gustave Eiffel was constructed entirely of iron, although like Eads' steel bridge it was also built using the cantilever principle of construction. This method involved the construction of arches beginning at the piers, working outwards towards the centre, supporting the construction on cables hung from temporary towers at each pier and thus avoiding the necessity for scaffolding.

The use of steel also made possible the building of complete bridges on the cantilever principle. The Forth Railway Bridge, 1890, by Benjamin Baker and John Fowler, was the first; a tremendously strong bridge that remains in use over a century later.

Since the advent of the automobile, however, most of the world's bridges have been for roads not rails; because road bridges are not required to be as massive or as rigid, even longer and more elegant suspension bridges could be developed. The world's first long suspension bridge was built over the River Ohio at Wheeling, West Virginia, USA, in 1852 by Charles Ellet. Unfortunately this blew down in 1854, only to be replaced immediately by a improved, stiffer model. By 1883, when the New York Brooklyn Bridge was completed it was the world's longest single span at 488m (1,600ft), it was also the first bridge to use steel cables.

Below: *the Brooklyn Suspension Bridge, New York, by John Roebling, completed in 1883 after his death by his son, W A Roebling*

Glasshouses

Markets were among the earliest buildings to employ iron for architectural effect, including those by Charles Fowler at Covent Garden, London, 1828; Hungerford, London, 1831–33; Exeter, 1837–38; also, most notably the Syon House conservatory, 1827–30, which has a 11.59m (38ft) diameter glazed dome.

The first glass dome of the Victorian era was at Chatsworth, where the Duke of Devonshire built a conservatory known as the Great Stove. Designed by Joseph Paxton, it was 75.34m (247ft)

long, 37.52m (123ft) wide and 20.44m (67ft) high and was completed in 1840, but is now demolished. Paxton created a span of 21.35m (70ft) across the central nave of the building using a system of ridge and furrow in laminated timber for its main ribs.

Decimus Burton had been consulted about its construction and was approached to prepare plans for the proposed Palm House at Kew, in 1844. Burton designed with the aid of Richard Turner a structure which was to be one of the most perfect examples of glasshouses ever built, completed in 1846. With its wrought-iron ribs, the roof spanned a central area 30.5m (100ft) wide and 42.09m (138ft) long. The entire building was 110.41m (362 ft) long and 19.22m (63ft) high, giving a clear demonstration of how to cover large spaces without an internal array of columns and buttresses.

Richard Turner with Joseph Locke erected a single-span train shed 46.67m (153ft) wide, supported on both sides by a line of Roman Doric columns, at Lime Street Station, Liverpool, 1849–50. This type of structure reached its zenith with the Crystal Palace, 1850–51, by Sir Joseph Paxton for the Great Exhibition of 1851. Its name was coined by *Punch*, a popular illustrated magazine.

Paxton sat on the Board of Directors of the Midland Railway, and must have been aware of the latest developments in railway architecture, but his magnificent glasshouse was on a scale far larger than anything that had preceded it. Its floor area was 563.64 x 124.44m (1,848 x 408ft) with an internal gallery and a central transept that rose 32.94m (108ft) into the air and had a span of 22m (72ft). The columns and girders were of cast iron, while the transept ribs and most of the glazing frames were of timber. The building was prefabricated, and constructed to schedule in just nine months. It was moved to Sydenham in 1852–54 where it served as a cultural centre for south London until it burnt down in 1936, from its original site in Hyde Park, London, south of the Serpentine.

It is likely that the success of the Crystal Palace influenced

Facing page, top left and centre, *Covent Garden as it is today;* top right, *the Duke of Devonshire's Chatsworth conservatory, and* bottom, *the south entrance of the barrel-vaulted Crystal Palace transept*

Left, *the west entrance;* below and bottom, *the Palace, which enclosed an area of about 74,000m² (796,536sq ft) and used 3,500 tons of cast iron for the 3,230 columns and 2,141 girders, plus 550 tons of wrought iron and 83,238m² (895,974sq ft) of glass, under construction*

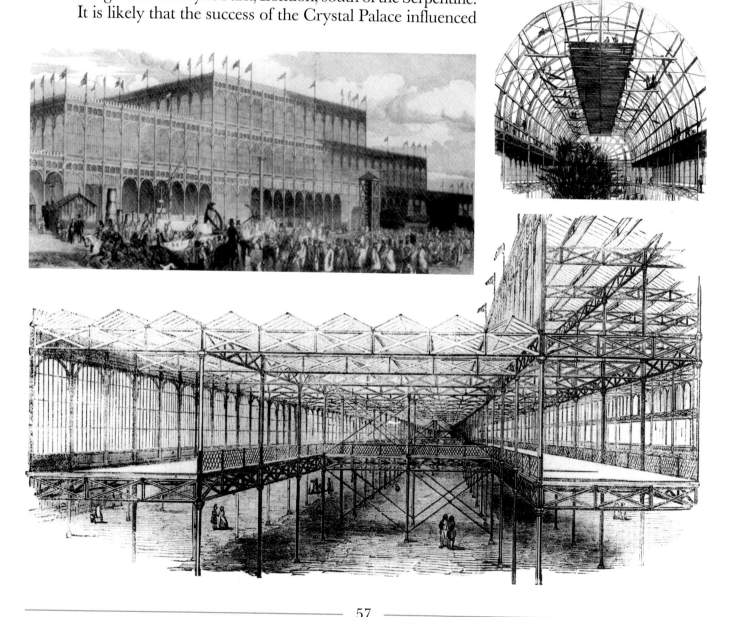

This page, right, *Paddington Station, London;* below, *St Pancras Station, London; and* bottom, *King's Cross Station today, fronted by its modern booking hall*

Facing page, top left, *King's Cross Station as first built;* top right, *the Grand Hall, Euston Station, London;* centre left, *Central Station, York; and* centre right, *the steel and glass concourse of Pennsylvania Station, New York, 1902–11, by McKim, Mead and White*

the twin train sheds, one for arrivals and one for departures, at King's Cross Station, 1850–52, by Lewis Cubitt and the engineer Joseph Cubitt. The span here was 32.03m (105ft). The ribs at King's Cross were made originally of laminated wood as at the Great Stove. They had to be replaced in 1869–70 by steel ribs, though these were housed in the original decorative cast-iron shoes.

Matthew Digby Wyatt, who had previously been employed as superintendent architect at Crystal Palace, designed Paddington Station, 1852–54, with Isambard Kingdom Brunel. Its three train sheds have arched roofs of wrought iron 20.74m, 31.11m, 21.96m, (68ft, 102ft and 72ft) wide. These were linked by two transepts which formed a path for the locomotives to be turned around, accentuating the length and breadth of the vast hall. The columns at Paddington are octagonal with Saracenic motifs.

The success of the span at Kew also encouraged twin sheds

Facing page, bottom left, *the Roundhouse, Camden Town engine shed; and* bottom right: *the former Gare d'Orsay (Orsay Station), Paris. Built in 1900 by Victor Laloux, it was converted to an art museum following plans drawn up in 1973*

Glasshouses

Euston Station, London, 1835–39, by Robert Stephenson; its central span was 12.2m (40ft)

Derby Tri-junct Station, 1839–41, by Robert Stephenson assisted by Francis Thompson; three tie-beam, cast-iron sheds, the central one having a span of 17.08m (56ft)

Winter Garden, Regents Park, London, 1840–46, by Richard Turner for the Botanic Society of London (demolished); a huge structure 96.08 x 50.33m (315ft x 165ft) covering 1,767m² (19,000 sq ft) with curving roofs supported on cast-iron columns and heated by 100mm (4in) pipes

Palm House, Glasnevin near Dublin, 1843, by Richard Turner for the Royal Dublin Society; a large rectangular central building articulated by glazed pilasters, linked to lower houses with rounded ends covered by curving roofs which swept down from a centrepiece of Greek floral design

New Street Station, Birmingham 1850–54 by E A Cowper and William Baker (demolished); 329.4m (1,080ft) long with a 64.36m (211ft) span. Sickle girders were used, which each weighed 25 tons

Manchester Central Station, 1876–80, by Sir John Fowler, where the arch is supported by brick buttresses without tie-bars

with a circular plan, such as that at Gorton, *c.* 1845, by Richard Peacock and the engineer Alfred S Jee for the Sheffield and Manchester Railway. They based a cast-iron structure on a central column with radiating bars to support a straightforward tie-beam roof. The Roundhouse, the Camden Town engine shed by Robert B Dockray, followed in 1847. Stephenson was consulted on this, which with a diameter of 48.8m (160ft) was not only much bigger but also architecturally more satisfying than Gorton. Its outer walls of light-yellow bricks were reinforced by buttresses, and the roof was supported on 24 cast-iron pillars arranged in an inner circle of 12.2m (40ft) diameter.

The world's largest single arched structure by 1865, and the most spectacular, was William Barlow's St Pancras train shed. Its span of 74.12m (243ft) was constructed from a lattice of wrought-iron ribs which rise in an elegant curve from the level of the platforms to meet in a point. The shed is 210.15m (689ft) long and rises to a height of 30.5m (100ft). It has tie bars that connect the spring lines of the arch concealed beneath the rail deck.

Iron architecture reached its climax with the Paris *Exposition Universelle* of 1889, where a Machinery Hall (now demolished) was constructed for industrial exhibits. The hall was a pure three-part arch, akin to that employed by Johann Wilhelm Schwedler in 1863 for his Berlin furnace house for the Imperial Continental Gas Association. It was 420m (1,378ft) long, with a ridge height of 43.5m (142.72ft) and a span of 115m (377.32ft), and covered a surface area of 46,000m² (495,144sq ft) without supports.

Right and far right: the Machinery Hall by Victor Contamin and Charles-Louis-Ferdinand Dutert ranks among the most important iron constructions of the nineteenth century

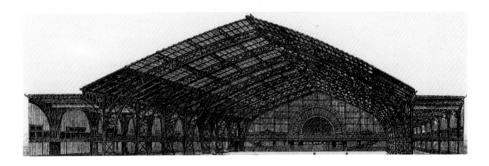

Below: Taut's Glass Pavilion

Bruno Taut (1880–1938) had a passionate deep-rooted belief in the advantages of glass, a material which he thought expressed a new self-awareness in mankind that would eventually rid the world of evil. He built the fantastic Glass Pavilion, which he said had been designed in the spirit of a Gothic cathedral, on behalf of the glass industry for the 1914 Deutscher Werkbund Exhibition in Köln. It was a pineapple-shaped, multi-faceted glass dome of rhomboid prisms set in a spaceframe, rising from a 14-sided base of glass bricks. The prisms were faced with coloured glass on the inside of the seven-tiered chamber, where there was an ambitious cascade of water animated by the play of coloured lights from a kaleidoscope.

The Eiffel Tower under construction; above, *in May 1888;* below, *July 1888;* and bottom, *September 1888*

The show-stopper of the Paris *Exposition Universelle* of 1889 was the Eiffel Tower, a structure that required 12,000 drawings to represent every section and every iron strut in two-dimensional form, and more than one million rivets to build, all of which were driven in by hand.

Gustav Eiffel drew up the plan in collaboration with the engineers Nougier and Koechlin, both members of his staff, who supplied the preliminary drawings. These drawings were made after meticulously accurate calculations were made, using logarithms, for the position of every individual rivet hole. The tolerances for these holes were calculated to one-tenth of a millimetre.

The sides of the square base area of the tower were 129.22m (423.97ft) long. The first platform, the four sides of which measured 65 x 65m (213.27 x 213.27ft), was constructed at a height of 57.63m (189.08ft). On this platform were situated four restaurants and twelve sales stands. A second platform was positioned at 115.73m (379.71ft). It was similarly square-shaped but with sides of 30m (998.43ft). At 276.13m (905.98ft) there is a third platform of 16.5 x 16.5m (54.14 x 54.14ft), a lookout from which it is possible to see a distance of 140km (86.94 miles) on a clear day.

This astonishing monument to its age and to the (then) prevailing high-tech building material, iron, was erected in a mere two years and two months and yet has become universally the symbol of Paris, and indeed of France.

Right: *the finished article in May 1889 and,* far right, *with a few days to go before the end of the millennium*

Factories, mills and warehouses

The picturesque Gothic style flowered in England from the 1840s, when it was most popular with the church architects. It established some favour among the country-house designers but failed to do so in the industrial building sector, with very few factories or warehouses displaying Gothic features.

In the early nineteenth century the style had featured in some essentially Palladian structures, though serving merely as decoration such as at Castle Grinding Mill, Sheffield, which was given a medieval air simply by the addition of turrets.

Left: *the Castle Grinding Mill, Sheffield*

Perhaps it was because the picturesque Gothic required irregular and intricate compositions that it held little attraction for the designers of factories and warehouses, where needs were easily satisfied by simple box-like structures of regular dimensions, certainly in the early years of industrialisation. Perhaps also it was the association of the Gothic style with Augustus Welby Northmore Pugin that dissuaded architects from adopting it when building mills and warehouses. Pugin had stirred things up a little with his publications, in which he argued that pointed architecture should be the basis of all true church architecture. In his later publications he even specifically accused the factory builders of aspiring to a lofty elevation far above the use to which the building was put. Whether or not we blame Pugin for it, there is very little industrial architecture in the picturesque Gothic style worthy of note.

Another of Pugin's overriding ideas was his insistence on sound structure, that the appropriate materials should be used, and that they should suit the design. He advocated the use of stone for non-ecclesiastical architecture, particularly in buildings of heavy mass. Demand for these was an aspect of the 1840s and the adoption of his 'advice' can be seen in Jesse Hartley's Albert Dock, Liverpool, 1841–45, where Pugin's ideas are expressed.

The Albert Dock covered 2.84ha (7 acres) and was comprised of a non-tidal basin surrounded on all four sides by fireproof brick warehouses. These were built with groups of Greek Doric cast-iron columns supported beams carrying the four floors above. Between the groups of columns, brick arches rose to the height of the first storey. Hartley was also responsible for the Stanley Dock, 1850–57, where a row of warehouses was of similar external appearance to those at the Albert Dock, also being five-storey buildings of iron and brick.

Below: *the Albert Dock, Liverpool, 1841–45, was surrounded on all sides by fireproof brick warehouses*

The origins of the Gothic revival lay in the eighteenth century but it attained its fullest development in the third quarter of the ninteenth century, when it influenced a whole range of buildings, painting, literature and social attitudes. Coincidentally during the same period, Britain's industrial performance reached its zenith. It was a time when demand for factory and warehouse premises rose to a new level, while there were also sufficient funds available with which to pay for quality materials and craftsmanship.

Whereas Pugin's ideas had influenced the ecclesiastical Gothic revival earlier in the century, now it was the published works of John Ruskin that influenced such builders as William Butterfield, George Edmund Street and Sir George Gilbert Scott. Although they were not themselves much concerned with industrial architecture, their creativity and practice did permeate down.

The theories of Ruskin and his contemporaries were based on a refusal to accept a rigid hierarchy in building. In contrast to the Ecclesiologists, they argued in favour of the Italian medieval style as opposed to the patriotic northern Gothic. They advocated the application of the Gothic style to much more than Pugin's churches, and held that buildings should be made with due attention to their operation and to the materials chosen, stating that 'all good architecture is the expression of national life and character'.

Fortunately there were now, in the mid-nineteenth century, enough architects in the country practising in an increasingly organised profession for the beliefs of the individual architect not to be unduly pervasive. The Institute of British Architects had been formed in 1834 and in 1862 was amalgamated with the provincial societies in a general organisation. Hence large commissions for mills and warehouses became worthy of attention as a means of attracting notice, opening up contracts for all manner of architectural work to competition on both price and reputation. Furthermore the industialists were increasingly well-educated men, some of whom wanted to participate in the designs of their buildings. Another consideration was that the outward appearance of such buildings was important symbolically, even if only as a means of impressing the shareholders.

It was also at this time that the use of colour increased, inspired by Ruskin and his contemporaries. The application of polychromy in Italian architecture was making its mark, and the demand for different coloured bricks and the wider application of various stones was now far more easy to fulfill because of improved access offered by the development of the railways. The high Victorian period therefore yielded a range of very interesting buildings.

Lavers & Barraud's Painted-Glass Manufactory, 22 Endell Street, London, 1859–60, by Robert Jewell Withers, was Gothic in style but effected in a variety of materials that included red, black and yellow bricks and Bath stone dressings. The London Printing & Publishing Co, Smithfield, London, 1860, by George Somers Leigh Clarke was a classical composition with Gothic decorative elements. It also used coloured brick, but with Cheesewring granite and Bath stone. It had an internal framework of cast-iron beams and columns, a feature that was to become more common as architects rebelled against the show of iron, a tool of the engineer. Although they were happy to utilise the strength of iron, and later steel, in their structures, they were at pains to conceal it behind masonry or brick walls.

Mills were not commonly built in the Gothic style although quite naturally there are some notable exceptions. These include the Anglo-Scotian Mill, Beeston, 1871, a castellated red-brick factory which had lancet windows, a central stepped gable, turrets and arrow loops. Far more impressive was the Venetian Gothic style used in constructing Templeton's carpet factory, Glasgow, 1889, by William Leiper. A large-scale mill, it owed much to the high Victorian movement and was said to have been based on the Doge's Palace, Venice, having an extravagant façade of red, light-green and cream bricks, and blue glass mosaic in the windows. It boasted

Italianate factories and mills 1855–1900

Highgate Mills, Clayton Heights, Yorkshire, enlarged 1851 and 1862 with a grand dressed stone entrance added in 1865

T Houldsworth & Co's Mills, Reddish, Lancashire, 1865, by Abraham Henthorn Scott; a very large brick building divided into three sections by twin Italianate staircase towers. The central nine-bay block was surmounted by a clock pediment. Each of the bays was linked vertically by pilasters

Messrs Rylands & Sons' Gidlow Works, Wigan, 1865, by George Woodhouse; a three-storey mill in red, blue and cream bricks 119.56m (392ft) long and 32.94m (108ft) wide, with Italianate towers

Messrs Listers' Manningham Mills, Patent Street, Bradford, 1871–73, by Thomas G Andrews and Joseph Pepper; six storeys high in dressed stone topped by an ornamental and panelled parapet. There was a staircase in the front which stood proud of the main walls. Its campanile-style chimney rose to 75.95m (249ft) and this gradually widened towards the top internally. Each floor had concrete arching resting on iron beams supported on massive iron pillars. The internal staircases were of stone and the window frames of cast iron, all of which created as fireproof a building as possible. There were good lighting and ventilation to the rooms, and proper sanitary arrangements were provided by the enlightened mill owners

Industrial buildings in the high Victorian Gothic style 1855–1900

John Perry carriage factory, 194 Stokes Croft, Bristol, 1862, by E W Godwin; based on medieval Florentine buildings, with subtly contrasting coloured stones

Skilbeck's drysalters' warehouse, 46 Upper Thames Street, London, 1865–66 remodelling, by William Burges; a medieval composition with a ground floor entrance supported by an exposed wrought-iron beam. The pointed gables were enlivened by sculptures relevant to the company's business. The building was regarded as a major success in the adaptation of Gothic for commercial premises

Messrs Hill, Evans & Co vinegar warehouse, 33–35 Eastcheap, London, 1868, by R L Roumieu; French Gothic five-storey warehouse and offices, richly ornamented exterior of red and blue bricks and Tisbury stone dressings

Wait & James' Granary, Welsh Back, Bristol, 1869 by Archibald Ponton and William Gough; a splendidly detailed polychrome warehouse in castellated Florentine style, it was capable of storing 125 tonnes of grain. The various brick perforations below the window openings provided ventilation

Abbey Cloth Mill, Bradford-on-Avon, 1875, by Richard Gane who used masonry blocks and fortress-like fenestration combined with narrow columns of pointed windows to provide an imposing medieval image

Doulton Pottery Works, Lambeth, London, 1876–77, by Waring & Nicholson and R Stark Wilkinson; a large building in Venetian Gothic with colourful decorative elements in blue Staffordshire and red Fareham bricks, complemented by red-and-buff dressings of terracotta. Its chimney, 71.07m (233ft) high, was based on the campanile of the Palazzo Vecchio, Florence

Paint warehouse, Tradeston Street, Glasgow, 1900, by William F McGibbon. A red-brick variation of the Bargello, Florence, with a square corner tower complete with quatrefoils, battlements and machicolations

High Victorian office buildings

Printing and Publishing Co, West Smithfield, London, 1860 (demolished very soon afterwards), by George Somers Leigh Clarke; smooth, solid brickwork elevations with brick polychromy

59–61 Mark Lane, London, 1864, by George Aitchison Jnr; three storeys of round-arched arcades, above a ground floor with segment-headed windows

General Credit and Discount Co, Lothbury, London, 1866, by George Somers Leigh Clarke; windows and decorative motifs derived from Venetian Gothic. The roof is slightly pitched with large ornate chimneys

Mappin and Webb, Queen Victoria Street, London, 1870, by J and J Belcher; in the Gothic arcaded mode

Albert Buildings, 39–49 Queen Victoria Street, London, 1871, by F J Ward; also Gothic arcaded but with the arcades continuing around all the main façades. It has bold Italian medieval style cornices

Iron and steel-framed buildings

Royal Navy Foundry ship-fitting shop and boat store, Sheerness, Kent, 1858–60, by Col Godfrey Green; considered to show the first use of simple H-section columns and beams

Chocolat Menier factory, Noisel-sur-Marne, France, 1871–72, by Jules Saulnier; considered to be the first factory built with an unconcealed iron skeleton

Home Insurance Building, Chicago, USA, 1883–85 (demolished 1929) by William Le Baron Jenney; used steel beams in the upper four storeys of a nine-storey building, with cast iron columns used for interior and exterior walls. Although the beams were to have been of wrought iron, Bessemer steel was substituted for some of them

Sears, Roebuck & Co's Leiter Building, Chicago, 1889–90 (*illustrated right*, demolished 1972) by William Le Baron Jenney and W B Mundie (1863–1939); the first entirely steel-framed building

Great Northern Railway Goods warehouse, Watson Street, Manchester *c.* 1895–98; a five-storey building with an internal frame of steel box-pillars and beams but with solid brick outer walls

Robinson's Emporium, West Hartlepool, 1896, by Daniel Scott. Britain's first example of a completely steel-framed building

Ritz Hotel, London, 1903–06, by Mewès and Davis; London's first major steel-framed building

Ornate Italianate chimneys

Messrs Townsend's Alkali Works, Port Dundas, 1857–59, by Duncan Macfarlane; its brick chimney, circular in section, rose to 138.47m (454ft)

Camperdown Linen Works, Lochee, Dundee, 1865–66, by James MacLaren; ornate chimney based on a Renaissance campanile. Known as 'Cox's Stalk', it rose to 86.01m (282ft) and consisted of two principal sections, a square tower of bands of red and white brick supporting an upper octagon. An ornamental iron balcony was placed at their meeting point

Sir Titus Salt's Saltair Mills, Yorkshire, 1851, by Lockwood and Mawson; in 1868 the original chimney was replaced by a copy of the bell tower of Santa Maria Gloriosa, Venice

Washer Lane Dyeworks, Halifax, 1871–75, by Isaac Booth; originally had a conventional chimney, remodelled by Richard Swarbrick Dugdale. He incorporated balustraded balconies, surmounted by a lantern dome and finale. Eventually was used as a viewing tower, the dyeworks having been sold during its construction. The tower rose to 77.17m (253ft)

Dalton Mills, Keithley, Yorkshire, by Sugden; built in the Roman-Italianate style, it had a staircase that wound around the shaft, up to a balcony near the top

Harding's Tower Works, Leeds, 1899, by William Bakewell; a chimney shaft in red brick, based on Giotto's campanile beside Florence cathedral. The bell louvres, which formed part of the dust extraction plant, were decorated with gilded panels. It stood near an 1864 tower by Thomas Shaw based on the Lamberti Tower, Verona

a whole range of colour and ornament including battlements and fanciful towers. Another adaptation of the Doge's Palace, but on a much smaller scale, was the Fryer and Binyons' warehouse, Manchester, 1856 (now demolished), by Alfred Waterhouse.

The majority of industrial buildings in the second half of the century were Italianate or neoclassical in style and the Gothic, often continental in style, achieved new heights in popularity and variety at a time of much contrast and development. During the high Victorian period the Italianate style became more ornate, and there is no lack of examples. One of the more impressive was the Eccles, Shorrock, Brothers & Co's India Mill, Darwen, 1859–67, by Ernest Bates, a six-storey building measuring 101.57 x 30.2m (333 x 99ft). This housed 67,968 spindles and had a magnificent campanile chimney that rose 94.55m (310ft) into the air, and was constructed of red, white and blue bricks with gritstone dressings. Each of the mill's four corner and two staircase towers rose to a loggia echoing the upper part of the chimney, and the several window forms that it exhibited created an overall effect that contrasted sharply with the simpler factories of earlier in the century.

Many other ornate chimneys were constructed (*see left*); generally during the eighteenth century chimneys had been short and square in plan. They were built higher in order to increase the draught, but because their flat surfaces generated greater levels of wind resistance, these chimneys were made circular in cross-section. This would require the use of specially shaped and therefore more expensive bricks, so a compromise was found in the form of the octagonal tower, although they were never as successful.

Another element in the chimney's design was the effect of noxious gases on the shaft towards its cap. Although it was claimed that ornamented caps were designed so as to assist the chimney's draught, cast-iron coronets were added to combat the corrosive effects of the escaping gases concentrated at the top of the shaft.

Many mills were built during the period: the cotton industry in Oldham alone housed 10.5 million spindles by 1890. Manufacturers wanted to build quickly; basically the mill owner was interested only in the number of spindles necessary to establish a going concern, and no doubt reasoned that ornamentation did not assist in the paying of dividends to shareholders. There was intense competition within the industry, and so the need for a quick return on investment showing on the bottom line of the accounts led to the construction of very few picturesque structures.

The architect thus had to produce designs to a specific budget. It is also true to say that here the prevailing dictates of architectural theory took second place to the practical requirements of the plant. It was therefore easier for the mill owners to turn to an established mill architect such as Abraham Henthorn Scott. His group of family practices claimed to have built 20–30 mills between 1885–88; they also held shares in the majority of those

Above: *the elevation of a staircase tower of Eccles, Shorrock, Brothers & Co six-storey India Mill, Darwen, Lancashire, 1859–67, by Ernest Bates*

companies for whom they built. In this way, the mill owners could have confidence in their architects without having to be concerned with a plethora of details. It was apparently quite normal practice for most of the shareholdings held by the architects to be sold once the mill had entered profitable production.

There are also recorded instances where the architects even acted as speculative builders, such was their confidence and such was the demand for mills towards the end of the nineteenth century.

Meanwhile, it is worth detailing some of the technical advances being made in mill architecture. Steel joists and concrete were being used in constructing some more fireproof and watertight floors, while other fireproof floors were built of rolled-iron girders with an unusual arch construction supported by brackets attached to the pillars, thus allowing broader windows. Brick window arches had been rejected, in favour of iron lintels bolted between the brick piers and flush with the level of the ceiling, to admit the maximum amount of daylight. The large increase in the area of glass being used meant that any ornamentation was more or less limited to the corners and the staircase towers.

Hollow cast-iron columns were common by the 1880s. They were spaced about 6.41m (21ft) apart, held together laterally by wrought-iron tie rods and cast-iron attached ribs, and supported cast-iron beams. The ceiling would be formed of brick arches covered by concrete to form a flat surface for the floor boards. The arch of the brick ceiling corresponded with the top of the windows.

Concrete floors became increasingly common in the 1890s as replacements for brick arches because they were quicker to build and more compact, while cast-iron beams were giving way to beams of wrought iron or steel. Mill development during the period was thus more concerned with technical considerations of construction rather than the application of styles or aesthetic ideas.

Edwardian industrial architecture

The preceding Victorian era had its underlying Gothic trend and the later emergence of Italian-derived treatments that could be readily identified and explained, whereas it is not easy to define any one style which characterised the short Edwardian era. If anything, the period produced a more diverse and searching approach which sowed the seeds of the modern movement.

While architects in the later Victorian period were prepared to utilise iron and steel in their constructions, yet they had been at pains to conceal its use within masonry. The new century saw the slow introduction of rationalism, defined as the expression of a steel or concrete structure in a building's outward form, in British industrial buildings. It had already appeared sporadically throughout the nineteenth century in miscellaneous buildings.

Cheap steel was available during the last two decades of the nineteenth century, although in Europe architects exhibited a reluctance to specify it, and it was left to the Americans to exploit its properties. The first entirely steel-frame building appeared in Chicago in 1890, and in 1892 the same city claimed the twenty-two storey Masonic Building (demolished 1931) by Burnham and Root as the tallest building in the world. It was to be another two years before New York built its first skyscrapers.

The use of steel skeletons for buildings coincided with extensive experiments with reinforced concrete. However, in this case the innovation was spearheaded by the French, with the first reinforced concrete factory being the Charles Six Spinning Mill, Tourcoing, 1895, by François Hennébique, which was built on the post and beam system.

Facing page, top: *one of Sir Robert Rawlinson's ornate chimney designs; and* bottom, *the Manhattan Building, Chicago, 1891, by William Le Baron Jenney, was one of the first tall buildings to use skeleton construction throughout, and was the world's first set-back skyscraper*

Left: *Weaver's flour mill in Swansea was the first building in Britain to be constructed using reinforced concrete*

Reinforced concrete

Iron-reinforced concrete was first used by the Parisian builder François Coignet in the 1850s. In 1862, he built his own house in Paris with the roofs and floors reinforced by small wrought-iron I-beams.

The next development came in 1867 when the French gardener, Joseph Monier, patented large flower pots that were made of concrete reinforced by a cage of iron wires. A French builder, François Hennébique, applied Monier's ideas to floors, using iron rods to reinforce concrete beams and slabs. He had been the first to realise that the rods had to be bent upwards to take negative movement near supports, when he set out in 1879 to fireproof a metal-frame house being built in Belgium. Hennébique later became a consultant engineer, advising on many structures with concrete frames composed of columns, beams and slabs.

His work was paralleled in North America by Ernest Ransome, who constructed concrete factory buildings. High-rise concrete structures followed the paradigm of the steel frame.

Britain's first multi-storey reinforced-concrete building was the Weaver & Co flour mill, Swansea, 1897–98, also designed by Hennébique but with Napoleon Le Brun (1821–1901). Although the Edwardian architects had available to them such new materials as steel for beams or reinforced rods and concrete, unfortunately many of them were ill-equipped to exploit these new materials. This was because using them made it necessary to employ the services of an engineer, and between the two professions there was little understanding of each other's art.

The Edwardian period therefore acted as a turning point, a transitional stage from the widespread popular Gothic to a host of styles, and from wrought and cast-iron, bricks and timber to steel and reinforced concrete. Architects had to pioneer construction techniques in order to exploit these new materials but conservative wisdom clung to loadbearing outer walls and the steel frame remained relatively unexploited in Britain. Just as both the USA and Germany stole the manufacturing initiative from Britain towards the end of the nineteenth century, so did their architects produce the most innovative designs for the factories that were constructed in the early years of the twentieth century.

Below: *a drawing of a monolithic concrete construction as used by Hennébique*

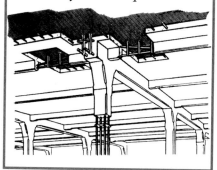

The work of Peter Behrens and Walter Gropius clearly showed the gap that had opened between mainland Europe and the UK, while Albert Kahn's car factories in the USA were also far ahead of contemporary UK practice.

Above: *AEG Turbine Factory Assembly Hall, Berlin, 1908–1909, by Peter Behrens with the engineer Karl Bernhard. The side façade had full-length horizontal girders, with the large glazed areas between them slightly recessed*

Above right: *other commissions undertaken by Behrens for AEG included this High Tension Plant, also in Berlin, 1909–1910, in which a glass-roofed double hall was inserted between the two parallel six-storey wing buildings*

Shops, arcades and stores

The shop front as we know it today has its origins in the Georgian period, with the Burlington Arcade and bazaars such as the Pantheon, Oxford Street, London. In both of these there were a large number of individual shops united within the one building, much like shopping malls or hypermarket complexes now.

Bow-fronted high street shops already had large windows by the early Victorian period, but the first-floor frontage was recessed, so that the shop front was not loadbearing. Using iron supports and better-produced, stronger and cheaper sheets of plate glass enabled the shop front to be taken back flush with the façade of the storey above by mid-century so that the retailer could create a very visible and alluring window display, while at the same time introducing a greater amount of light onto the shop floor.

Facing page, centre: a rear view of the Model Factory, exhibited at the Werkbund Exhibition, Köln, 1914, by Walter Gropius; and, bottom, the Glass Plant, Ford Motor Company, Dearborn, Michigan, 1924, by Albert Kahn. This was one of Kahn's later factories at Dearborn for Ford, with a symmetrical layout of the shed in which there were four furnaces and glazing that could be opened to release any excess heat

Above, left: Burlington Arcade, London, 1819, by Samuel Ware; and, right, the Royal Arcade, London, 1879. The nineteenth century was the great age of the arcade, the covered market and the department store. The arcade, the upmarket development of the shopping street as a glazed internal street, is an invention belonging to Paris and London, then the two richest cities in the world, in the early nineteenth century. Department stores and covered retail markets were the century's re-invention of the market-place. All depended on iron and glass

Left: Les Halles Centrales, Paris, 1853–58, by Victor Baltard (demolished 1971), a great iron and glass market in which tunnel-vaulted avenues connected pavilions

Above: *Galleria Vittorio Emanuele II, Milan, 1877, by Giuseppe Mengoni, which established itself as Europe's grandest arcade; and* below, left and right: *Au Bon Marché department store, Paris, 1876, by Louis-Auguste Boileau, depended on glass and iron to direct light into the middle of the store, as may clearly be seen in both the drawing and the photograph*

Architects were now attracted to the shop unit, and began to apply more detailing such as extra pilasters which were often added to carry a fascia board in order to advertise the shop or the proprietor's name. Ornate stucco-work also enabled a building to stand out and to be more noticeable; the favoured style for this was a rococo revival style.

The arcades had their origins in France, but by the second half of the nineteenth century Italy had developed them to their most splendid form. British arcades were never to emulate those of the warmer Mediterranean regions, but one of Britain's more spectacular buildings, Victoria Buildings in Victoria Street, Manchester, of 1874 by William Daws (now demolished), was a forerunner of the modern shopping centre. This large complex that included a hotel and offices was a triangular building with a spacious glazed courtyard. Not only was the courtyard lined with shops, but also there were shops around the outside.

The department store began to replace the arcade in the mid-nineteenth century, pioneered and promoted by the co-operative societies. Many of the large London stores were an extension of successful drapers' businesses, one of the first of which was the Marshall and Snelgrove store in Oxford Street, 1876, by Sir Horace Jones (now demolished).

The main part of the present Harrods store, Brompton Road, Knightsbridge, London, was built by Stevens and Hunt 1901–05, and its exterior is faced entirely with Doulton's yellow terracotta. Inside, the store had installed Britain's first public escalator, in 1898. This sensational novelty prompted the store to position an assistant at the top of the escalator, primed to offer a glass of brandy to customers in order to restore their shattered nerves. In addition, the store provided a variety of restaurants and a hairdressers.

Above left: *the interior of the Charles Jenner & Co department store, Edinburgh, 1895, by W H Beattie*

Above right: *A l'Innovation department store, Brussels, 1900–03 (demolished 1967), thought to be one of Victor Horta's masterpieces*

Below: *the Carson Pirie Scott and Company Store, Chicago, 1899–1904, by Louis H Sullivan, originally only nine storeys high*

Chapter Six

Government and Institutional Buildings

Halls, exchanges, law courts and markets

THE MUNICIPAL CORPORATIONS ACT of 1835 signalled the beginning of a more efficient and more democratic town administration, although the initiative remained largely with the town committees and with ratepayers. Thus there existed a great deal of civic pride and rivalry, and just as the rivalry between the trading cities of Italy led to their beautiful cathedrals, so the town halls or exchanges, especially in the north of England, fostered large and ornate civic buildings.

These buildings were intended to serve a variety of different functions and thus required a variety of different rooms: large halls for public meetings and concerts, municipal offices for officials such as the town clerk and treasurer, and a council chamber. Town halls of the smaller towns also housed the courts, in addition to these.

Probably most of the new industrial towns already had town halls by 1820, mostly in the Greek revival style and rapidly becoming old fashioned, and soon they were to be outshone by their Victorian successors in a variety of styles. The protagonist of this new civic pride was unquestionably the city of Birmingham. A competition was advertised in 1830 and won by the enigmatic Joseph Hansom; building of the Town Hall began in 1832. Its style is classical and it is completely surrounded by Corinthian columns. It stands in isolation in the centre of an area that once included the Midland Institute and Public Library which housed the first Museum (1855 by E M Barry and now demolished) and the Council House (1874 by Yeoville Thomason), which extends back along Congreve Street where the City Museum and Art Gallery were built in the 1880s by Thomason. The area also includes 'Big Brum', a Renaissance version of Big Ben, and the Post Office of 1891, by Sir Henry Tanner. Further civic buildings

Facing page: *the interior of the University Museum, Oxford, 1855–60, by Sir Thomas Deane and Benjamin Woodward. Here, Woodward tried to develop the idea of a glazed courtyard on a large scale, with delicate Gothic ironwork*

Below: *Birmingham Town Hall, which was completed in 1835*

Above: *'Big Brum', with the City Museum and Art Gallery to the right and behind them the dome of the Council House*

Below: *Manchester Town Hall, with Albert Square on the right, symbolized the new opulence of the city*

in the classical style were to follow in the other industrial towns of the midlands and the north of England.

Meanwhile, a competition for the design of a new Town Hall in Manchester was held in 1867. The result of this was that Alfred Waterhouse obtained a commission for a building that was erected in 1868–77. It was composed entirely of municipal offices, apart from the great public hall, the hall itself being sited in the centre as a quasi-independent structure around which he grouped three wings. Waterhouse's thoughtful design on this irregular site was influential insofar as much of the later Victorian picturesque aesthetic, and the idea of flexible planning, are based upon it. In Liverpool, the third of England's large-city rivals outside of the capital, there was already a prominent eighteenth-century town hall. The city fathers decided therefore to construct a new 'forum' to the east of the town centre, on a sloping area called the plateau. Here they built St George's Hall, a large and splendid building which forms an epitaph to neoclassicism in Britain and that incorporates a public hall, courts and a concert hall.

The public hall occupies the centre of the building, and is flanked by two courts, with the concert hall located at the northern end. A huge portico of sixteen Corinthian columns marks the main entrance, which faces Lime Street station. The Corinthian order is continued to each side of the portico by square pillars, behind which are the halls of the two courts. Internally the hall is no less splendid, with red granite columns supporting part of the elaborately coffered vault and a richness of detail and colouring.

This forum complex, which is a masterpiece of sophisticated planning, includes such other buildings as the Picton Reading Room, 1874, and the Walker Art Gallery, 1875, both by Cornelius Sherlock; the William Brown Library and Museum, 1875, by Thomas Allom; the Sessions House, 1882, by F and G Holme, and the College of Technology, 1896–1902, by Edward William Mountford.

In order not to be outdone by Liverpool, Leeds built a Town Hall, 1853–58, by Cuthbert Brodrick. Its giant Corinthian order is topped by a deep cornice running right around the building to form rectangular façades on all four sides of its square plan. Urns dot the top balustrade above each of the serried columns. Above all, the central clock tower with its Corinthian colonnade is crowned with a dome of European baroque style. Its main entrance is recessed behind a row of columns and inside much of the space is occupied by the Great Hall, which in yet another attempt to outpoint Liverpool has double rows of columns supporting its vaulted roof.

Leeds had many imitators, among them two of the most impressive classical civic structures of the Victorian period: Bolton Town Hall, 1866–73, and Portsmouth Guildhall, 1886–90. Both were designed by William Hill and both buildings were constructed on a square plan with their elevations consisting mainly of a giant Corinthian order with a clock tower above the entrance.

The aspiration to a magnificent town hall was not exclusively the preserve of the cities; for example, the town of Todmorden, Yorkshire, built a magnificent Town Hall in 1860–75 by John Gibson. The template for the Todmorden building was a simplified copy of St George's Hall, a plain rectangle with an apse at one end being surrounded by a giant attached Corinthian order.

Such ambitions did not really cross the border into Scotland. Glasgow, which is a city rich in Victorian architecture, already had its civic panoply comprising the Royal Exchange (later Stirling's Library), 1828–30, by David Hamilton and the County Buildings and Courthouses, Wilson Street, 1842–71, by Clarke and Bell, so there was no rush to invest in further buildings. However, when St Andrew's Hall was built by James Sellars for the city in 1873, it was graced by a building in the geometric neoclassicism of the very early nineteenth century. Later still came the Glasgow City Chambers in George Square of 1883–85, by William Young. Here there are vague resemblances to the Leeds group, with a central tower set back behind the main entrance portico, but the elevations follow sixteenth-century Italian precedents.

Whereas the larger English cities and many towns also followed the classical path others followed the Gothic style, possibly in an attempt to associate themselves with the New Palace of Westminster, known to most of us as the Houses of Parliament. The old Palace had been burnt on 16 October 1834, from which conflagration only the Westminster Hall and the cloisters and undercroft of St Stephen's Chapel had survived. Following the decision to rebuild on the same site in 1835, the rules of the competition for a new building stipulated that only the Gothic or Elizabethan styles were deemed appropriate for a great national monument. This restriction provides a sure indication of the strength of the tradition of associational architecture that had developed in the eighteenth century.

Facing page, right: *the exterior of St George's Hall, Liverpool, 1839–40, by Harvey Lonsdale Elmes*

Right: *an early design for the Palace of Westminster, by Charles Barry*

Below: *Big Ben; the soubriquet was originally given to the Great Bell of Westminster, and has since been extended to include the bell, clock and St Stephen's Tower of the Houses of Parliament. The clock and bell became operational on 31 May 1859*

There were 97 entries to the competition, of which 91 were designs in the Gothic style. Charles Barry won the competition with a series of drawings executed with the help of the young Pugin. The foundations of Barry's great building were begun in 1837 and the first stone of the superstructure was laid in 1840. The House of Lords was opened in 1847, the clock tower completed in 1858, the Victoria Tower in 1860 (the same year as Barry's death), with the work continuing in the 1860s under the direction of Barry's son, Edward Middleton Barry. Eventually the building cost almost three times the estimated amount, reaching a total of £2m. The symbolic potency of this particular building, however, far outweighed its architectural influence in those days of an extensive British Empire.

Both its plan and its elevations emphasise Gothic drama and classic planning. An enclosed porch to the south of Westminster Hall leads through a gallery, which is on the site of St Stephen's Chapel, to the central lobby. From here the main axis runs at right angles, and contains lobbies, the House of Lords and the Royal Gallery to the right, while to the left are more lobbies, the House of Commons and Big Ben. The river front runs parallel to the main axis and contains libraries and committee rooms that overlook a terrace.

Externally a regular fenestration is carried around the building regardless of the internal spatial arrangement, and the pinnacles and numerous turrets help a rather unclassical appearance. We owe a debt to Pugin for the abundance of decorative detail. He produced sheaves of designs, claiming that over 2,000 were made for the House of Lords alone. These included designs for metalwork, tiles, woodwork, furniture, wallpaper and even inkwells and calendars; it should be no surprise that he died from overwork and nervous strain at the age of 40, in September 1852.

Before the emergence of the high Victorian Gothic style, only one other major public building echoed the style of the Houses of Parliament. This was the unremarkable Public Record Office, Chancery Lane, London, 1851–59, by Sir James Pennethorne.

Left: *the river façade of the Palace of Westminster, which contains the Commons' and Lords' libraries, separated by committee rooms. Big Ben is on the right, the entrance porch on the opposite side of the building*

The Palace of Westminster had little other immediate influence over the style of either public or major civic buildings, as by the time it had been completed already it was deemed to be old fashioned by the eminent architects of the day, although there were undeniably many copies of the clock tower. The Palace had been built in what many now regard as a restrictive English Perpendicular style, at a time when a wider palette was being sought that permitted French, German and Italian Gothic influences on style. Similarly there was a desire to combine materials such as marble and brick with classical elements such as mansard roofs.

The most eminent example of this move to the high Victorian Gothic in public buildings outside London is the University Museum (now the Oxford University Museum of Natural History). In London, although a competition for the building had been held and designs selected in 1856, political argument and government changes resulted in such delay and alterations to the much-needed Foreign Office that building work did not commence until 1862.

Left: *the building originally known as the University Museum, Oxford, 1855–60, by Deane and Woodward; another Gothic building but of very different character to that of the Palace of Westminster. Its high slate roof and the metal finial that crowns the central tower are of French / Flemish influence, while the constructional polychromy is Italian Gothic. Woodward developed the idea of an internal glazed courtyard on a large scale, which is both functional and decorative* (pictures pp 74, 92)

Sir George Gilbert Scott's eventual compromise for the Foreign Office was an Italian sixteenth-century Renaissance style, with the buildings grouped around courtyards. The façades are in Portland stone with coloured granite. It was an influential design that led to Scott being awarded the commission for St Pancras Station Hotel, for many the most successful high Victorian building.

Following this success, Scott was chosen by the Queen to design the memorial to her beloved Albert, who had died in 1861.

Right: *St Pancras Station Hotel*

Far right: *London's Albert Memorial during restoration, which took seven years to complete at a cost of £11 million. The 61m (200ft) Memorial, by Sir George Gilbert Scott, was originally unveiled in 1872; following its repair, the Memorial was formally reopened by Queen Elizabeth II on 21 October 1998*

Right, *The Guildhall, Broad Street, Bristol, and* far right, *its Small Street entrance*

Although Scott vigorously advocated Gothic for civic buildings, and more specifically the Gothic of Italy, Germany and the Low Countries, prior to his Foreign Office there had been very little civic Gothic architecture in Victorian England. One major exception that still remains perhaps is the Guildhall, Broad Street, Bristol, 1843, by Richard Shackleton Pope. Also, Sir George Gilbert Scott did build the Town Hall at Preston, Lancashire, 1862 (now demolished), but by this time some of the younger architects whom he had influenced were more vigorously challenging for the few commissions that were being offered.

One such large commission, won through a competition by Alfred Waterhouse, was that for the Manchester Town Hall, 1868–77. Here, apart from the obligatory great public hall which has an elaborate hammerbeam roof and frescoes by Ford Maddox Brown, the entire building is taken up by municipal offices. The structure is of triangular plan with the front wing, which contains the main entrance under a clock tower, to Albert Square. The windows vary both in size, although they are often large, and in type. There are many bay windows, and the outline is further enlivened by gables and chimneys. Manchester also benefitted from the works of Thomas Worthington who, like Waterhouse, practised the combination of Gothic expression and practicality. His most important contribution was the Police Court (now Magistrates' Court), Bloom Street, 1867–71, with its 'Big Ben' type clock tower.

New Gothic buildings were becoming rarer by the late 1870s, with late Victorian mixed styles more prominent. One of the last very ornate provincial civic Gothic buildings was the Town Hall at Middlesborough, 1883–89, by G O Hoskins, the Royal Courts of Justice being the capital's last great monument in the style.

Other town halls, exchanges and markets

in classic style
Corn Exchange, Diss, Norfolk, 1854, by George Atkins
Loughborough Town Hall, 1854–55, by William Slater
Halifax Town Hall, 1859–63, by Sir Charles Barry
Municipal Offices, Liverpool, 1860–66, by John Weightman and E R Robson
Corn Exchange, Leeds, 1861–63, by Cuthbert Brodrick
Mechanics' Institute (*now* Art School), Leeds, 1865, by Broderick
Exchange Building, Liverpool, 1865, by Thomas Henry Wyatt
Royal Exchange, Manchester, 1869–74, by the firm of Mills and Murgatroyd

in Gothic style
Assize Courts, Manchester, 1859–64 by Alfred Waterhouse (now demolished)
Northampton Town Hall, 1860, by Edward Godwin
Chester Town Hall, 1864, by William Henry Lynn
The Exchange, Bradford, 1864–67, by Lockwood and Mawson
Town Hall, Rochdale, Lancashire, 1866–71, by W H Crossland
Town Hall, Bradford, 1869–73, by the firm of Lockwood and Mawson
Town Hall, Barrow-in-Furness, Lancashire, 1878–87, by William Henry Lynn

in late Victorian style
Sheffield Town Hall, 1890–97, by Edward William Mountford
Oxford Town Hall, 1893–97, by Henry Thomas Hare

Left: *Manchester Assize Courts, 1859–64, by Alfred Waterhouse, were opened for the holding of criminal and civil trials in the Hundred of Salford, following Manchester's elevation to the status of a city by royal charter in 1853*

Above: *the Royal Courts of Justice, London*

Below: *the Great Hall of the Victoria Assize Courts, Birmingham, 1886–91, by Aston Webb and Ingress Bell*

The competition for the Royal Courts of Justice, held in 1866, had brought forth only Gothic designs and was won by George Edmund Street. Building work had begun in 1874, but the architect had died before the building was completed in 1882, and it was necessary for his son, A E Street, together with Arthur Blomfield, to supervise the final stages.

The freer styles of the late Victorian period were quickly accepted. Styles such as the Queen Anne revival combined elements of outward form, in this case English renaissance, with a relaxed planning, with the function being more fully expressed through the materials that were used. An early example of this informality can be seen in Leicester Town Hall, 1874–76, by F J Hames. It was constructed in warm red brick with some buff stone details. The sash windows have wooden frames, and when these are painted white their large size creates an impression of domestic informality in this public building.

Another town hall with characteristically large windows is at Wakefield, Yorkshire, 1877, by Thomas Edward Collcutt, though here there are three oriels with rounded corners. They extend three storeys into the roof and terminate in Jacobean gables.

The culmination of this late Victorian montage of styles appears in one of the finest civic structures of the 1880s. The Victoria Assize Courts, Birmingham, 1886–91, by Aston Webb and Ingress Bell, is furnished in terracotta and brick and has a profusion of styles both inside and out, all nestling side by side.

Such 'free styles', however, by the 1890s were being spurned by younger architects, as being too whimsical and insincere for public buildings. In reaction, there followed a tendency towards a baroque revival. One early expression of this new attitude was the Battersea Town Hall, London, 1892, by Edward William Mountford where stone dressings are combined with red brickwork in a formal tripartite façade on two storeys. There is a tripartite window in the centre of each block, above which, set in the parapet, is a curving pediment filled with low-relief sculpture.

A later essay in this late Victorian baroque, which is far more successful, is the elaborate composition in brick and stone of Colchester Town Hall, Essex, 1898–1902, by John Belcher. Here the ground floor is faced in Portland stone with banded rustication, and above this giant columns support the triangular central, and two flanking, segmental pediments. The entire façade is a profusion of baroque architectural decoration and allegorical sculpture. Its slender tower, a local landmark, rises from one end.

The very best examples of the style can be seen in Cardiff, where the City Hall by Henry Vaughan Lanchester, James Stewart and Edward Alfred Rickards is part of a civic complex which grew in response to the city's new-found status and its position as the capital of the principality of Wales. Here the elevations of European baroque are quite wonderful.

The City Hall, Cardiff, opened on 29 October 1906, is a symmetrical composition that consists of two-storey buildings surrounding a huge quadrangle. The quadrangle is split in two by the assembly hall. The ground floor is given over mainly to council offices, which also form the lower part of the perimeter rooms at first-floor level. On both floors the perimeter ranges consist of single rooms on the outer face of the building with a corridor around facing into the inner courtyards.

The court to the south, which is sub-divided by the entrance hall, contains the mayor's parlour, various committee rooms, and the council chamber itself in the centre. A clock tower some 59m (194ft) high rises from the centre of the west range. The external skin of the building is constructed in traditional Portland stone ashlar, although the floors are supported on steel stanchions. Steel joists spanning in between are embedded in concrete.

The south façade in particular is lavishly endowed with sculpture, largely allegorical, while the corner pavilions which terminate the main façades support sculpture groups.

Schools and education

Illiteracy was still very widespread when Victoria succeeded to the throne, even though the Church had made noble efforts to provide what it could afford in terms of elementary education. It was not until the Elementary Education Act of 1870 that the great Victorian achievement of an elementary education for all of the nation's children became available, at least in theory. Secondary education remained available only to the more fortunate, while higher education was the preserve of the very few.

At the base of the education system was the parish school, usually comprised of a small house occupied by a single teacher. The instruction was carried out in a single large schoolroom, although sometimes one or two smaller rooms adjoined, for the teaching of smaller groups. Larger parish schools did segregate the boys from the girls, and attempts were made, especially by the clergy, to separate the school from the master's house.

The Church was at the forefront of elementary education, and at the same time promoted the idea that the school building should be the most attractive (after the local church) in town. It also expected the school to be built in the Gothic style, thus it is not surprising that the high Anglican architects such as James Brooks, William Butterfield, George Edmund Street and William White should produce a number of parish school buildings along the same lines of construction and detailing that they had developed for their church architecture.

The parish schools that were built within the larger towns were more constrained in their plot size, and thus multi-storeyed

Above: *the Assize Courts, Small Street, Bristol, 1867, by T S Pope and J Bindon*

Below: *Vine Street, Hulme, 1875, was one of the first Board Schools to be built in Manchester*

Above: *St Giles-in-the-Fields National Schools, London, 1860, by Edward Middleton Barry*

buildings were necessary. One example was the Northern District School, St Martin's-in-the-Fields, London 1849–50, now demolished, by James William Wild. The building was constructed of brick with arcades of Gothic arches. Classrooms were arranged on the first two floors, above which was a covered playground. This tendency to build upwards on the confined town sites was developed by William Butterfield with his All Saints' Choir School, Margaret Street, London, 1850–53, where he included a dormitory, master's study, classroom and refectory. Edward Middleton Barry, meanwhile, opted for five storeys when building the St Giles-in-the-Fields National Schools, Endell Street, London, 1860, which were to accommodate 1,500 pupils on a cramped corner site.

The Elementary Education Act of 1870 resulted in the construction of large numbers of Board Schools, mainly in the more crowded urban areas. One indication of the scale of this building is that there were over 400 such Board schools in London by 1895. The London School Board appointed E R Robson as its first architect, and both his work and his book *School Architecture*, published in 1874, were to became very influential.

Mainly for these reasons, the London Board schools were usually multi-storeyed buildings, constructed from yellow bricks with red brick used as quoins and for dressings. The window frames were wooden, had glazing bars, and were painted white. There were distinctive brick gables and tall chimney stacks, and quite often a crowning bellcote or cupola. It is true to say, however, that outside of London a more Gothic style of design was preferred. Despite the Victorians' tremendous effort to provide universal elementary education during this period, the provision of secondary and tertiary levels of education still remained the preserve of the upper and middle classes as there was no public funding.

The effect of this new-found energy to educate did penetrate upwards, however. The ancient public schools, which had been generally in a state of depression during the eighteenth century, were once again the focus of the provision of a Christian education fit for a gentleman's son. While the existing schools were forced to rebuild and extend, many new schools were founded as demand grew for this type of education. Here, too, Gothic tended to be the predominant style, being promoted by both the Oxford and Cambridge Societies, although later in the period there came a tendency to favour renaissance styles.

Augustus Welby Northmore Pugin promoted a school style that was centred on a large and preferably ornate chapel. This style was followed by most Anglican public boarding schools, where the Gothic chapel was the dominant feature, emphasising the importance of religion in daily life.

The colleges and universities tended traditionally to be arranged around a courtyard. St Augustine's, Canterbury, Kent, begun in 1844 by William Butterfield, was typical of this arrangement. It was founded to train missionaries for overseas work and was part of St Augustine's monastery. Its courtyard is open to one side, the buildings on the other three sides each being afforded emphasis in line with their importance. The chapel and library buildings are the most elaborate.

Of all of the university buildings of the period, it is perhaps William Butterfield's Keble College, Oxford, that best exemplifies the idealism and originality of high Victorian polychromy architecture. Work on the college was begun in 1867 and completed in 1883. Whereas for centuries Oxford's colleges had been built of stone, here, much to the surprise of everyone, Butterfield used red brick. As he explained later, he had wanted to use materials that were both local and of the age, while also being free to design a building devoid of tradition. Although the rooms are arranged around quadrangles in the traditional manner, their composition was different. The hall does not face the entrance gate, but is located on the first floor of a block set at right angles to it. Next to the hall is the library, with a staircase to the upper rooms that is lit by an oriel window.

The chapel, with its elaborate polychromy, faces the library and dominates the entire complex.

Girton, Cambridge's first womens' college, was begun a little later in 1872. Designed by Alfred Waterhouse in a Gothic style with red brick and red terracotta, it was based on the corridor plan. Waterhouse repeated this formula in the colleges that he built

Parish schools

Roman Catholic School, Spetchley, Worcestershire, 1841, by A W N Pugin; red brick with mullioned windows and a gabled roof

Probus School, Cornwall, 1849, by William White; constructed from local granite rubble, with some dressed stone

Inkpen School, Berkshire, 1850, by George Edmund Street; constructed from local flint and red brick, with a few Gothic details, a tiled roof and wooden window frames

School and School House, Boyne Hill, near Maidenhead, 1854, by George Edmund Street; the complex also includes a church, a vicarage and almshouses

Church Preen School, Shropshire, 1870, by Richard Norman Shaw; its tall windows, designed to provide as much light as possible, extend into the roof as dormers

Public schools

King Edward VI, Birmingham, 1833–37, by Sir Charles Barry (demolished); a traditional symmetrical façade was decorated with Perpendicular Gothic motifs by A W N Pugin

Radcliffe College, Leicestershire (parts only), 1843, by A W N Pugin; a massive layout with cloisters, dormitories and outbuildings, all different in plan and elevation and dominated by a large chapel

Lancing College, Sussex, begun in 1854 by R C Carpenter and completed after his death by his son R H Carpenter and William Slater; a restrained Gothic building executed in stone and local flint, essentially early Victorian in detail although the Great Chapel, which was completed much later, is in the early Decorated style

Marlborough, Wiltshire, founded 1843, additions after 1844 by Edward Blore; an existing house altered to the William and Mary style

Wellington College, Berkshire, 1856–59 by John Shaw; in a classical style, the school buildings of red brick with stone dressings being arranged around a courtyard

Left: *Keble College chapel, Oxford, 1867–83, by William Butterfield*

Above right: *the Examination Schools, Oxford, 1876–82, by Sir Thomas Graham Jackson* Facing page, top left: *West Street School, London Fields, c. 1870, by Edward Robert Robson, which boasted terracotta decorative details and Dutch gables, all part of the Queen Anne idiom that became the hallmark of the London Board Schools; and,* top right, *St Nicholas School, Enmore Road, Newbury, 1859, by William Butterfield, which has a tower set back from the two wings between which it stands*

in the north of England, giving rise the term 'red-brick universities'.

Oxford and Cambridge dispensed with the services of Butterfield and Waterhouse respectively as the late Victorian period came on, turning to new architects in search of a less assertive new style. At Oxford, Thomas Graham Jackson built the Examination Schools Building of stone between 1876–82 in a seventeenth-century renaissance style, while Cambridge employed George Gilbert Scott for the new building at Pembroke College, which was in a similar renaissance style.

Possibly the most spectacular of all of the late-Victorian educational establishments is Royal Holloway College, Egham, Surrey, 1879–87, by William H Crossland. In this large building of some 168 x 115m (550 x 376ft), the accommodation for the students and their maids is arranged around two courtyards. The college was constructed by skilled Italian masons in red brick with lavish stone dressings and the glass in the windows of the corner turrets is curved. The overall effect is that of a François I château. One of the few early colleges for women, it was founded by Thomas Holloway, who had made his fortune from patent medicines. He also built an asylum for the mentally ill at Virginia Water, Surrey.

If Royal Holloway, now part of London University, was the most grandiose college building of the Victorian period, then Charles Rennie Mackintosh's Glasgow School of Art was in many ways the most interesting. To its basically symmetrical north front of 1896–99, Mackintosh introduced several asymmetrical elements, such as variations in both the size and shape of the windows. The whole character of the façade is determined by the large studio windows divided by metal mullions and transoms. The centrally-placed doorway has a curved pediment, but to its left there is a bay window with a small turret. The delicate ironwork is *art nouveau*.

Below left: *Wellington College, 1856–59, by John Shaw, was founded as a school for the orphans of officers. It was built in red brick with stone dressings*

Above: *the north front of the School of Art, Glasgow, 1897–1907, by Charles Rennie Mackintosh. One of the finest examples of contempory modernity, it is a complete fusion of aestheticism and the Arts and Crafts movements*

Left: *the grand-ducal Saxon School of Arts and Crafts, Weimar, Germany, 1906, by Henri van de Velde. The large windows recall Mackintosh's Glasgow School of Art*

Workhouses, asylums, hospitals and prisons

Workhouses were reintroduced following the Poor Law Amendment Act of 1834. They were buildings where poor unemployed people could be gainfully employed, and the vast majority of districts and towns had built their workhouses during the first fifteen years that followed the Act.

In the main each was composed of a series of two-storeyed buildings grouped around an open courtyard, and built in a sort of simplified classical style, or a related Tudor or Elizabethan style.

Once the initial rush to comply with the new law was over, a new generation of workhouse began to appear in the 1850s. Workhouses such as that at Winson Green, Birmingham (now the Dudley Road Hospital), 1852, by J J Bateman were large enough to enable the segregation of men, women and children, while providing modern conveniences such as heating by means of hot water pipes and the lighting of individual rooms by gas. The complex also benefitted from having its own infirmary.

Above: *the workhouse at Abingdon, Oxfordshire (now demolished) was the first to be completed after the 1834 Poor Law Amendment Act. It was built to accommodate 500 paupers, at a cost of £9,000. The external walls formed a hexagonal plan: the three main buildings met in the centre to form a Y. At this centre were the governor's rooms, for easy control of the whole establishment. The six yards made possible more precise classification of the inmates*

Right: *Chorlton Union Workhouse, 1856, by Hagley Son and Hall. The 1834 Act had removed control from individual parishes, and formed groups of parishes into Unions for ease of administration. It was only in these new workhouses that able-bodied paupers, and their families, could now obtain relief. The sexes were strictly segregated, and conditions made less acceptable than the most unpleasant way of earning a living outside*

Asylums

It was also at about this time that it was considered that the mentally ill who could not be cared for by their own families, the 'pauper lunatics', should be accommodated in separate institutions from healthy people who were merely without paid employment. It was thought that an ideal size of building would be able to house 350 inmates. Although views differed concerning the form of the building, some asylums were built on the same radiating principle that had been introduced for prisons because it was agreed that ease of control was of paramount importance. Others thought that separate wings at right angles were perfectly satisfactory.

Hospitals

It was not until the late 1860s that care for the sick became at all organised, following the Crimean War of 1853–56 when 4,600 soldiers died in battle, 13,000 were wounded and 17,500 died of disease. Public opinion was outraged by the daily reports on conditions by W H Russell of *The Times*, and Florence Nightingale did much to encourage good practice with her book *Notes on Hospitals* of 1859. The Royal Victoria Military Hospital, Netley, Hampshire, was constructed in 1856–61 by a War Department surveyor called Mennie. This vast structure was heavily criticized when it was built, especially because it had windows only to one side of the wards. The Victorians intended that through judicious planning basic requirements of patients, such as light and air, would be met.

It was considered that an efficient hospital should be based on the pavilion model, where each ward is a building of one or two storeys only, provided with sufficient light and cross-ventilation. The entrances, stairs and WCs should be located at the end of each ward, which should consist of between 24 and 30 beds. The ward entrances should ideally be connected to each other via covered walkways, while the kitchens and the administrative blocks should be centrally placed. For the smaller to medium-sized hospitals an H-plan layout was preferred, with the administrative building occupying the centre and wards to both sides. These principles were first adopted with the building of the Herbert Royal Military Hospital, Woolwich, begun in 1860 by Captain Galton.

Prisons

Apparently at the beginning of the nineteenth century there was a consensus of opinion that a system of solitary confinement should be adopted in Britain's prisons. It followed that the structures should be composed of as many cells as possible, and combined with a plan that facilitated supervision. The panopticon plan was preferred, when the cells are placed around a central observation core. This evolved into the radial plan, was comprised of several wings or arms each with a central top-lit corridor radiating from a control point.

The first such example of the plan had been the Eastern Penitentiary, Philadelphia, Pennsylvania, 1823, and the style was widely used and developed in the UK until the central governemnt decided to take over direct control of the running and financing of prisons in 1865.

It appointed Sir Edmund Du Cane to be in charge of the buildings and his Wormwood Scrubs, London, 1873–85, was built on the pavilion principle similar to that used for hospitals and asylums. This was the arrangement that gradually came to replace any others.

Workhouses

Great Dunmow, Essex, 1840, by Sir George Gilbert Scott and W B Moffatt; a Jacobean-style building constructed in red brick with yellow brick dressings

Asylums

Devon Asylum, Exminster, 1843–46, by Charles Fowler; based on the radiating principle

Colney Hatch, Middlesex, 1847–51, by Samuel Daukes; now converted to apartments. It was built to house 1,300 inmates on a scale that included its own railway siding

The Lunatic Asylum, St Anne's Heath, Virginia Water, Surrey, 1871–84, by William H Crossland; built by the same philanthropist as Royal Holloway College and so also known as the Holloway Sanatorium, to accommodate 100 middle-class patients. It was decorated in fairly lavish Gothic, has a prominent tower and a distinctive Great Hall with a hammerbeam roof

Hospitals

St Thomas' Hospital, London, 1868–71, by Henry Currey; designed to care for 588 patients, with 44 wards in six blocks

Leeds Infirmary, 1864–68, by Sir George Gilbert Scott; similar to St Thomas', but smaller

Royal Infirmary, Edinburgh, 1870–79, by David Bryce

Norwich and Norfolk Hospital, 1879, by Thomas Henry Wyatt; a medium-sized hospital based on an H-plan

Royal Hampshire County Hospital, Winchester, 1863–68, by William Butterfield; an individualistic longitudinal arrangement of wards

University College Hospital, Gower Street, London, 1897–1906, by Alfred Waterhouse; built on a small square site, its four wings are arranged in a diagonal cross with four wards on each floor

Prisons

Pentonville Prison, London, 1840–42, by Sir Joshua Jebb; four radiating arms behind a monumental entrance. Each cell was individually heated

Reading Goal, Berkshire, 1842–44, by Sir George Gilbert Scott and W B Moffatt; in castle style

Holloway Prison, Camden Road, London, 1849–52 (*now* demolished), by J B Bunning; built to accommodate 300 women prisoners, in six radiating wings each of four storeys with top-lit central corridors

Walton Goal, Liverpool, 1848–55, by John Weightman; in Norman castle style

Chapter Seven

Museums, Theatres, Clubs, Inns and Hotels

Museums

BOTH LONDON AND EDINBURGH are blessed with grand neoclassical museum buildings, and although some of them were neither completed nor opened to the public until Victorian times, their origins are firmly rooted in the previous era.

The British Museum in its solid Greek revival style was begun in 1823 by Sir Robert Smirke, but it was not until 1842 that work started on the grand entrance front. Although the massive Doric structure of the Royal Scottish Institution was begun at almost the same time in 1822 by William Henry Playfair, it was enlarged and remodelled between 1832–35. Its neighbour, the National Gallery of Scotland, with its Ionic order also by Playfair, was built somewhat later, between 1850–54.

Facing page: the main entrance to the Ashmolean Museum, Oxford, 1841–45, by Charles Robert Cockerell

Left: *work began on a new front for the British Museum in 1842, involving the demolition of Montagu House and its substitution by this fine classical Greek façade with its portico, decorated on its pediment with an ornamental group representing the progress of civilization*

Right: *the Ashmolean Museum and Taylorian Institution (right), Oxford, was the result of a competition won by Charles Robert Cockerell. His Greek revival design included Ionic capitals that were rounded at the top*

Below left: *inside the University Museum, Oxford, where the central court is surrounded by cloisters on two storeys, their column shafts of different stones or marbles, all of which are carefully labelled and have individual capitals*

Below right: *the University Museum in the course of erection, 1859–61. It was structurally complete in 1860 but not finished internally until some years later. Much of the labour was performed by Irishmen brought over from Dublin by Benjamin Woodward. The building, which then stood in splendid isolation, is now hemmed in by laboratories*

Together with the Ashmolean Museum and abutting Taylorian Institution, Oxford, 1841–45, by Charles Robert Cockerell, these represented the last important examples of public architecture in the Greek revival style. The façade of the Taylorian has Ionic columns with capitals, rounded at the top, which stand proud of the wall, with their entablatures breaking forward above them. Each of the orders is crowned by a statue and linked to the next by an arch.

The Fitzwilliam Museum, Cambridge, was begun in 1837

by George Basevi. Its clever, perhaps even profligate, use of internal space represents a shift in taste towards a richer architectural effect, with its portico of eight Corinthian columns flanked by colonnades that terminate in elaborate pavilions.

When the competition was held for the University Museum, Oxford, now called the Oxford University Natural History Museum, attitudes had begun to change, bringing the advent of high-Victorian Gothic eclecticism with its inclusions of European Gothic, brick and marble and even classical elements. The building was begun in 1855 by Sir Thomas Deane and Benjamin Woodward, and completed in 1860. Internally rooms are grouped around a central glazed courtyard, and surrounding this open space are cloisters on two storeys, their column shafts of different British stones and marbles. The walls are faced with stone with Venetian early renaissance details, while the external façade is relatively flat, the walls enlivened with bands of stone of different colours. In the centre of the main front above the entrance porch is a tower, and the windows, which are placed slightly asymmetrically, each have a different capital carved appropriately with leaves, animals and birds.

At the same time as the construction of the Oxford museum a group of buildings was being built in South Kensington, London. The design for the first of these, the Victoria and Albert Museum, was begun by Captain Francis Fowke in 1859, but when he died in 1865 he was succeeded by Lieutenant-Colonel Henry Young Darracott Scott, who saw it through its initial stages to the completion of the impressive Quadrangle in 1872. The style of the Quad is Italian renaissance, but north Italian, rather than the normal Venetian or Florentine. It has fine red brick and buff terracotta elevations, replete with ornamental piers and columns that divide the many arches.

Above: *the Victoria and Albert Museum main entrance, London*

Below left: *the Royal Albert Hall, opened in 1870 by the Prince of Wales, pays a annual rent of one shilling (£0.05) because of the difficulty in raising building funds*

Below right: *the Albert Memorial, photographed after extensive restoration work*

The Victoria and Albert Museum was actually completed between 1899 and 1909. The designs for the final work by Aston Webb included the red brick and Portland stone façade, which was crowned by an elaborate octagonal cupola in a baroque revival or late-Victorian baroque style.

The complex, which also included the Royal Albert Hall which was begun 1867 and the Albert Memorial, also encompasses the other major museum in the area, the Natural History Museum. A competition was held for its design and won by Fowke in 1864, but following his death the commission was given to Alfred Waterhouse. New designs were produced and work began in 1873, concluding in 1881. The Cromwell Road façade extends to

Right: *the Natural History Museum, Cromwell Road, London, was built to house the natural history collection of the British Museum as a cheaper alternative to building extensions to the British Museum in Bloomsbury. A competition was held, won by Captain Francis Fowke, but Fowke died before his work was finished and the Trustees approached Alfred Waterhouse, whose varigated terracotta design for the building, opened in 1881, displays a characteristically Victorian determination to provide a fitting repository for the wonders of creation. It has a central nave like that of a cathedral, embellished externally with towers and spires*

205.88m (675ft) and is punctuated by central towers 58.56m (192ft) high and by high-roofed pavilions at both extremities. It is entirely faced in terracotta, with yellow walls enlivened by bands of blue-grey and decorated with figures of animals. Between the twin central towers is an arched portal which leads directly into a glazed hall.

The aristocracy and the landed gentry had dominated English towns until the nineteenth century by virtue of funding any amenities provided to local society. The museum, often with a library attached, was an innovation in civic building that needed two Acts of Parliament, in 1845 and 1850, to empower the municipalities to levy a special rate for the building and maintenance of such buildings, which for the most part were unremarkable. Their building continued into the last Victorian decades, and even into the Edwardian period.

Other museum buildings and libraries were financed either completely or in part by benefactors such as Andrew Carnegie and Passmore Edwards during the 1890s. These tended to be constructed either in the late-Victorian picturesque or in the baroque grand manner, albeit on a small scale, which represented a shift away from the informal use of renaissance styles of the 1880s. The last decade of the century included a wealth of original styles that combined renaissance with Arts and Crafts and *art nouveau* elements such as at the Horniman Museum, London, 1898–1901, by Charles Harrison Townsend. Its façade is dominated by a curving pediment, with the entrance sited at the side of the building and set at the foot of an unusual tower which has rounded corners and rises to cylindrical pinnacles decorated with leaf carvings.

Theatres and places of entertainment

Theatre, which included the music hall, reigned supreme in the field of entertainment during the Victorian and Edwardian eras. As its architecture was closely linked to this prevailing social climate, theatre design attained a summit of achievement during the period.

The changes wrought in theatre architecture were instigated initially by the set designers and then by the theatre directors. This led to the realisation of some masterpieces of fantasy, where a superb handling of space created a setting for the magical illusion of theatre.

Britain then had no tradition of state subsidy to the theatre. Companies of actors had regularly performed at Court and in the great houses, and later on theatres were built by entrepreneurs who let them for seasons to troupes of actors, who performed for the fee-paying public. Thus the commercial theatre was left to flourish or fail at the public whim, and the buildings in which actors performed were usually makeshift, cheaply constructed and off the main streets. It was not until 1705 that Sir John Vanbrugh's Queen's became the capital's first opera house.

Below: *the Horniman Museum, London Road, Forest Hill, London, was founded by Frederick J Horniman, the head of a well-known tea company, who assembled a large general collection during his travels abroad. This collection was opened to the public three times a week at his home, Surrey House, in Forest Hill, in 1890. The house was demolished in 1898 and replaced by a new museum, designed by Charles Harrison Townsend. Constructed of stone and red brick, the building consisted of North and South Halls and a clock tower. A decorative mosaic panel stretching the length of the main façade depicts an allegory on the course of human life. When completed in 1901, the museum was presented with its 8.51ha (21 acres) of park and gardens to the London County Council, as a gift to the people of London*

Charles II had granted the sole rights to perform drama in London to the Drury Lane and Covent Garden Theatres in 1662. Drury Lane, however, burnt down in 1809, Covent Garden in 1856, and this exclusivity had ended in 1843. Theatre architecture benefitted from the ensuing progress in practical matters such as the organisation of exits, fireproofing and comfortable seating. Until this point, British theatres had been simply an enclosed space with an enticing façade in the street, rather than offering a safe and comfortable evening out, or the appearance of a prominent civic building. Their foyers and main stairways were inadequate and underdeveloped because of the restrictions in licensing, and no new theatres were constructed in London between 1840 and 1858.

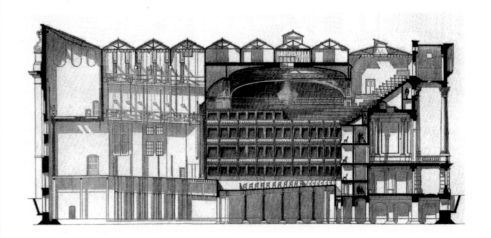

There was some rebuilding and reconstructing, though without a coherent style. Sadlers Wells, for instance, was altered in 1846 to include open semi-circular balconies which extended over the pit. The Lyceum was redecorated in 1847, when it had open balconies and stage boxes within a giant order. In 1856 when it was used by the Covent Garden Theatre Company, the stage was pushed back and the ceiling heightened to provide greater gallery capacity and the open balconies were separated into private boxes.

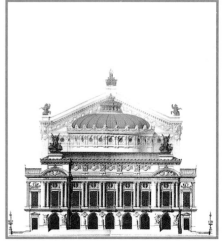

Left, *the portico of Covent Garden; and,* facing page, *a sketch made for the rebuilding, said to have been based on the auditorium,* right, *of La Scala, Milan*
Facing page, bottom, left and right: *the Théâtre de l'Opéra, Paris, 1875. Now known after its architect, Charles Garnier, as the Opéra Garnier, it has been cleaned and regilded as part of the city's millennium facelift*

The auditorium of Covent Garden was refurbished in 1846 to resemble La Scala, Milan, and the theatre reopened the following year as the Royal Italian Opera House, with seating for over 3,000 people. After it burnt down it was rebuilt in a neo-Palladian style in 1858 by Edward Middleton Barry with a more spacious auditorium and a larger stage yet within a smaller building. It is now the oldest surviving Victorian theatre in Britain; known as the Royal Opera House, Covent Garden, it has recently undergone another major redevelopment.

The boom in theatre building began in 1858. The Theatre Royal, Adelphi, London, by Thomas Henry Wyatt was completed in that year. Here the grand tier balcony was cantilevered six feet out from the balcony columns, a feat only made possible by using iron. Wrought-iron roof trusses were used that were rivetted in parts and carried on stanchions continuing right down to the foundations, so that the entire ceiling was suspended. Although the new Adelphi was far grander and more spacious than any other commercial theatre in London, its auditorium was sited well back from the main street, the Strand. It was approached by a series of corridors, because the value of frontage on main thoroughfares was still far too high to be wasted on theatres.

These traditionally designed buildings for use specifically as theatres or opera houses were gradually afforded more attention, with foreign styles such as French Empire, Viennese baroque and Bavarian rococo becoming increasingly prevalent. Others were designed in a modified Gothic style, and theatre architecture generally became more florid.

Fuelled by easier travel and increased prosperity as well as a growing population, the boom in theatre building had reached its height by the end of the century. The major railways had already been completed by the middle of the century, and the skilled acting companies of London were able to tour in speed and comfort; thus commercial theatres were in demand for the provinces.

A whole spate of regulations had been introduced in 1878 to control door entrances and exits, staircases, seating capacities,

London theatres in the 1870s and 1880s

Criterion, Piccadilly Circus, 1870–74, by Thomas Verity; ornate neo-renaissance façade, rebuilt internally 1884, remodelled and redecorated 1902–03. Its auditorium is entirely underground
Haymarket (built 1821), remodelled 1879 by Charles John Phipps; taken over by the Bancroft family in 1879 when the remodelling abolished the pit under the first balcony, although this was later restored in 1904 when the theatre was again rebuilt, and added the theatre's first complete four-sided picture frame for its proscenium
Comedy, 1881, by Thomas Verity
Savoy, 1881, by Charles John Phipps; the first public building to be lit entirely by electric light. Its exterior was in red brick in a sort of Queen Anne manner
Trocadero Palace, 1882
Empire, Leicester Square, 1882, by Thomas Verity; tiers and corridors constructed of fireproof material, a spacious staircase provided access to a large foyer and to two promenades surrounding the tiers
London Pavilion, Piccadilly Circus, 1885, by the firm of Worley and Saunders
Lyric, 1888, by Charles John Phipps
Shaftsbury, 1888; bombed during the Second World War
Garrick, 1888–89, by Walter Emden
Royal English Opera House, Cambridge Circus, 1889–91, by G H Holloway and Thomas Edward Collcutt for Richard D'Oyly Carte; sold in 1892 to Augustus Harris who reopened it as the Palace Theatre of Varieties. It featured cantilevered balconies, which eliminated view-obstructing pillars, and hot and cold air ventilation

Victorian music halls

Concert Room, St George's Hall, Liverpool, begun in 1836 by Harvey Lonsdale Elmes and completed in 1847 by Charles Robert Cockerell

Philharmonic Hall, Liverpool, 1846–49, by John Cunningham

Colosseum, Liverpool, converted from a Unitarian Chapel *c.* 1850

The Alhambra, London, 1851, by T Hayter Lewis; originally conceived as the Panopticon of Science and Art, it had a rotunda 29.59m (97ft) in diameter and a hydraulic passenger lift. It was renamed the Royal Alhambra Palace Music Hall in 1860 but was destroyed by fire in 1882, rebuilt in the same style the following year and remodelled in 1888, 1892, 1897, 1907 and 1912 before finally being demolished in 1936, when the Odeon Cinema was erected on the site

Lord Nelson Tavern, St Pancras, London; licensed from 1852

Surrey Zoological Gardens Concert Hall, Southwark, 1856, by Horace Jones; known as The Music Hall, and built at a cost of £18,200, it had seating capacity for 10,000 spectators plus room for 1,000 musicians

Evans late Joy's, Covent Garden, London, 1857; a long room with a stage at one end

McDonald's Music Hall, Hoxton, London, 1864; constructed from mass-produced parts with cast-iron columns, ornamental capitals, decorative railings and galvanised iron roofing

Grecian, Shoreditch, London, rebuilt 1876–77; combined a pleasure garden with a theatre and a variety saloon which was called the Eagle. It was purchased by General Booth for the Salvation Army, 1882; demolished 1901

Royal Victoria Hall and Coffee Tavern, now Old Vic, London; it was renamed in 1880 when taken over by Emma Cons

Paragon Theatre of Varieties, Mile End Road, London, 1884–85; advertised as the best-ventilated theatre in London, it had air intake vents 1.83m (6ft) above ground level and was the model for some 200 further theatres

Tivoli, London, 1888–90, by Charles John Phipps; combined theatre with restaurant, the street façade of which boasted a giant order of French Empire pilasters surmounted by an attic storey of romanesque arcading, topped by a mansard roof

Empire Music Hall, Newcastle-upon-Tyne, 1891, by Oliver and Leeson. The façade was in the style of early Flemish renaissance

Empire Palace Music Hall, Leeds, *c.*1897 by Frank Matcham

Later Victorian and Edwardian places of entertainment

Daly's, Cranbourn Street, London, 1891–93, designed by Spencer Chadwick with Charles John Phipps' assistance

Hippodrome, London, 1889–1900, by Frank Matcham; built in an ornate and remotely English baroque style, it was converted into a Palace of Varieties in 1909 and refurbished as the Talk of the Town in 1958

Her Majesty's Theatre, London, 1896–97, by Charles John Phipps

Imperial, London, 1901, by Frank Thomas Verity; originally opened in 1876 as the Royal Aquarian theatre. Lily Langtry bought it in 1900 and employed Verity to reconstruct the interior completely. The theatre was dismantled in 1906

Playhouse, London, 1905–06; originally erected in 1881–82, it was rebuilt by F M Fowler but was damaged before opening when part of Charing Cross Station fell on it. It was rebuilt by Detmar Blow and Fernand Billerey, although Fowler's façade remained

Coliseum, London, 1904, by Frank Matcham; neo-baroque building originally advertised as the Theatre De Luxe of London with a seating capacity of 4,000 (but actually licensed for 3,389). Later became the home of English National Opera

London Opera House, 1910–11, by Bertie Crewe; conceived by Oscar Hammerstein I, but too grand in every sense and not successful. Oswald Stoll gained control in 1916 and the following year converted it to Stoll Picture Theatre

Shaftsbury, 1911, by Bertie Crewe; formerly the Prince's Theatre

Golders Green Hippodrome, 1913, by Bertie Crewe

Sprague's London theatres

The Coronet, Notting Hill Gate; 1898; converted into a cinema

Wyndham's, Charing Cross Road, 1899; could accommodate about 1,200 when opened

Camden, Camden Town, 1901

Albery, Piccadilly, 1903

The Strand, 1905; originally called the Waldorf

Aldwych, 1905; a twin of the Strand theatre with an identical façade and a mixture of Georgian and French baroque classicism

Globe, Shaftsbury Avenue, 1906; twinned with the Queen's, from which it was separated by a commercial block with shops

Queen's 1907; a complete mix of styles. The Shaftsbury Avenue frontage was damaged during the Second World War and replaced in 1958

Ambassadors, West Street, 1913

St Martin's, West Street, 1916

Notable pier pavilions

The Britannia Pier, Great Yarmouth, 1858

West Pier, Brighton, 1863–66, by Eugenius Birch

Pavilion, Winter Gardens, Blackpool, 1876–78, by Mitchell and Macleod

Empress Ballroom, Winter Gardens, Blackpool, 1896, by Mangnall and Littlewood

Palace Pier, Brighton, 1898

Below: *the portico of the Lyceum, by Samuel Beazley, dates from 1834; the interior, which was frequently remodelled, dates from 1856*

stages and operating equipment. More importantly, the buildings had to be sited so that at least one half of the theatre would abut onto a public highway. Corner positions therefore became standard after the 1890s, and the theatres more comfortable, especially with the introduction of electric lights and air conditioning.

On the other hand, the music hall was quite a different building. Victorian popular music had originated in the taverns, which had vied with the minor theatres in the presentation of serious entertainment interspersed with song and dance until 1843. The Act of 1843 prohibited dramatic entertainment accompanied by eating and drinking in the auditorium. As this had been an essential element of the tavern, these saloon theatres were now forced to confine themselves to the music hall proper. Many taverns very soon built extensions. These were long rooms, with a stage at one end or with a balcony above for non-drinking customers. These extensions developed into the purpose-built music hall, hundreds of which were built all over the country between 1880 and 1910.

Above: *the Theatre Royal, Nottingham, 1865, by Charles John Phipps, was to be one of this famous theatre architect's first and greatest buildings*

Left: *the Surrey Zoological Gardens, Southwark, 1856, by Horace Jones; it was known as the Music Hall and, rather incredibly, was erected in just four months. It had a seating capacity of 10,000 and further space for 1,000 musicians*

These halls, flourishing in the poorer areas, borrowed from many other traditions, combining the entire cornucopia of architectural history: baroque, oriental, Gothic, Flemish and middle-eastern.

Another aspect of Victorian theatrical life was the show at the end of the pier. These pavilions provided many people with their first experience of the theatre, and hundreds of pavilions were erected around the coast of Britain. Typically they consisted of a flat floor, with a stage at one end and a single balcony around the other three sides of the room. At the more populated and prosperous resorts, these entertainment centres were extravagant conceptions such as the baroque opulence of the flamboyant ballroom of Blackpool's famous Tower Pavilion.

Theatre architecture flowered during the Victorian and Edwardian periods, but then died as the cinematograph, the first 'moving pictures', became popular. The earliest buildings to provide this new form of entertainment, such as the Majestic Picturedrome, Tottenham Court Road, London, 1910, looked for something plainer and even dispensed with side boxes and balconies.

Below: *the Savoy Theatre, which opened in 1881 with a performance of Gilbert and Sullivan's* Patience, *was designed by Charles John Phipps for Richard D'Oyly Carte and was the first public building to be lit entirely by electric light*

Clubs

The London clubs had their roots in the seventeenth-century coffee houses, and set out to provide a convivial atmosphere for a select membership in a building that was a cross between a private house and a public building. Its large rooms usually comprised the dining hall, a library, lounge, smoking room and billiard room.

The era of the private club really began with the opening of the Travellers' Club in 1829. This was followed by the Reform Club, which opened its doors a few years later, next door in Pall Mall. The Reform was a Liberal institution, and was important architecturally for having Britain's first major palazzo elevation of the nineteenth century. It is almost square in plan, with a large central court that is top-lit by a glazed roof. In addition, its façade of Portland stone gives equal prominence to the ground floor, thus reflecting the internal arrangement.

Other early clubs

Western Club, 147 Buchanan Street, Glasgow, 1841, by David and James Hamilton

Conservative Club, St James, London, 1843–45, by George Basevi and Sydney Smirke

Carlton, Pall Mall, London, 1845–56, by Sydney Smirke; later considerably altered and since demolished

Army and Navy Club, Pall Mall, London, 1845–51, by Charles Octavius Parnell and Alfred Smith; demolished

Later Victorian clubs

Junior Carlton Club, Pall Mall, London, 1866, by David Brandon; demolished

Constitutional Club, Northumberland Avenue, London, 1884, by Robert Edis

National Liberal Club, Whitehall Place, London, 1884, by Alfred Waterhouse

Union Club, Newell Street/Colmore Row, Birmingham, 1869, by Yeoville Thomason

Manchester Reform Club 1870 by Edward Salomons

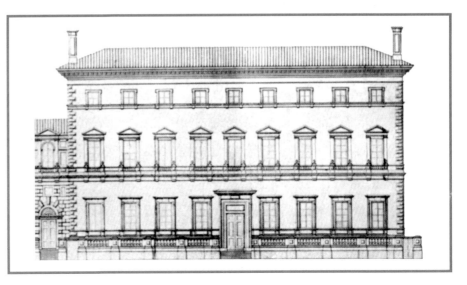

Above and right: *the Reform Club, 104–105 Pall Mall, London, was founded in 1832. The competition held for the design of the club building in 1837 was won by Charles Barry. There was to have been an open courtyard surrounded by corridors on both of the main floors, but the club insisted that it was covered in. It opened in 1841*

Inns and hotels

It was inevitable that the hotel would undergo much drastic change during the Victorian period, given the epic advances made in the mode and speed of transport. A new group of inns rapidly appeared from 1830, and became the new hotels, their aim to service travellers on the new, improved turnpike roads.

However they were soon to be eclipsed in turn by the needs of the intrepid railway traveller. The majority of all new journeys being undertaken by rail were scheduled to be completed within a day, and thus accommodation was needed at the terminals. Huge hotels, many of them financed by the railway companies, were built from the late 1830s onwards. These new establishments catered on a par with the London clubs, while also providing a number of cheaper rooms; by the 1860s they were unrivalled.

The Great Western Hotel at Paddington Station, 1851–53, by Philip Charles Hardwick, can be seen as the hotel that heralded the real boom. It accommodated guests in a choice of 150 rooms, ranging from the large apartments that were located on the first floor and were equipped with W Cs, at a cost of 22s 6d (£1.12) per day, to smaller bedrooms on the fourth floor at 1s 6d (7p).

The Great Western was followed by the Grosvenor Hotel, 1860–62, by James Knowles (Snr). It adjoined the Brighton Company's station, which is Victoria today. This impressive building of seven storeys was quickly followed by others such as the Canon Street Hotel, 1861, by Edward Middleton Barry but since demolished. Barry also designed the Charing Cross Hotel, 1864, which offered 214 beds. This was about half the size of the Midland Grand Hotel at St Pancras Station, 1868–74, by Sir George Gilbert Scott, with space for 400 guests but closed since 1935. This memorable building has a brick elevation decorated by arcaded Gothic windows with polished granite shafts, and inside, an utterly

Facing page, centre: *the National Liberal Club, Whitehall Place, London, 1884, by Alfred Waterhouse. The interior has much glazed patterned tiling, and boasts a wide marble staircase rising unsupported through three storeys, designed by Clyde Young and Eagle in 1950–51. The club was established in 1882 with W E Gladstone as President*

Below left: *the Grosvenor Hotel, 101 Buckingham Palace Road, London, was built in Bath stone by James Thomas Knowles in 1861. It has five storeys and two further storeys of dormers. There are French pavilion roofs on the angles, with much carved foliage. In the spandrels of the arches are medallion portraits of, among others, Queen Victoria, Prince Albert and H J T Palmerston, all in Portland stone*

Below right: *the Great Central Hotel, Marylebone Road, London, 1899, by Robert William Ellis, was the last of the railway terminus hotels to be built in London*

Above: *the Great Northern Hotel, King's Cross, London, 1854, by Lewis Cubitt; a crescent-shaped hotel with 66 bedrooms, which is set apart from the station*

Below right: *the Great Western (later the Great Western Royal) Hotel, Praed Street, London, by Philip Hardwick, was opened in 1854 as the largest hotel in England, with 103 bedrooms*

extraordinary staircase that is supported on exposed iron beams.

Another new category of places where hotels were required was at those spas and seaside resorts that the Victorians made popular. The Grand, Brighton, 1862–64, by John Whichcord, was one among this group. It was bedecked with gilded balconies, but more importantly it also boasted five lifts. Lifts had become one of the major technical advances of the period and, since their first use by Elisha Otis in New York in 1857, had an everlasting effect on both the scope available to, and the attitudes of, architects.

The Grand was later eclipsed by the nearby Metropole, 1888, by AlfredWaterhouse, but another Grand, built on a cliff at Scarborough, Yorkshire, 1863–67, by Cuthbert Brodrick, was perhaps the most spectacular of the era.

The majority of hotels built during the first half of the

century were in the classical or renaissance style, but later on combinations of styles proliferated. Many hotels were constructed in the picturesque or French renaissance style, but always with a continual striving to retain the classical proportions.

As the end of the century approached, hotelliers tended to concentrate on providing an air of sophisticated refinement rather than one of grandeur, and the style turned towards domestic revival. The Savoy, London, 1884–89, by Thomas Edward Collcutt for instance, was not only lit by electricity but also offered 67 bathrooms, and when the Carlton was built, 1891–99, by Charles John Phipps, every bedroom had a bathroom – the first such arrangement in London.

Above left: The Grand, Brighton, 1862–64, by John Whichcord

Above right: the Cavendish Hotel, Eastborne, Sussex, c. 1866, by Thomas Edward Street

Below left: the Russell Hotel, Russell Square, London, 1898, by Charles Fitzroy Doll, is a fantasy François-I château hotel in red brick and terracotta, and does overlook Russell Square. It opened in 1900, boasts 324 rooms and has a main entrance and restaurant resplendent with marble pillars and chandelier. The hotel has recently undergone a £10m refurbishment

Overleaf: Hector Guimard's internationally-acclaimed Paris métro entrance pavilion, officially opened to coincide with the Paris Exposition Universelle of 1900, when their design shocked lovers of the traditional Paris cityscape

Chapter Eight

The Wider Picture

Adler and Sullivan: the High Rise

CHICAGO WAS BOOMING in the 1880s; having been destroyed by fire in 1871 it was being rebuilt as the midwestern capital, and architects were being encouraged to master advanced new methods of construction. Major factors included the lift, which enabled user-friendly structures to be built high, and the steel frame, which enabled them to be built higher still.

In 1886 Adler and Sullivan (the firm of Dankmar Adler and Louis Sullivan) was commissioned to design the Auditorium Building, Chicago, a multi-use complex occupying a half-block site in the city. It was to include an opera house, flanked by two eleven-storey buildings that were part-hotel and part-offices.

The auditorium itself was designed for a variable capacity, a feat achieved by Adler by means of a series of folding ceiling panels and vertical screens, enabling the size to be limited to 2,500 for a concert or 7,000 for a convention.

The whole complex was housed in a massive masonry and iron structure that had to be ballasted during construction so as to compensate for differential loading of its foundations. Sullivan varied the facing material to take account of the building mass, by changing from rusticated blocks to smooth ashlar above the third floor.

However, Sullivan cannot be credited with the invention of the skyscraper, as multi-storey structures of great height had already been achieved in load-bearing brick, most notably in the firm of Burnham and Root's sixteen-storey Monadnock Block, Chicago, 1889–92. He may be credited, though, with the evolution of an architectural language appropriate to the high-rise frame.

His famous phrase 'form follows function' found its ultimate expression in the concave cornice of the thirteen-storey Guaranty Building, 28 Church Street, Buffalo 1895.

Above: *the Auditorium Building*
Below: *the Guaranty Building*

Frank Lloyd Wright: the myth of the prairie

Above: *the remodelled lobby of the Rookery Building, Chicago, 1905, by Frank Lloyd Wright*
Below left: *the Robie House, Chicago, 1908–10, the epitome of Wright's Prairie House style in which horizontal lines imitated the flat ground plane of the midwest*
Below right: *the Sagrada Familia cathedral, Barcelona, 1883–1926, by Antoni Gaudí*
Facing page, left: *Gaudí's Bishop's Palace, Astorga, Spain, commissioned in 1887; and,* right, *Casa Montero, Bilbao, Spain, 1901–04, by Luis Aladrén and Darroguy, who were disciples of Gaudí*

Frank Lloyd Wright worked for Adler and Sullivan as a draftsman involved with Sullivan's domestic work during the early 1890s. He left Sullivan's office in 1893, at the time of the Columbian World Exposition in Chicago.

Wright had erected his own house in 1889, adopting a formulaic style, and before the end of the century he had outlined the fundamental principles underlying his entire oeuvre. He considered that everything that had no need to be seen in order to fulfill its function should be hidden, even such necessities as central heating radiators being hidden within the construction. This premise was also applied to industrial buildings, compounded by his mistrust of the building trade's working practices and tendency to save money by cutting corners and economising on materials.

Wright set up his own office in Oak Park, Chicago, in 1889, and his early homes were named after the flat prairies of the American midwest. Their exteriors were influenced by his respect for the quiet, wide-open countryside, using low-pitched, over-hanging roofs, low eaves, wide-set fireplaces and extensive garden walling to achieve his effects.

The houses were multi-storey, with narrow stairs and narrow entrances which were often hidden away. In plan the rooms were often grouped in a cruciform arrangement, with staggered axes around a large central fireplace.

His Prairie Houses reached their climax in the Robie House, Chicago, 1906–10, for Frederick C Robie, where the living room and the dining room were separated by the stairs and the fireplace inside the house, but are reconnected visually by the wide window band which optically enlarges both rooms.

Gaudí, Horta, Guimard and Berlage: structural rationalism

The great French architectural theorist Eugène-Emmanuel Viollet-le-Duc advocated a return to regional building as early as 1853, in his lectures at the École des Beaux-Arts in Paris. His later *Entretiens*, in which certain aspects of his illustrations anticipated *art nouveau*, came to serve as an inspiration to the *avant garde* during the last quarter of the nineteenth century.

His ideas influenced such men as Sir George Gilbert Scott, Alfred Waterhouse and Richard Norman Shaw in England, but his most pronounced impact was on the works of the Catalan Antoni Gaudí i Cornet, the Belgian Victor Horta, and the Dutch architect, Hendrik Petrus Berlage.

Gaudí's achievements appear to have sprung from two compulsions: the desire to revive indigenous architecture, and the struggle to express this in the creation of totally new forms.

Both Gaudí and his patron, Eusebi Güell i Bacigalupi, grew up under the influence of the Catalan separatist movement, Gaudí having been involved with the Mataró Workers co-operative for which he designed a workshop in 1878. In the same year he built the exotic Casa Vicens in a quasi-Moorish style, which testifies to the influence of Viollet-le-Duc. It is a Mudéjar pastiche planned around a conservatory, which in its banded brick, glazed tiles and decorative ironwork was more exuberant than any house of comparable date. Here for the first time Gaudí used the traditional Catalan or Roussillon vault, in which arch-like forms are achieved through corbelling out laminated layers of tiles. The vault became a key feature of his style, appearing in its most delicate form in the thin-shell structure of his Sagrada Familia School, Barcelona, 1909.

Viollet-le-Duc (1814–1879)

Born in Paris, France, his immense reputation was based on his writings and theories of rational architectural design which linked the revivalism of the romantic period to twentieth-century functionalism. He was also a French Gothic revival architect, and a restorer of medieval buildings.

A pupil of Achille Leclère, his career was influenced by the architect Henri Labrouste. In 1839 he was put in charge of the restoration of the abbey church of La Madeleine at Vézelay which was the first edifice to be restored by a modern state commission. In 1840 he worked with F-L-J Duban on restoring the Sainte-Chapelle in Paris, and in 1845, together with J B Lassus, was appointed to restore Notre-Dame de Paris and to build a new sacristy in the Gothic style. This commission was regarded as an official sanction for the Gothic revival movement in France. Another important early restoration was the work done in 1846 on the abbey church of Saint-Denis. After 1848 he was associated with supervising the restoration of numerous medieval buildings, the most important being the cathedral of Amiens (1849), the synodal hall at Sens (1849), the fortifications of Carcassonne (1852), and the church of Saint-Sernin at Toulouse.

His many written works, all finely illustrated, provide the foundation on which Viollet-le-Duc's distinction rests. He wrote two great encyclopedic works containing exact structural information and extensive design analysis: the 16-volume *Dictionnaire raisonné de l'architecture française du XIe au XVIe siècle*, 1845–68, and the *Dictionnaire raisonné du mobilier française de l'époque carlovingienne à la Rénaissance*, 1858–75.

He envisaged a rational architecture for the nineteenth century based on the coherent system of construction and composition that he had observed in Gothic architecture, but which would in no way imitate its forms and details. He considered that architecture should be a direct expression of current materials, technology, and functional needs.

Viollet-le-Duc's general theory of architecture, which affected the development of modern organic and functional concepts of design, was set forth in his book *Entretiens sur l'architecture* (1858–72), published in English in 1875 as *Discourses on Architecture*. This work, containing information on the construction of iron skeletons enclosed by non-bearing masonry walls, especially influenced the late nineteenth-century architects of the Chicago School, particularly John W Root.

Above: *Park Güell, Barcelona, by Gaudí*

Below: *three of Victor Horta's masterpieces in Brussels;* left, *Horta's house, 1898–1901;* centre, *the main entrance, Hôtel Deprez, 1895–97; and* right, *the façade of Hôtel Tassel, 1893*

Facing page, top: *29 Avenue Rapp, Paris, 1901, by Jules Lavirotte*

Gaudí was commissioned to design the Park Güell in 1900. It was to emerge as the uninhibited crystallisation of his ecstatic vision, although the only buildings to be completed were the gate-house, the grand stairway leading to the covered market above, and Gaudí's own house. The irregularly-shaped undulating vault of the market was carried on 69 grotesque Doric columns, while its roof, bounded by a continuous serpentine bench, was intended to function as an arena or open-air stage. This exotic, mosaic-faced perimeter terminated in an esplanade which in turn merged into the naturalistic random rubble construction of the rest of the park. The park itself was divided by serpentine pathways, which were supported on vaulted buttresses where necessary, shaped so as to suggest petrified tree trunks.

Meanwhile, in Brussels the situation at the end of the century was similar in many respects to that in Barcelona. Here, too, there was a conscious desire to be modern and to tempt architecture away from traditional values and towards fashionable trends. At the time, both cities were blessed with a prosperous middle class which was seemingly obsessed with surface decoration. Brussels was enjoying an economic boom, and this, combined with the strength of the middle classes and the Socialist Party, produced a new breed of architectural patrons who were prepared to award contracts to a favoured circle of young architectural friends.

The form of the city, however, was rigidly governed by municipal building regulators. The heights of buildings and even rooms, the measurements of plinths, cornices and balconies were all monitored. It was the very existence of these mountains of regulations that, combined with the lack of overall city planning, that was to stretch the imaginations of the architects.

Their new theories and approaches allowed the use of all

available building materials, as long as they were openly exposed and their integration within the building was logical and stylistically harmonious. The façades of Victor Horta's buildings blended quietly into their surroundings, being relatively conservative, but their novelties were revealed inside. Steel and marble were combined with precious woods and flat iron was coiled artistically into banisters and lamps. Elaborate ornamentation was combined with a sensitive use of colour, and load-bearing supports were revealed to the world. His own house is now a museum of his work.

Horta's inspiration was drawn from the graphic art of the day, such as the lively posters of Toulouse-Lautrec (1864–1901), the book illustrations of Arthur Heygate Mackmurdo and Walter Crane (1845–1915) and even those of Aubrey Beardsley (1872–1898). Many *art nouveau* works were inspired by the pictorial world of the Far East, as prints by such graphic artists as Hokusai and other more formal stylists became available. The style was also influenced by forms taken from nature, which could be extremely vigorous but quickly tended to elongate and curl towards the decorative. Soon they appeared only as decoration and were used almost exclusively in the applied arts, for example by Louis Comfort Tiffany (1848–1933), failing to meet the long-term challenge of architecture. The *art nouveau* style gained immense popularity very quickly, appearing as *Jugendstil* in Germany, *Sezessionstil* in Austria, *Stile floreale* (or *Stile Liberty*) in Italy, *Modernismo* or *Modernista* in Spain.

The fashionable nature of *art nouveau* surfaced in Paris in Hector Guimard's Castel Béranger. Here he animated the façade with mainly floral natural forms as motifs, similar to those which he had seen in Horta's buildings. He acknowledged his debt to Voillet-le-Duc by declaring that 'Decoratively, my principles are perhaps new but they derive from those already in use with the Greeks ... I have only applied the theories of Viollet-le-Duc without being fascinated by the Middle Ages'.

In 1899 Guimard was awarded the commission for the design of the Paris métro stations. The entrances were made up of interchangable standard iron pieces cast in the form of naturalistic elements, framing enamelled steel and glass. Thereafter, over the next four years, these masterpieces of apparently natural emanations from a wondrous subterranean world erupted over the streets of Paris, making Guimard notorious as the creator of the '*style métro*'.

This notoriety overshadowed Guimard's masterpiece of structural rationalism, the Humbert de Romans concert hall, Paris, 1901 (but demolished in 1905), which must rank alongside Horta's Maison du Peuple, Brussels, 1897–1900 (also demolished), as major achievements of the period.

This age of so many imitated styles and forms would not, it seemed, provoke any permanent change, and the future appeared therefore to lie with the systematic reductions of Hendrik Petrus Berlage and Henry van de Velde.

Above: *the frontispiece of Guimard's* Castel Béranger *album, 1898* Below: *Horta's Maison du Peuple, Brussels, 1897–1900*

In accordance with the principles of structural rationalism, the Dutch architect Petrus Josephus Hubertus Cuijpers sought to rationalise his own eclecticism in evolving a new national style, an attempt that resulted in his neo-Flemish Rijksmuseum, Amsterdam, 1855. This work had a strong influence on Berlage, and a group called *Architectura et Amicitia* was centred on this pair of architects.

Berlage's major work was the Amsterdam *Beurs*. Placed only fourth in the design competition of 1883, he was awarded the commission twelve years later. Here he seems to have been guided by complex theoretical ideas, some drawn from Viollet-le-Duc and others from the originator of the Amsterdam School of Mathematical Aesthetics, Jan Hessel de Groot. The Exchange, a load-bearing brick structure which was precisely articulated in accordance with the principles of structural rationalism, was opened in 1903. Granite abutments, quoins, corbels and cappings consistently mark the points of structural transference and bearing inside. The same dressed stones which in one instance are corbelled out to receive a steel truss, in another articulate the keying of an arch. In this way, the ethos and the logic of Viollet-le-Duc pervade the very fabric as in no other structure of the nineteenth century.

The Vienna Secession: reaction

Part of the influence of *art nouveau* was absorbed in Germany and Austria as an important early twentieth-century development that became known as the Vienna Secession. Otto Wagner became professor at the school of architecture in the Academy of Fine Arts, Vienna, in 1894, and two years later published his first theoretical work, *Moderne Architektur*. Wagner's polytechnical education had made him aware of the technical and social realities of the last quarter of the nineteenth century, but at the same time his romantic imagination was drawn towards the radical stirrings of his more talented pupils. His assistant at the time was Joseph Maria Olbrich, his most brilliant pupil Josef Hoffmann, and together with two young Viennese painters, Gustav Klimt and Koloman Moser, they revolted against the Academy in 1897, and founded the Vienna

Top: *interior view, commodities floor of Amsterdam* Beurs *(Stock Exchange), 1896–1903, by Berlage*

Above: *Joseph Maria Olbrich's poster of 1898 for the Secession, using the Exhibition Building for the Secession*

Right: *title page from Otto Wagner's* Moderne Architektur *(1896)*

Left: *Secession Exhibition Hall, 1897–98, by Olbrich*

Above: *the second Villa Wagner, Vienna, 1912–13, by Otto Wagner, who designed the building for a widow in 1905*

Secession with Wagner's blessing. Wagner formally declared his approval of the movement in the following year and became a full member in 1899.

Olbrich built the Secession Exhibition Hall in Vienna in 1898, apparently after a sketch by Klimt, but by then the focus of the evolution of the group's style had switched to Darmstadt, where Olbrich had been invited by the Grand Duke Ernst Ludwig. In 1899 he was joined by six other artists: the painters Peter Behrens, Paul Bürck and Hans Christiansen; the architect Patriz Huber, and the sculptors Ludwig Habich and Rudolf Bosselt. Two years later this 'artists' colony' exhibited its lifestyle and habitat as a total self-contained work of art. The Ernst Ludwig House, 1901, without question was the pinnacle of Olbrich's work. A most progressive building, it consisted of eight studio living spaces, four to each side of a common meeting hall.

Peter Behrens was ever-present throughout Olbrich's career. Behrens had arrived in Darmstardt from the Munich Secession in 1899 and was then a graphic artist and painter, but he was to emerge as an architect and designer and a more powerful creator of form than was Olbrich. He urged Olbrich towards a return to the kind of crypto-classicism that characterises Olbrich's work in his final years.

Josef Hoffmann was influenced by the Secession's exhibition of Charles Rennie Mackintosh's furniture in 1900. In the same year he replaced Olbrich both as the designer of the elite Hohe Warte suburb on the outskirts of Vienna, and therefore also as the leading architect of the Secession.

Below: *Wiener Werkstätte poster, 1905, by Josef Hoffmann*

Above: the Palais Stoclet, Brussels, 1905–10, by Josef Hoffmann, is an art nouveau *gem, built for the Belgian banker Adolphe Stoclet. Its smooth external surfaces of Norwegian marble are framed with bands of bronze; note the upper floor windows, which break through the line of the eaves, emphasising the weightlessness of crystalline planes.*

Hoffman founded the Wiener Werkstätte craft studio in Vienna in 1903; it was based on the William Morris conviction of the importance of a unity between architecture and the crafts. It survived until 1932

Right: the centrepiece of the north front of the Glasgow School of Art, 167 Renfrew Street, 1896–99

Far right: the west wing, with the Scott Street entrance, Glasgow School of Art

Facing page, bottom: the Salon de Luxe, Willow Tea Rooms, Sauchiehall Street, Glasgow, 1903

Hoffmann's style evolved and by 1902 he was already beginning to move towards a more spartan and classical mode of expression that was based largely on the work of Otto Wagner. Together with other Secessionists, including Moser, he became interested in the craft production of decorative and applied art objects, as in Charles Robert Ashbee's Guild of Handicraft.

The high period of the Secession was over by 1903; at the same time the magazine *Ver Sacrum* ceased to be published and Hoffmann began his work on his masterpiece, the Palais Stoclet, Brussels, 1905–10. Here he used thin polished sheets of Norwegian marble facing which, with its metal seams, has all the hand-crafted elegance of a Wiener Werkstätte object on a larger scale.

Mackmurdo and Mackintosh: the Glasgow School

The main practitioners of the *art nouveau* style in Britain were Arthur Heygate Mackmurdo and Charles Rennie Mackintosh. The former perpetuated the ideas of John Ruskin and William Morris through the Century Guild, founded in 1882 for architects, artists and designers, and the *Hobby Horse*, an *avant garde* periodical.

Mackmurdo published his drawings of Sir Christopher Wren's City of London churches in 1883. His sinuous, tendril-like lines had a formative influence on *art nouveau* in Britain and marked the beginning of a style with international influence.

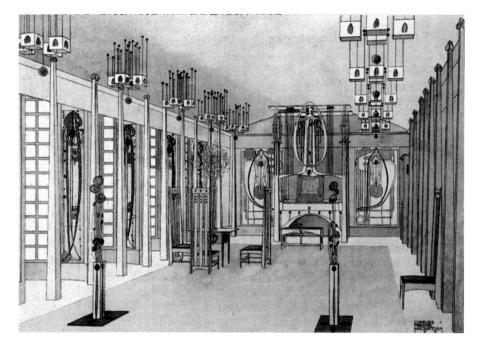

Mackintosh's masterpiece was his 1896 design for the Glasgow School of Art, which combined the sinuous curves of *art nouveau* and crisp regular forms that synthesised the free-playing character of *art nouveau* ornament with functional considerations, and demonstrated a rare sense of spiritual interpenetration.

His innovative fusion of the old with the new is most dramatically expressed along the west wall, where he took the traditional oriel window, compressed its glass into a modern pilaster, framed it in an iron grid, and opened up the wall in a design never before contemplated.

Mackintosh's tea rooms for Kate Cranston in Glasgow, begun in 1897, uniquely expressed the synthesis of his sympathy with the Scottish past and his daring innovation. The only surviving example, The Willow Tea Rooms, Sauchiehull Street, Glasgow, was restored in 1981.

The diversity of Mackintosh's work and his innovations made a deep impression on contemporary architecture outside the United Kingdom. The brief and brilliant, violet and silver period of organic ornamentation set against plain white surfaces, commonly regarded as the touchstone of the Mackintosh style and eulogised as such by Kala in 1905, came to its full maturity at the end of the nineteenth century. It was already developed in full in the furniture and décor of Mackintosh's Glasgow apartment, designed in 1900. It was further elaborated in the Scottish section of the Viennese Secession Exhibition in that same year, and in the music salon built for Fritz Wärndorfer in Vienna in 1902. The 'Hatrack' building in St Vincent Street, Glasgow, 1899–1902, by the architects James Salmon and Son, reflects Mackintosh's interpretation of the *art nouveau* style in the blend of curve and grid of its narrow façade, only 7m (22.97ft) wide; hence the nickname.

Above left, an illustration depicting the drawing room and music room from A House for an Art Lover, *published by Alexander Kock (Darmstadt, 1902) and,* right, *the Lunch Gallery, Miss Cranston's Tea Rooms, Buchanan Street, Glasgow, 1896–97*

Architects and Buildings of the Period

The years of birth and death of each architect are given in parentheses where they are known; page numbers are indexed in bold for text and *italic* for illustrations

Facing page: *Keble College, Oxford, 1867–83, by William Butterfield*

Baker, Benjamin *see* **Fowler, Sir John**

Baker, William *see* **Cowper, E A**

Bakewell, William (1839–1925) **66**
Harding's Tower Works, Leeds, 1899 **66**

Ball, J H (1861–1931)
A pupil of **Alfred Waterhouse**.
Parish Hall, Grantham Road, Eastleigh,
    Hampshire, 1891
St Agatha's Church, Landport, Portsmouth,
    1893–95 (decoration by Heywood Sumner)
Undershaw House, Hindhead, Surrey, 1896

Baltard, Victor (1805–75) **71**
Studied painting at the École des Beaux Arts,
    Paris, and was the winner of the Grand Prix de
    Rome for architecture, 1833.
Les Halles Centrales, Paris, 1853–58
    (demolished) 1971 **71**
St Augustin, Paris, 1860–71

Barbour, James (1835–1912)
24–36 Buccleuch Street, Dumfries, 1877
Militia Barracks, 109–113 English Street,
    Dumfries, 1877

Barclay, Hugh (1828–92)
A school specialist, he was a pupil of **W Spence**
    and a partner of his brother, David Barclay
    (1846–1917).
Ewing Place Church, Glasgow, 1858
    (demolished)
Municipal Buildings, Greenock, 1881–89
St George's in the Fields, Glasgow, 1886
Coats Thread Agency, Bothwell Street, Glasgow,
    1891–1901
Hunter Barr's, Queen Street, Glasgow, 1899

Barlow, William H 60
Train shed, St Pancras station, London, 1865–68
    59, 60

Barnsley, Sidney Howard (1865–1926) **51**
He entered the Royal Academy Schools in 1885
    and the following year was articled to Richard
    Norman Shaw; published *Byzantine Architecture in
    Greece* with Robert Weir and was a member of
    the Art Workers' Guild.
St Sophia's Church, Lower Kingswood, Surrey,
    1891 **51**

Barry, Sir Charles (1795–1860) **78, 81, 100**
His buildings range from the timid Gothic of the
    1820s to the splendour of his work with
    Augustus Welby Northmore Pugin for the
    Palace of Westminster. His use of classicism
    was often flamboyant, typical of the Victorian
    age, although his churches, built of brick with
    stone detailing, are in simple Gothic manner
    without the burning conviction of later Gothic
    revival work by architects such as Pugin. He
    was awarded the RIBA Gold Medal in 1850.
City Art Gallery, Manchester, 1824–35
St John's National Schools, Holloway Road,
    London, 1830
Travellers' Club, Pall Mall, London, 1830–32
    below **100**

King Edward VI School, Birmingham, 1833–37
    (ornament by **Augustus Welby Northmore
    Pugin**; demolished) **85**
St Peter's Church, St Peter's Street, London, 1834
Horsey Place (*now* Towers), Surrey, 1834
Trentham Hall, Staffordshire, 1834–42 (demolished)
Bowood House, Wiltshire, 1834–57 (alterations
    and additions)
Royal College of Surgeons, Lincoln's Inn,
    London, 1835–36 (altered) *below*

New Palace of Westminster (Houses of
    Parliament), London, 1835–60 (ornament by
    Augustus Welby Northmore Pugin) *above 3,
    77, 78, 78, 79, 79*
Athenaeum (*now* part of Art Gallery), Princess
    Street, Manchester, 1837–39
Unitarian Chapel, Upper Brook Street,
    Manchester, 1837–39
Reform Club, Pall Mall, London, 1839–41 **26,
    100,** *100*
Trafalgar Square, London, 1840 (terrace and
    steps, opposite National Gallery)
Highclere Castle, Hampshire, 1842 (alterations)
    32, *32*
Holy Trinity Church, Hurstpierpoint, Sussex,
    1843–45
Dunrobin Castle, Sutherland, 1844–50
Treasury, Whitehall, London, 1845 (façade)
    12, 18–19 and 20 Kensington Palace Gardens,
    London, 1845–47
Bridgewater House, Cleveland Row, London,
    1845–54
Façade Pentonville Prison, Caledonian Road,
    London, 1847 (altered)
St John's Lodge, Regent's Park, London, 1847
    (additions and alterations)
Shrubland Park, Suffolk, 1849–54 (additions
    and alterations)
Cliveden, Buckinghamshire, 1850–51

Canford Manor, Dorset; additions, 1854–55
Schools, Dowlais, Glamorgan, 1855
Town Hall, Halifax, 1859–63 **81**

Barry, Charles (Jnr, 1823–1900)
The eldest son and pupil of **Sir Charles Barry**,
    he was President of RIBA between 1876–79
    and was awarded the RIBA Gold Medal in
    1877. He was in partnership with Robert
    Richardson Banks (1813–72).
Bylaugh Hall, Norfolk, 1849–51
Dulwich College, College Road, London,
    1866–70
St Stephen's Church, College Road, London,
    1868–75
Façade of Burlington House, Piccadilly, London,
    1869–73
Stevenstone House, Devon, 1869–74 (partly
    demolished)
Great Eastern Hotel, Liverpool Street, London,
    1884

Barry, Edward Middleton (1830–80) **35, 75,
    78, 84, 96, 97, 101**
The third son of **Sir Charles Barry**, he worked
    in the offices of **Thomas Henry Wyatt** before
    joining his father, whose practice he inherited
    in 1860. He was Professor of Architecture at
    King's College, London, between 1873–80.
Birmingham and Midland Institute,
    Birmingham, 1855 (demolished) **75**
St Saviour's Church, Hampstead, London, 1856
Royal Opera House, Bow Street, London,
    1857–58 **96, 97,** *97*
Floral Hall, Bow Street, London, 1858–60 *below*

St Giles-in-the-Fields National Schools, Endell
    Street, London, 1860 **84,** *84*
Cannon Street Station Hotel, London, 1861
    (demolished) **101**
Charing Cross Station Hotel, Strand, London,
    1863–64 (since altered) **101**
Mansion Hotel, Richmond, Surrey, 1864
    (demolished)
Crewe Hall, Chester, 1866–71
Fitzwilliam Museum, Cambridge, 1870–75
    (staircase)
Wykehurst Park, near Slaugham, Sussex,
    1871–74 **35,** *35*
Temple Gardens Building, Middle Temple Lane,
    London, 1878

Basevi, George (1794–1845) **16, 92, 100**
A pupil of Sir John Soane (1753–1837) who
    unfortunately fell to his death while inspecting
    the west tower of Ely Cathedral.
Belgrave Square, London, 1827–44 **16**
Truesdale's Hospital, Scotgate, Stamford,
    Lincolnshire, 1832
Fitzwilliam Museum, Trumpington Street,
    Cambridge, 1837 **92**
Holy Trinity Church, Twickenham, Middlesex,
    1839–41
St Matthew's Church, Eye, Cambridgeshire,
    1845–46

with Sydney Smirke
Conservative Club, St James's Street, London,
  1843–45 **100**

Bassett, Henry (*b.* 1803)
Burton Park, near Petworth, West Sussex, 1831

Bateman, J J 88
Winson Green Workhouse, (*now* Dudley Road
  Hospital), Birmingham, 1852 **88**

Bates, Ernest (*d.* 1877) **67**
Eccles, Shorrock, Brothers and Co's India Mill,
  Darwen, Lancashire, 1859–67 **67**, *67*

Batterbury, Thomas (*d.* 1922)
In partnership with Huxley.
Hampstead Hill Gardens, London, 1877 (houses)
Warnham Lodge, Warnham, Surrey, 1894
  (demolished)

Bazalgatte, Sir Joseph William (1819–91)
Metropolitan drainage system, London, 1858–75
  (including Crossness Sewage Works, 1865, and
  Abbey Mills Pumping Station, 1867)
Thames Embankment, London, 1862–74
Hammersmith Bridge, London, 1884–87

Beattie, William Hamilton (1840–98) **73**
Paper Warehouse, West Register Street,
  Edinburgh, 1865
Jenners Department Store, 47–52 Princes Street,
  Edinburgh, 1893–95 **72**, *73*
North British Hotel, Princes Street, Edinburgh,
  1896–1900
Carlton Hotel, North Bridge, Edinburgh, 1898

Beazley, Samuel (1786–1851) **98**
Theatre Royal, Drury Lane, Covent Garden,
  London, 1831 (external colonnades and porch)
Leys Castle, Highlands, 1833
Lyceum Dance Hall, London, 1834 *98*

Beckett, Edmund *see* **Grimthorpe, Lord**

Behrens, Peter (1868–1940) **41**, **70**, **111**
A graphic artist, painter and designer, he was
  educated at Karlsruhe and Düsseldorf, Germany.
  He moved to Munich in 1890, and helped to
  found the Munich Sezession in 1892. In 1897
  he joined the United Workshops for Arts and
  Crafts, and in 1899 the Artists' Colony in
  Darmstadt, invited by Grand Duke Ernst
  Ludwig of Hesse, where he taught until 1903.
  He was the Director of the School of Applied
  Arts in Düsseldorf from 1903 until 1907, when
  he became the artistic advisor to AEG (General
  Electric Company), Berlin. **Le Corbusier,**
  Walter Gropius and Mies van der Rohe all
  worked in his offices in the coming years. From
  1922 to 1927 he was head of architecture at the
  Vienna Academy of Arts, and in 1936 he was
  made head of the department of architecture at
  the Prussian Academy of Arts, Berlin.
Own house, Darmstadt, Germany, 1901 *41*
Obenauer house, Saarbrücken, Germany, 1905–06
AEG Turbinenfabrik (turbine factory), Berlin-
  Moabit, 1908–09 **70**
AEG high-tension plant, Humboldthain, Berlin-
  Wedding, 1909–10 **70**
Housing complex for AEG workers,
  Henningsdorf, 1910–11
AEG small motors factory, Humboldthain,
  Berlin-Wedding, 1910–13
Gasworks, Frankfurt-am-Main, 1911–12
IG-Farben dye factory, Höchst, Frankfurt-am-
  Main, 1920–24
House, Mathildenhöhe, Darmstadt, 1901 (with
  Artists' Colony; built for *A Document of German*
  Art exhibition)

Belcher, John (Jnr, 1841–1913) **28, 29, 66, 82**
The son and pupil of John Belcher Snr
  (1816–90), this London architect and surveyor
  became a partner in his father's practice in

1865 and a partner of **John James Joass** in
  1905. He was President of RIBA between
  1904–06 and awarded a Gold Medal in 1907.
Mappin & Webb, Queen Victoria Street,
  London, 1870 **66**
Rylands and Sons warehouses, Wood Street,
  London, 1885 (demolished)
Institute of Chartered Accountants, Great Swan
  Alley, London, 1890–93 **28**, *29*
Convent of the Good Shepherd, Wargrave,
  Berkshire, 1894
Pangbourne Tower, Pangbourne, Berkshire,
  1897–98
Town Hall, Colchester, Essex, 1898–1902 **82**
Electra House, Moorgate, London, 1902 **28**
Mappin & Webb, Oxford Street, London, 1906–08
Royal Society of Medicine, Henrietta Street,
  London, 1908 **28**

Bell, George *see* **Clake, William**

Bellamy, Thomas (1798–1876)
Emmanuel Church, Camberwell Road, London,
  1841–42
St Anne's Church, Brookfield, Highgate West
  Hill, London, 1852–53
Law Fire Insurance Office, Chancery Lane,
  London, 1857–58 and 1874–76

Bellamy, Pearson
A partner of J Spence Hardy in Lincoln from
  c. 1855.
Town Hall, Louth, Lincolnshire, 1854
Corn Exchange, Spalding, Lincolnshire, 1854
Corn Exchange (*now* Transport Museum), Hull,
  1856
Town Hall, Grimsby, Lincolnshire, 1863
Town Hall, East Retford, Nottinghamshire, 1864
Town Hall, Ipswich, 1867
Corn Exchange, Lincoln, 1880

Bentley, John Francis (1839–1902) **46, 47, 51**
A pupil of **Henry Clutton** who converted to
  Catholicism in 1862. His greatest work,
  Westminster Cathedral, was not consecrated
  until eight years after his death.
St Francis of Assisi R C church, Pottery Lane,
  London, 1861–63 (additions)
235 Lancaster Road, London, 1863
Sunnydean, 108 Westwood Hill, London, 1868–70
Ellerslie, Sydenham Hill, London, 1870
St Thomas' Seminary, Hammersmith, London,
  1876–88
St Mary's Church, Cadogan Street, London,
  1877–82
Our Lady of the Holy Souls church, Hazlewood
  Crescent, London, 1881
Holy Rood R C church, Watford, Hertfordshire,
  1883
Church of Corpus Christi, Brixton Hill,
  London, 1886–87
St John's Preparatory School, Beaumont,
  Windsor, Berkshire, 1886–88
Redemptorist Monastery buildings, Clapham
  Park Road, London, 1891–93
Cathedral of the Most Precious Blood
  (Westminster Cathedral), London, 1894–1902
  45, 46, *47*, 51

Berlage, Henrik Petrus (1856–1934) **107, 109,**
110
Educated at the Polytechnikum, Zurich, between
  1875–78, returning home to Amsterdam only in
  1882, establishing his own practice there in
  1889. He worked on city development plans for
  Amsterdam in 1902 and 1925, The Hague in
  1908 and 1924, Rotterdam in 1922, Utrecht in
  1924 and Groningen between 1927–28.
  He moved to the Hague in 1913 following
  commissions from the Kröller-Müllers shipping
  company, published *Thoughts on style in Architecture*
  in 1905, *Principles and Development of Architecture*
  in 1908, and from 1924 he taught at the
  Technical University, Delft.
Focke & Melzer building, Amsterdam, 1885

De Algemeene Insurance offices, Amsterdam,
  1893
De Nederlanden Fire Insurance offices,
  Amsterdam, 1893–95
De Nederlanden Fire Insurance offices,
  The Hague, 1895
Amsterdam Beurs, 1896–1903 (stock exchange)
  110, *110*
House, The Hague, 1898 (for Carel Henny)
Diamond workers' union building, Amsterdam,
  1899–1900
Offices for Kröller-Müllers, London, 1914–16
Sint Hubertus hunting lodge, Otterlo,
  Gelderland, the Netherlands, 1915

Bidlake, William Henry (1861–1938)
The son of the church architect George Bidlake
  of Wolverhampton, he was a pupil of **George**
  Frederick Bodley and later **Thomas Garner**.
  He entered the Royal Academy Schools in
  1883, and won the RIBA prize in 1885.
St Oswald's Church, Small Heath, Birmingham,
  1892–99
St Agatha's Church and vicarage, Sparkbrook,
  Birmingham, 1898–1901
Branch School of Art, Moseley Road,
  Birmingham, 1899
Garth House, Edgbaston Park Road,
  Birmingham, 1901
Bishop Latimer Church, Handsworth,
  Birmingham, 1904

Billings, Robert William (1813–74)
A pupil of John Britton, he was a noted architectural
  draughtsman, antiquarian and restorer.
St John the Evangelist's Church, Crosby-on-
  Eden, Cumbria, 1854
Dalziell Castle, near Motherwell, North
  Lanarkshire, 1859 (restoration)

Blackburne, Edward Lushington (1803–88)
St Mark's Church, St Mark's Rise, London,
  1877–80 (tower)

Blanc, Hippolyte Jean (1844–1917)
A pupil of **Robert Matheson**.
Mayfield North Church, Edinburgh, 1876–79
Coats Memorial Church, Paisley, 1885–94
Edinburgh Café, 70–71 Princes Street,
  Edinburgh, 1886
60 Princes Street, Edinburgh, 1903

Blomfield, Sir Arthur William (1829–99) **82**
The son of the Bishop of London, he was a
  pupil of **Philip Charles Hardwick**. He was
  knighted in 1889, and awarded the RIBA Gold
  Medal in 1891.
St Paul's Church, Shoreditch, London, 1859–60
  (demolished)
St Luke's Church, Torquay, Devon, 1861
All Saints' Church, Windsor, Berkshire, 1863–64
All Saints' Church, Fulham, London, 1880–01
Selwyn College, Cambridge, 1882–89
St Mary's Church, Portsea, Portsmouth,
  1884–89
Royal College of Music, Prince Consort Road,
  London, 1890–94

Blore, Edward (1787–1879) **85**
The son of a Derbyshire antiquary who began
  as an illustrator of topographical and
  architectural books.
Westminster Abbey, London, 1827–49 (survey
  and repair work)
Market House, Woburn, Bedfordshire, 1830
Bishop's Palace (former), St Asaph, Clwyd,
  1830–31 (west wing)
University Press, Trumpington Street,
  Cambridge, 1831–33
Bedford Modern School, Harpur Street,
  Bedford, 1833–37
Ramsey Abbey, Cambridgeshire, 1838–39
  (additions)
Merevale Hall, Warwickshire, 1838–44
Worsley Hall, Lancashire, 1840–45 (demolished)

St James the Great church, Bethnal Green,
London, 1842–43
Chapel of St Mark's College, Chelsea, London,
1843–47
Marlborough College, Wiltshire, 1844–50 **85**
Buckingham Palace, London, 1846–47 (east front)

Bodley, George Frederick (1827–1907) **50, 51**
A relative of **Sir George Gilbert Scott**, he
trained in Scott's offices before becoming a
partner of **Thomas Garner** from 1869 to 1897.
He was awarded the RIBA Gold Medal in 1899.
St John the Baptist's Church, France Lynch,
Gloucestershire, 1855–57
St Michael's Church, Ship Street, Brighton,
1858–62 *below*

All Saints' Church, Selsley, Gloucestershire,
1859–62
St Martin's Church, Scarborough, Yorkshire,
1861–63
All Saints' Church, Dedworth, Berkshire, 1863
St Wilfred's Church, Hayward's Heath, Sussex,
1863–65
All Saints' Church, Cambridge, 1863–69
St Saviour's Church, Dundee, 1865–70
St Martin's vicarage, Scarborough, Yorkshire,
1867
St John the Baptist's Church, Liverpool, 1868–70
St Augustine's Church, Pendlebury, Lancashire,
1870–74
St Germain's Church, Roath, Cardiff, 1883–84
Hewell Grange, Worcestershire, 1884–91
Church, Clumber, Nottinghamshire, 1886–89
St John the Baptist's Church, Epping, Essex,
1889 (not built until 1908)
Queens' College Chapel, Cambridge, 1890–01
St Mary's Church, Eccleston, Cheshire, 1894–99
Cathedral of SS Peter and Paul, Washington
DC, USA, 1906
with Thomas Garner 50
Holy Angels church, Hoar Cross, Staffordshire,
1872–76 **50**
River House, 3 Chelsea Embankment, London,
1876–79
St Michael's Church, Camden Road, London,
1880–94
St Mary of Eton Mission Church, Hackney
Wick, London, 1890
Holy Trinity Church, Prince Consort Road,
London, 1902–03

Bonomi, Ignatius (*c.* 1787–1870)
Windleston Hall, Co Durham, *c.* 1834 (thought
to be by)
St Cuthbert's R C church, Wigton, Cumbria,
1837
St Paulinus R C chapel, Brough Hall, North
Yorkshire, 1834–37 (with Sir W Lawson)

Boileau, Louis-Auguste *see* **Eiffel, Gustave**

Booth, Isaac (1823–91) **66**
Dyeworks, Washer Lane, Halifax, 1871–75 **66**

Boston, W J *see* **Burnet, Frank**

Boucher, James (1832–92) and **James
Cousland** (*c.* 1832–66)
Renfield Free Church, Bath Street, Glasgow,
1857 (demolished)
St George's Free Church, Elderslie Street,
Glasgow, 1864 (demolished)
Teacher Building, 18 St Enoch Square, Glasgow,
1875
998 Great Western Road, Glasgow, 1877

Bowman, Henry (1814–83) and **Joseph Stretch
Crowther** (1832–93)
The partnership operated from Manchester.
Unitarian Church, Stockport Road, Hyde,
Cheshire, 1846–48
Mill Hill Unitarian Church, Park Row, Leeds,
1847–48
St Mary's Church, Hulme, Manchester, 1856–58
St Alban's Church, Cheetham, Manchester,
1857–64
St Mary's Church, Bury, Lancashire, 1871–76
St Wilfrid's Church, Northenden, Manchester,
1873–76

Brakspear, William Hayward (1818–98)
Exchange (*now* a cinema), Blackburn,
Lancashire, 1863–65

Brandon, David (1813–97) **100**
A pupil of the Royal Academy Schools and partner
of **Thomas Henry Wyatt** from 1838 to 1851.
Colesbourne House, Gloucestershire, 1853–56
St Mary's Church, Wallingford, Berkshire, 1854
Junior Carlton Club, Pall Mall, London, 1866
(demolished) **100**
Sidbury Manor, Devon, 1879
with Thomas Henry Wyatt
SS Mary and Nicholas church, Wilton,
Wiltshire, 1840–46
16 Kensington Palace Gardens, London,
1846–47

Brandon, John Raphael (1817–77)
Practised with his brother Joshua Arthur
Brandon (1822–47); together they published
An Analysis of Gothick Architecture (1844, 1847).
Croydon and Epsom Atmospheric Railway
Station, Epsom, Surrey, 1844–45
Church of Christ the King, Gordon Square,
London, 1850–54
St Mary's Church, Datchet, Buckinghamshire,
1858–60
1 Clement's Inn, London, 1874

Briant, Henry
Royal Berkshire Hospital, London Road,
Reading, Berkshire, 1837–39
Barclay's Bank, King Street, Reading, Berkshire,
1838–39 (with Nathaniel Briant)

Briggs, Wolstenhome and **Thornley 29**
Mersey Docks and Harbour Board offices, Pier
Head, Liverpool, 1907 **29**

Brodrick, Cuthbert (1822–1905) **77, 81, 102**
Trained with **Henry Francis Lockwood**.
Town Hall, Leeds, 1853–58 **77**
Hydropathic hotel, Ilkley, Yorkshire, 1860 (later
College of Housecraft)
Corn Exchange, Leeds, 1861–63 **81**
Town Hall, Hull, 1862 (demolished, parts re-
used in memorial at Brantingham, Yorkshire)
Grand Hotel, Scarborough, Yorkshire, 1863–67
102
Mechanics Institute (*now* Art School), Leeds,
1865 **81**
Turkish Baths, Cookridge Street, Leeds, 1866
(demolished)

Brooks, James (1825–1901) **49, 83**
The son of a Berkshire farmer, he was a pupil of
Lewis Stride. He moved to London, entered the
Royal Academy Schools in 1849, and established
his own practice in 1851; awarded the RIBA
Gold Medal in 1895.
Parish School, Henley-on-Thames, Oxfordshire,
1856
Baptist Chapel, Wantage, Berkshire, 1860
The Grange, 42 Clissold Crescent, London,
1861–62
St Michael's Church, Mark Street, London,
1863–65 (redundant)
Parish School, Headington Quarry, Oxford, 1864
St Saviour's Church, Hoxton, London, 1865–66
(demolished)
St Andrew's Church, Plaistow, London, 1867–70
(redundant) **49**
St Columba's Church, Kingsland Road,
London, 1868–69
St Chad's Church, Dunloe Street, London, 1868–69
Church of the Annunciation, Chislehurst, Kent,
1868–70
National Schools, Wolstanton, Staffordshire,
1871–72
St Saviour's Church, Mortomley, Yorkshire, 1872
St John the Baptist's Church, Holland Road,
London, 1872 **49**
W W F Hume Dick Mausoleum, Kiltegan,
Co Wicklow, Ireland, 1875
St James' Church, Marston Meysey, Wiltshire,
1875–76
Church of the Ascension, Lavender Hill,
London, 1876–83
St Modoc's Church, Doune, Perth, 1877–78
Church of the Transfiguration, Algernon Road,
London, 1880–86
St Peter's Church, St Leonard's-on-Sea, Sussex,
1883–85
Church of the Holy Innocents, Paddenswick
Road, London, 1889–1901
SS Peter and Paul church, Dover, Kent, 1891–93
All Hallows church, Savernake Road, London,
1892–1901 (chancel completed by **Giles
Gilbert Scott** 1913–15)

Brown, J Palmer
Christ Church, High Street, Tunbridge Wells,
Kent, 1836–41

Brown, John (1805–76)
He lived in Norwich and became Norfolk
County Surveyor in 1835.
St Michael's Church, Stamford, Lincolnshire, 1835
Bignold's yarn mill (*now* Jarrolds Print Works),
Cow Gate, Norwich, 1836
Workhouse (*now* Vale Hospital), Swainthorpe,
Norfolk, 1836
St Margaret's Church, Lee Terrace, London,
1839–41 (altered by **James Brooks**)
Christ Church, New Catton, Norwich, 1841
St John's Church, Eastover, Bridgewater,
Somerset, 1843

Browne, Sir George Washington (1854–1939)
Born in Glasgow, articled to **John James
Stevenson** and a pupil of **James Sellars**. He
worked with a wide range of partners including
Sir Robert Rowand Anderson, **Sir Arthur
William Blomfield**, **William Eden Nesfield**
and **John James Stevenson**. He was the first
Scot to win the RIBA Pugin prize, and was the
President of the Scottish Academy in 1926, the
same year in which he was knighted; *see also*
Peddie, John More Dick.
Central Library, Edinburgh, 1887–89
Redfern's shop, Princes Street, Edinburgh, 1892
(demolished)
Miss Cranston's Tea Rooms, 91 Buchanan
Street, Glasgow, 1897 (later Clydesdale Bank)
British Linen Bank, George Street, Edinburgh, 1905

Browning, Bryan (1773–1856)
Stamford Institution (*now* YMCA), St Peter's
Hill, Stamford, Lincolnshire, 1842

Barn Hill House, Stamford, Lincolnshire, 1843
(north front)

Brunel, Isambard Kingdom (1806–59) **7, 11,
54, 58**
A famous engineer and entrepreneur, especially
of the Great Western Railway.
Clifton Suspension Bridge, Bristol, 1836–59 **54**
Railway bridge, Maidenhead, Berkshire, 1838
Temple Meads Station, Bristol, 1839–40 *below*

Station, Bath, Avon, 1840
Chepstow Bridge, Monmouthshire, 1852
(demolished) **54**
Royal Albert Bridge, Saltash, Cornwall, 1859 **54**
with Richard Shackleton Pope
Royal Western Hotel (*now* offices), Bristol 1837
with Sir Matthew Digby Wyatt
Paddington Station, London, 1852–54 *11*

Bryce, David (1803–76) **26, 89**
A pupil of **William Burn** before becoming his
partner, 1841–50.
St Mark's Unitarian Chapel, Castle Terrace,
Edinburgh, 1834–35
Edinburgh and Leith Bank, Edinburgh, 1841
(later Clydesdale Bank)
British Linen Bank, St Andrew's Square,
Edinburgh, 1846–51 **26**
Western Bank, St Andrew's Square, Edinburgh,
1846 (later Scottish Widows' Fund offices, since
demolished)
Kinnaird Castle, Farnell, Angus, 1854
(reconstruction work, castle since demolished)
Queen's Theatre, Edinburgh, 1857
Fettes Cottage, Edinburgh, 1863–70
Castlemilk, Lockerbie, Dumfries, 1864
Bank of Scotland, Edinburgh, 1864–70
Post Office, College Green, Dublin, 1868
Edinburgh Infirmary, 1870–79 **89**
Union Bank, 62–6 George Street, Edinburgh,
1874–78 (later Bank of Scotland)
The Glen, Innerleithen, Peebles, 1875

Brydon, John McKean (1840–1901)
Trained under **David Bryce** in Edinburgh
before working as an assistant to **Richard
Norman Shaw** and to **William Eden Nesfield**.
Chelsea Vestry Hall, Chelsea Manor Gardens,
London, 1885–87 (later Town Hall; municipal
offices from 1965)
Chelsea Polytechnic and Library, Manresa
Road, London, 1891–95
Local Government Offices, Parliament Square,
London, 1898–1912

Buckeridge, Charles (1832–73)
A pupil of **Sir George Gilbert Scott**.
Holy Trinity Convent (*now* St Anthony's
College), Oxford, 1865–68

Buckler, John Chessell (1793–1894)
Son of the architectural draftsman John
B Buckler (1770–1851), he specialised in church
restoration and was a noted antiquarian writer.
Butleigh Court, near Glastonbury, Somerset,
1845
Museum, Wisbech, Cambridgeshire, 1847
Choristers Hall (*now* Library), Magdalen
College, Oxford, 1849–51
Jesus College, Turl Street, Oxford, 1854–56 (façade)

Buckler, Charles Alban (1824–1905)
The son of **John Chessell Buckler**.
Our Lady of the Immaculate Conception
church, Stroud, Gloucestershire, 1858
St Dominic's Priory, Southampton Road,
London, 1874
Arundel Castle, Sussex; rebuilding, 1890–1903

Bucknall, Benjamin (1833–1895)
Our Lady and St Michael's church,
Abergavenny, Monmouthshire, 1858
Woodchester Park, Gloucestershire, *c.* 1858
St George's R C church, Taunton, Somerset,
1861
Seamen's Church, Swansea, 1868

Bunning, John Bunstone (1802–63) **89**
The son and pupil of a London surveyor,
architect to the City of London 1843–63.
Chapels and Lodges, Nunhead Cemetery,
London, 1844
Coal Exchange, London, 1847–49 (demolished)
Holloway Prison, London, 1849–52
(demolished) **89**
Caledonian Market, Islington, London, 1855
(demolished)

Burges, William (1827–81) **31, 35, 36, 49, 66**
The son of a civil engineer who trained initially
as an engineer also himself, before joining first
Edward Blore then **Sir Matthew Digby Wyatt**.
Lille Cathedral, France, 1855 (unexecuted design)
Crimean Memorial Church, Constantinople,
1857 (unexecuted design)
Gayhurst House, Buckinghamshire, 1859–60
(alterations)
All Saints' Church, Fleet, Hampshire, 1861–62
St Finnbar Cathedral, Cork, Ireland, 1863
Warehouse, 46 Upper Thames Street, London,
1866 **66**
St Michael's Church, Lowfield Heath, Surrey,
1867
Cardiff Castle, 1868–81 **35, 36**
Knightshayes Court, Devon, 1869–71
Christ the Consoler church, Skelton-upon-Ure,
Yorkshire, 1870–76 **49**
St Mary's Church, Studley Royal, Yorkshire,
1871–78 **49, 49**
Trinity College, Hartford, Connecticut, USA,
1873–80
Harrow School, Harrow-on-the-Hill, Middlesex,
1874–77 (Speech Room)
Castell Coch, Glamorgan, 1875–81 **30, 35, 36**
Tower House, 9 (*now* 29) Melbury Road,
London, 1876–81 (own house)

Burn, William (1789–1870)
The son of the Scottish architect **Robert Burn**
and a pupil of **Sir Robert Smirke**; inherited
his father's practice in 1820. Partner to **David
Bryce** in Edinburgh until moving to set up his
own practice in London in 1844. He was later
in partnership with J Macvicar Anderson.
Tyninghame House, near Dunbar, Lothian,
1829–30
Raehills, near Moffat, Dumfries and Galloway,
1829–34 (enlargements)
Spott House, Lothian, 1830 (remodelling)
Pitcaple Castle, Grampian, *c.* 1830 (additions)
Drumlanrig Castle, Dumfries and Galloway,
c. 1830–34 (wings; thought to be by)
Bowhill, near Selkirk, Borders Region, 1831
onwards (alterations, by Burn, 1870)
Auchmacoy House, Logie Buchan, Grampian,
1831–33
Kilconquhar Castle, Fife, 1831–39 (rebuilding)
Kirkmichael House, Dumfries and Galloway,
1832–33
Auchterarder House, Tayside, 1832–33
Posso House (*now* Dawyck House), Borders
Region, 1832–33 (enlarged 1898)
Bank of Scotland, Kirkcaldy, Fife, 1833
Bank of Scotland, King Street, Stirling, Central
Region, 1833
Ardanaiseig House, Loch Awe, Strathclyde,

1833
Netherby Hall, Cumbria, 1833 (remodelling)
Tyneholme House, Pencaitland, Lothian, 1835
Balcarres House, Fife, 1836–38 (alterations, by
Burn, 1863)
Invergowrie House, Tayside, 1837 (remodelling)
Lude, near Blair Atholl, Tayside, 1837–40
Finnart House, Loch Rannoch, Tayside, 1838
Harlaxton Manor, Lincolnshire, 1838–55
Bank of Scotland, High Street, Montrose,
Tayside, 1839
Stoke Rochford Hall, Lincolnshire, 1839–41
Whitehill House, Lasswade, Lothian, 1839–44
(in disrepair)
Falkland House, Fife, 1839–44
Prestwold Hall, Leicestershire, 1842–44
(remodelling)
Buchanan House, Stirling, 1851–53
Fonthill Abbey, Wiltshire, 1856
Montague House, Whitehall Gardens, London,
1857–59 (demolished)

Burne-Jones, Sir Edward Coley (1833–98) **8, 37**
A painter and designer, born in Birmingham; he
studied at Oxford, where he met **William
Morris**. He designed stained glass and
tapestries, and illustrated several books for
Morris.

Burnet, Frank (1848–1923) and **W J Boston**
(1861–1937)
St Vincent Chambers, St Vincent Place,
Glasgow, 1898
Castle Chambers, Renfield and West Regent
Streets, Glasgow, 1898
Castle Chambers, St George's Road and
Woodlands Road Junction, Glasgow, 1900
Gordon Chambers, Mitchell Street, Glasgow,
1906

Burnet, John (Snr, 1814–1901)
Elgin Place Congregational Church, Bath Street,
Glasgow, 1856
Clydesdale Bank, St Vincent Place, Glasgow,
1870–73
Stock Exchange, Glasgow, 1874

Burnet, Sir John James (1857–1938)
Worked initially for his father **John Burnet** in
Glasgow, then from 1885–1898 with John
Archibald Campbell (1859–1909).
Lanarkshire House, Ingram Street, Glasgow,
1876
Fine Art Institute, Sauchiehall Street, Glasgow,
1879–80 (demolished)
Barony Church, Castle Street, Glasgow, 1886
Athenaeum (*now* Music Academy), St George's
Place, Glasgow, 1891
Charing Cross Mansions, Sauchiehall Street,
Glasgow, 1891
Savings Bank, Ingram Street, Glasgow, 1894
Garner Memorial Church, Brechin, 1896–1900
Albany Chambers, Sauchiehall Street, Glasgow,
1896
Atlantic Chambers, 43–47 Hope Street,
Glasgow, 1899
King Edward VII wing, British Museum,
London, 1904–14
Garmoyle House, Dumbarton, 1890 (with John
Archibald Campbell)

Burnham, Daniel Hudson (1846–1912) and
Root, John Wellborn (1850–91) **69, 105**
Burnham was apprenticed to Carter, Drake and
Wright, where he met Root, and they became
partners in 1873. Burnham was appointed
President of the American Institute of
Architects in 1894.
The Rookery, Chicago, USA, 1886
Reliance Building, Chicago, USA, 1890
Monadnock Building, Chicago, USA, 1891 **105**
Masonic Building, Chicago, USA, 1892
(demolished 1931) **69**
Burnham, alone after Root's death
Flatiron Building, New York, USA, 1901

Union Station, Washington DC, USA, 1909 *above*
Filene's Store, Boston, USA, 1912

Burt, Henry (*d.* 1844)
Assise Court, Mount Folly, Bodmin, Cornwall, 1837–38

Burton, Decimus (1800–1881) **10, 11, 56**
The tenth son of the architect James Burton. He trained in his father's office together with **George Vaughan Maddox**. He contributed more gracefully charming buildings to London than any other architect of the neoclassical or Regency period, even though his career in public building spanned little more than twenty years. He retired early, and produced very little in the second half of his life.
Athenaeum Club, Waterloo Place, Pall Mall, London, 1827–30 *below*

Calverley Estate, Tunbridge Wells, Kent, 1828–52
Adelaide Crescent, Brighton, East Sussex, 1830–34
Charing Cross Hospital (former), Agar Street, London, 1831–34
Burrswood, near Groombridge, Kent, 1831–38
Bentham Hill, Southborough, Kent, 1832–33
Glevering Hall, Suffolk, 1834–35 (additions)
Newtown, including St Peter's Church and an hotel, Fleetwood, Lancashire, 1835–43
Holy Trinity, Eastbourne, Sussex, 1837–39 *below*

Grimstone Park, North Yorkshire, 1840–50
Palm House, Royal Botanic Gardens, Kew, Richmond, Surrey, 1845–48 **10, *11*, 56**
Museum, Royal Botanic Gardens, Kew, Richmond, Surrey, 1856–57
Temperate House, Royal Botanic Gardens, Kew, Richmond, Surrey, 1860–99
Winter Gardens, Regent's Park, London, 1845–46 (with **R Turner**; demolished)

Bury, Thomas Talbot (1811–77)
A pupil of **Augustus Charles Pugin**, he furnished drawings for the publications of both **Augustus Welby Northmore Pugin** and **Owen Jones**. He was a partner of Charles Lee between 1845–49.
St Paul's Church, Chipperfield, Hertfordshire, 1837
St Gregory's Church, Welford, Berkshire, 1852–55
St John's Church, Burgess Hill, Sussex, 1861–63
St Mary's Church, East Molesey, Surrey, 1864–67

Butterfield, William (1814–1900) **21, 34, 36, 43, 48, 64, 83-6, 89, 115**
The son of a London chemist and a pupil of **Edward Lushington Blackburne** from 1833–37, who worked for W and H Inwood before setting up his own practice in 1840; he was awarded the RIBA Gold Medal in 1884; *see also* **Cundy, Thomas** Jnr.
Highbury Chapel, Bristol, 1842
St Saviour's church and vicarage, Colpit Heath, Gloucestershire, 1844–45
St Augustine's College, Canterbury, Kent, 1844–73 **84**
St Bartholomew's Church, Yealmpton, Devon, 1848–49 (rebuilding)
SS James and Mary church, Alfington, Devon, 1849
St Mary's Church, Ottery St Mary, Devon, 1849–50 (restoration)
Cathedral of the Isles, Cumbrae, Bute, 1849–51
All Saints' Church, vicarage and choir school, Margaret Street, London, 1849–59 **42, 48, *48*, 84**
St Dunstan's Abbey, Plymouth, 1850
St Matthias' Church, Matthias Road, London, 1851–53
Vicarage, Cowick, Yorkshire, 1853 **36**
Milton Ernest Hall, Bedfordshire, 1853–56 **34, *34***
All Saints' Church, vicarage and school, Wykeham, Yorkshire, 1853–54
All Saints' Church, Braishfield, Hampshire, 1854–55
Church and school, Langley, near Maidstone, Kent, 1854–55
St Mary's Church, Milton, near Banbury, Oxfordshire, 1854–56
Balliol College chapel, Oxford, 1854–57
St James' Church, Waresley, Cambridgeshire, 1855–57
Church and cottages, 1855, and school, 1857, Baldersby St James, Yorkshire **21**
St Mary's Church, Etal, Northumberland, 1856–58
Church, Bamford, Derbyshire, 1856–60
School House, Trumpington, Cambridgeshire, 1857
Rectory, St Mawgan-in-Pydar, Cornwall, 1858
Rugby School, Warwickshire, 1858–84 (additions, including Chapel, 1870–72)
St John's Church, Glenthorne Road, London, 1858–59
St Nicholas' School, Enmore Road, Newbury, Berkshire, 1859 **86, 87**
Rectory of St Paul, 14 Burleigh Street, London, 1859–60 (demolished)
School, Castle Hill, Devon, 1859–64
St Alban's Church, Brook Street, London, 1861–62 (altered)
Royal Hampshire County Hospital, Winchester, 1863–68 **89**
St Augustine's Church, Penarth, Glamorgan, 1864–66
St Anne's Church, Dropmore, Buckinghamshire, 1865–66
All Saints' Church, Babbacombe, Devon, 1865–74
Keble College, Oxford, 1867–83 **85, *85*, 114**
Christ Church, Albany Road, London, 1867 (alterations)
St Augustine's Church, Queen's Gate, London, 1870–77
St Mary's Church, Brookfield, Dartmouth Park Hill, London, 1876
St Mark Dundela, Belfast, 1876–91
Grammar School, Exeter, Devon, 1877–87
St Paul's Anglican Cathedral, Melbourne, Australia, 1877–91
St Michael's Home, Axbridge, Devon, 1878
The Chanter's House, Ottery St Mary, Devon, 1880–83

Byrne, Patrick (1783–1864)
St Paul's R C church, Arran Quay, Dublin, 1835–37
St Audoen's R C church, High Street, Dublin, 1841–46
Rathmines R C parish church, Dublin, 1850

Caröe, William Douglas (1857–1938)
Born near Liverpool, the son of a Danish Consul, educated at Trinity College, Cambridge and a pupil of **John Loughborough Pearson**; worked for Ecclesiastical Commissioners and a partner to J H Christian and later to Herbert Passmore.
Congregational Church, Huyton, Lancashire, 1889–90
Martins Bank, junction of Brunswick and Castle Streets, Liverpool, 1890–94
St David's Church, Exeter, Devon, 1897–1900
Church Commissioners' Offices, 1 Millbank, London, 1903

Carpenter, Richard Cromwell (1812–55) **85**
Articled to **John Blyth** and a friend of **Augustus Welby Northmore Pugin**, he was closely associated with the Cambridge Camden Society; much of his work was with **William Slater**.
Lonsdale Square, London, 1842–45
St Andrew's Church, Bordesley, Birmingham, 1844–46
St Paul's Church, Brighton, 1846–48
St Peter's Church, Chichester, Sussex, 1848
St Mary Magdalene church, Munster Square, London, 1849–52
St John's College, Hurstpierpoint, Sussex, 1851–53
St John's Church, Bovey Tracey, Devon, 1852
Parsonage, Burntisland, Fife, 1854–56
Lancing College, Sussex, 1854 **85**

Carpenter, Richard Herbert (1841–93) **85**
The son of **Richard Cromwell Carpenter** and pupil of **William Slater**, he became a partner first of Slater then of Benjamin Ingelow.
Chapel, Lancing College, Sussex, 1868 **85**
Ellesmere College, Ellesmere, Shropshire, 1876–83 *and*
Denstone College chapel, Denstone, Staffordshire, 1879–87 (with Benjamin Ingelow)
with William Slater
Ardingly College, Sussex, 1864

Carter, Owen Browne (1806–59)
Corn Exchange (*now* Library), Jewry Street, Winchester, Hampshire, 1836–38

Carver, Richard (*c.* 1792–1862)
Holy Trinity Church, Bridgwater, Somerset, 1839

Cave, Walter Frederick (1863–1939) **23**
Born at Clifton, Bristol, he was educated at Eton and at Bristol School of Art. He was articled to **Sir Arthur William Blomfield** and entered the Royal Academy Schools in 1885. Cave set up in practice in 1889, and was appointed surveyor to the Gunter estate, Brompton, London.
Coleherne Court mansion flats, Old Brompton Road, London, 1901–03 **23**
The Wharf, Sutton Courtney, Berkshire, 1908–16, for the Prime Minister, Herbert Asquith
Burberry's, Haymarket, London, 1912

Cawston, Arthur (1857–94)
Ascension Church and vicarage, Malwood Road, London, 1883–84
St Luke's Church, Bromley Common, Bromley, Kent, 1886–90
Market, Fisher Street, Carlisle, 1887–89 (with J Graham)

Chamberlain, John Henry (1831–83)
He was a pupil in Leicester of H Goddard, strongly influenced by John Ruskin, and practised in Italy in 1856. He was a trustee of Ruskin's St George's Guild, and a partner to **William Martin** between 1864–83; responsible for the design of no fewer than 41 Board Schools for Birmingham between 1873–98.

28–29 Union Street, Birmingham, 1856 (demolished)
Eld House, Ampton / Carpenter Roads, Edgbaston, Birmingham, 1858
St Stephen's Church, Serpentine Hill, Selly Oak, Birmingham, 1870
Longbridge Pumping Station, Birmingham, 1870–80
St Cyprian's Church, Acock's Green, Birmingham, 1873
School Board Offices (*now* City Treasurer's Dept), Edmund Street, Birmingham, 1875
Oozells Street School, Birmingham, 1877 (later Food and Domestic Arts College)
The Grove, Harbourne, Birmingham, 1877 (demolished but interior of 'Harbourne Room' is in the Victoria and Albert Museum, London)
Highbury, Yew Tree Road, King's Heath, Birmingham, 1879
Chamberlain Memorial, Chamberlain Square, Birmingham, 1880
Central Library, Birmingham, 1880–82 (demolished)
Midland Institute, Paradise Street, Birmingham, 1881 (additions; demolished)
School of Arts, Birmingham, 1881–85 (later College of Arts and Crafts)
Library, Constitution Hill, Birmingham, 1883

Champneys, Basil (1842–1935) **86**
The son of the Dean of Lichfield, he was born in Whitechapel, educated at Trinity College, Cambridge, and articled to **John Prichard**; he was awarded the RIBA Gold Medal in 1912.
St Luke's Church, Caversham Road, London, 1868–70
Oak Tree House, Redington Gardens, London, 1872–73
Newnham College, Cambridge, 1875–1935 **86**
Selwyn Divinity School, Cambridge, 1878–79
Girls' High School, Bedford, 1878–82
Hall Oak, Frognal, London, 1881 (own house)
Indian Institute, Oxford, 1883–96
Butler Museum, Harrow School, Harrow-on-the-Hill, Middlesex, 1884–86
St Bride's Vicarage, Bridewell Place, London, 1885
Fawcett Memorial, Victoria Embankment, London, 1886
19–27 Copthall Avenue, London, 1890
John Rylands Library, Manchester, 1890–99
St Andrew and St Michael's church, Blackwall Lane, London, 1900–02
Bedford College, Regent's Park, London, 1910–13

Chantrell, Robert Dennis (1793–1872)
A pupil of Sir John Soane (1753–1837).
Parish Church of St Peter, Leeds, 1839–41
St Paul's Church, Shadwell, Leeds, 1841

Chatwin, Julius Alfred (1830–1907)
A pupil of **Sir Charles Barry**.
Lloyds Bank, Temple Row, Birmingham, 1864
St Augustine, Lyttelton Road, Edgbaston, Birmingham, 1868–76
Lloyds Bank, Colmore Row, Birmingham, 1871 (demolished)
SS Peter and Paul church, Aston, Birmingham, 1879
St Philip's Cathedral, Birmingham, 1883 (chancel)
Christ Church, Sommerfield Crescent, Winson Green, Birmingham 1883–85

Chesterton, Frank Sidney *see* **Coleridge, John Duke**

Christian, Ewan (1814–95)
Articled to **Matthew Habershon**, he later worked with **William Railton** and **John Brown** before establishing his own practice in 1842. He became the architectural adviser to the Ecclesiastical Commissioners from 1850 and President of RIBA between 1884–86. He received the RIBA Gold Medal in 1887; *see also* **Clarke, George Somers Leigh.**

St Peter's Church, Rochester, Kent, 1858–60
Manor House, Market Lavington, Wiltshire, 1865
St Mark's Church, Leicester, 1869–72
Holy Trinity Church, Scarborough, Yorkshire, 1880
St Dionis' Church, Fulham, London, 1884–85
National Portrait Gallery, London, 1890–95 *below*

Clake, William (1812–89) and **Bell, George** (1814–97) **77**
Pupils of **William Burn** and **David Bryce** respectively.
City and County Buildings, Wilson Street, Glasgow, 1842–71 **77**

Clark, William Tierney (1783–1852)
A civil engineer employed as a mechanic at Coalbrookdale Foundry; he became the engineer of West Middlesex Waterworks.
Suspension Bridge, Marlow, Buckinghamshire, 1831–36

Clarke, George Somers Leigh (Snr, 1825–82) **28, 65, 66**
A pupil of **Sir Charles Barry** who illustrated *The New Palace of Westminster*, 1849, with J Johnson.
Cowley Manor, Gloucestershire, 1854–62
Printing and Publishing Co building, West Smithfield, London, 1860 (demolished) **65, 66**
Merchant Seamens' Orphans' Asylum, Wanstead, London, 1861–63
General Credit and Discount Company (*now* Overseas Bankers Club), 7 Lothbury, London, 1866 **28, 66**
Wyfold Court, Oxfordshire, 1872–76
with Ewan Christian
Architectural Museum and Architectural Association building, 18 Tufton Street, London, 1869 (demolished)

Clarke, George Somers (Jnr, 1841–1926)
He was the son of Brighton town clerk and the nephew of **George Somers Clarke** Snr, a pupil of **Sir George Gilbert Scott**, and a partner of **John Thomas Micklethwaite** from 1876–92; surveyor of St Paul's Cathedral 1896–1906.
St Martin's Church, Brighton, 1871–75
Holy Trinity Church, Ardington, Berkshire, 1887

Clarke, Joseph (1819–88)
The author of *Schools and School Houses* 1852, and the diocesan architect for Canterbury, Rochester and St Albans.
Mental Hospital, Burwood, Surrey, 1840
Hockerill Training College, Bishops Stortford, Hertfordshire, 1851–52
Teachers' Training College, Culham, Oxfordshire, 1852
All Saints' Church, Cockermouth, Cumbria, 1852–54

Clarke, Thomas Chatfield (1829–95)
Unitarian Church, Upper Street, London, 1862 (demolished)
25 Throgmorton Street, London, 1869
Royal Bank of Scotland, Bishopsgate, London, 1877
66–67 Cornhill, London, 1880
385–97 Oxford Street, London, 1889
Central Foundation School for Girls, Stepney, London, 1891
77–78 Gracechurch Street, London, 1897
Clutton, Henry (1819–93)

A pupil of **Edward Blore**, friend of **William Burges**; they won the 1856 Lille Cathedral competition.
Quantock Lodge, Somerset, 1857
Minley Manor, Hampshire, 1858–62
St Francis of Assisi church, Pottery Lane, London, 1859–60
Oratory, Birmingham, 1860 (cloisters)
St Peter R C church, Leamington, Warwickshire, 1861–65
St Mary Magdalene R C church, Tavistock, Devon, 1865–67
St Mary's Church, Woburn, Bedfordshire, 1865–68
St Michael's Church, Apsley Heath, Bedfordshire, 1868
Bedford Chambers, Covent Garden, London, 1877–90

Cockerell, Charles Robert (1788–1863) **26, 91, 92, 98**
The second son and a pupil of Samuel Pepys Cockerell (1753–1827), he was employed as an assistant to **Sir Robert Smirke** in 1809, travelled extensively in Italy and Greece between 1810 and 1817, became the first recipient of the RIBA Gold Medal in 1848 and the President of RIBA in 1860.
Langton House, Langton, Long Blandford, Dorset, 1827–33 (demolished)
Holy Trinity Church, Hotwell Road, Bristol, Avon, 1829–30
Blaise Castle House, Henbury, near Bristol, Avon, 1832 (additions)
University Library, Cambridge, 1836–42
London and Westminster Bank, Lothbury, London, 1837 (demolished) **26**
Squire Law Library, Old School, Cambridge, 1837–42
Sun Fire and Life Assurance, Threadneedle Street, London, 1839–42 (demolished) **26**
Chapel, Killerton Park, Devon, 1840–41
Ashmolean Museum and Taylorian Institution, Oxford, 1841–45 **90, 91, 92, 92**
Caversfield House, Oxfordshire, 1842–45 (demolished)
Bank of England branches at Bristol (demolished), Liverpool and Manchester, 1844–47 **26**
Bank Chambers, Cook Street, Liverpool, 1846–49 (demolished)
St George's Hall, Liverpool, 1847–56 (completion)
with Frederick Pepys Cockerell
London and Globe Insurance, Dale Street, Liverpool, 1855–57

Cockerell, Frederick Pepys (1833–78)
The son of **Charles Robert Cockerell** and pupil of **Philip Charles Hardwick**, 1854–55.
Highgate School, London, 1865–68
Down Hall, Essex, 1871–73
Woodcote Hall, Shropshire, 1876
Crawley Hall, Hampshire, 1877

Coe, Henry Edward (1825–85)
A pupil of **Sir George Gilbert Scott**, he worked in various partnerships. He won the first prize for the design of the War Office in 1856, but his design was not built.
Agricultural Hall, Islington, London, 1861–62 (ironwork by Heaviside of Derby)
as **Coe, Peck and Stevens**
Guildhall (*now* part of the Public Library), Cambridge, 1862

Coleridge, John Duke (1879–1934) **23**
A pupil of Walter Cave and of **Sir Edwin Lutyens**.
Terraced housing, Hornton Street, London, 1904 **23**
Hornton Court, Kensington High Street, London, 1905 **23**

Collcutt, Thomas Edward (1840–1924) **82, 97, 103**
Employed in the offices of **George Edward Street** before setting up in practice on his own in 1873; a partner of Stanley Hamp, he was awarded the RIBA Gold Medal in 1902.

Town Hall, Wakefield, Yorkshire, 1877 **82**
Imperial Institute, Kensington, London, 1887–93
  (only tower remains)
Savoy Hotel, Strand, London, 1889–1903
  (altered) **103**
Royal English Opera House (*now* Palace
  Theatre), Cambridge Circus, London, 1889–90
  97
Midland Bank, Nos 45–47, Ludgate Hill,
  London, 1890
Wigmore Hall, London, 1890 *below*

Wraysbury Hall, Buckinghamshire, 1892
The Croft, Totteridge, Hertfordshire, 1895
Lloyds Register of Shipping, junction of Lloyds
  Avenue and Fenchurch Street, London, 1900

Colling, James Kellaway (1816–1905)
He worked in the offices of William Brooks
  (1786–1867), **Matthew Habershon**, **John
  Brown** (Norwich), **Sir George Gilbert Scott**
  and Moffatt. He published *Gothic Ornaments*,
  1848–50.
Albany Building, Old Hall Street, Liverpool, 1856
St Paul's Church, Hooton, Cheshire, 1858–62
Coxwold Hall, Lincolnshire, 1861

Contamin, Victor (1840–93) with Dutert,
  Charles-Louis-Ferdinand (1845–1906) **60**
Machinery Hall, *Exposition Universelle*, Paris, 1889
  60, *60*, *61*

Cooper, John James (*d.* 1839)
Congregational Chapel, Castle Street, Reading,
  Berkshire, 1837

Cooper, Thomas
Town Hall, Market Place, Brighton, East Sussex,
  1830–32

Corson, George (1829–1910) **96**
Scottish Widows Assurance office, Park Row,
  Leeds, 1869
Sun Buildings, Park Row, Leeds, 1877 (demolished)
Grand Theatre, Leeds, 1878–79 **96**
Municipal buildings, including library and City
  Art Gallery, Leeds, 1878–88

Cousin, David (1809–78)
A pupil of **William Henry Playfair**.
West (*now* Old) Kirk, Greenock, 1841
Corn Exchange, Edinburgh, 1847 (demolished)
Reid School of Music, Edinburgh, 1858
India Buildings, Victoria Street, Edinburgh, 1864

Cousland, James *see* **Boucher, James**

Cowper, E A with Baker, William **60**
New Street Station, Birmingham, 1850–54
  (demolished) **60**

Crewe, Bertie (*d.* 1937) **98**
The chief assistant and then partner of **W G R
  Sprague** until 1895, when he began to practise
  on his own account, becoming responsible for
  more than 100 theatres and music halls.
New Orient Theatre, Bedminster, Bristol, 1904
Mogador Palais, Paris, 1904
Alhambra, Paris, 1904
Alhambra, Brussels, 1907

The Hippodrome, Bedminster, Bristol, 1909
London Opera House, Kingsway, London,
  1910–11 (demolished) **98**
New Prince's Theatre *now* the Shaftesbury,
  Shaftesbury Avenue, London, 1911 **98**
Golders Green Hippodrome, London, 1911 **98**
Palace of Varieties, Manchester, 1913
The Coliseum, Dublin, 1913; destroyed 1918

Crickmay, George Rackstraw (1830–1907)
Diocesan surveyor to the Archdeaconry of
  Dorset, where he designed many churches and
  schools and carried out many restorations. He
  practised in Weymouth, where he was joined
  by his son, George Lay Crickmay (1858–1921).
  They opened London offices in the 1890s.
Eldridge Pope Brewery, Weymouth Avenue,
  Dorchester, Dorset, 1880
Horns public house, Kennington, London, 1886
Church House, Crane Street, Salisbury, 1887
Holy Trinity Church, Weymouth, Dorset, 1887
St Aldhelm's Church, Lytchett Heath, Dorset, 1898

Crossland, William H (1823–1909) **77, 81, 86, 89**
A pupil of **Sir George Gilbert Scott**.
Akroydon, Yorkshire, 1861 (model town, in
  succession to Sir George Gilbert Scott)
St Thomas's Church, Bradley, Yorkshire, 1861
St Stephen's Church, Copley, Yorkshire, 1863–65
Holy Trinity Church, Ossett, York, 1865
Town Hall, Rochdale, Lancashire, 1866–71 **81**
Holloway Sanatorium, Virginia Water, Surrey,
  1871–84 **86, 89**
Holloway College, Egham, Surrey, 1879–87 **86, 89**

Crowther, Joseph Stretch *see* **Bowman, Henry**

Cubitt, Lewis (1799–1883) **58, 102**
The pupil of **Henry Edward Kendall** Snr, he
  was a brother of **Thomas** and William **Cubitt**,
  designing many of the houses that they built.
Lowndes Square, London, 1841–44 (houses on
  south side)
Bricklayers' Arms Station, Bermondsey,
  London, 1842–44 (demolished)
King's Cross Station, King's Cross, London,
  1851–52 (rebuilt) **58**, *58, 59*
Great Northern Hotel, King's Cross, London,
  1854 *102*

Cubitt, Thomas (1788–1855) **16**
He was a brother of **Lewis** and William **Cubitt**.
Lewes Crescent, Brighton, 1825 **16**, *16*
Eaton Place, Eaton Square, Belgrave Place and
  Chester Square, Belgravia, London, 1825–53
Manchester Terrace, Barnsbury Estate, London,
  begun 1827
College Cross Street, Barnsbury Estate, London,
  1836–43 **16**

Cuijpers, Petrus Josephus Hubertus 109
Rijksmuseum, Amsterdam, 1855 **110**

Cundy, Thomas (Jnr, 1790–1867)
The son and pupil of Thomas Cundy Snr
  (1765–1825), whom he succeeded as surveyor
  to Earl Grosvenor's London estates (1825–66).
St Paul's Church, Wilton Place, London,
  1840–43
Holy Trinity Church, Paddington, London,
  1844–46 (partly demolished)
St Michael's Church, Chester Square, London,
  1846
St Mark's Church, Hamilton Terrace, London,
  1846–64
St Gabriel's Church, Warwick Square, London,
  1852–53
with **William Butterfield**
St Barnabas Church, Pimlico Road, London,
  1847–50

Cundy, Thomas (1820–95) **17**
The third son of **Thomas Cundy** Jnr, whom he
  succeeded as surveyor of the Grosvenor
  Estates.

Belgrave Mansions, Grosvenor Gardens,
  Grosvenor Place, London, 1868 **17**
Park Place House, Berkshire, 1870

Cunningham, John 98
Philharmonic Hall, Liverpool, 1846–49 **98**
Sailors' Home, Canning Place, Liverpool,
  1846–52 (demolished)

Currey, Henry (1820–1900) **89**
A pupil of **Decimus Burton**.
Baths, Buxton, Derbyshire, 1852 (altered)
London Bridge Terminus Hotel, London,
  1859–61 (demolished)
Hardwick Street Congregational Church,
  Buxton, Derbyshire, 1861
St Thomas' Hospital, London, 1868–71 (partly
  demolished) **89**
The Duke of Devonshire's Estate, Eastbourne,
  Sussex, 1870, 1874, 1889
Eastbourne College, 1889
St Peter's Church, Meads Road, Eastbourne,
  1894–96

Darbishire, Henry Astley 22, 23
Columbia Square, Bethnal Green, London,
  1857–60 (flats, demolished) **22**
Victoria Park, London, 1861 (fountain)
Peabody Trust Buildings, Commercial Street,
  London, 1862–64 **22**
Peabody Trust Buildings, Blackfriars Road,
  London, 1864 onwards
Peabody Trust Buildings, Greenman Street,
  London, 1865 **22**
Holly Village, Swain's Lane and Chester Road,
  London, 1865
Columbia Market, London, 1866–68 (demolished)
Peabody Trust Buildings, Wild Street, London,
  1881 *22*

Darby, Abraham 53
Iron Bridge, Coalbrookdale, Shropshire, 53, *53*

Daukes, Samuel Whitfield (1811–80) **89**
A specialist in railway stations and churches, he
  was articled to **James Pigott Pritchett** Snr of
  York but practised mostly in Gloucester and
  Cheltenham.
St Andrew's Church, Old Church Lane,
  London, 1845–47 (originally in Wells Street,
  taken down and rebuilt 1932)
Royal Agricultural College, Cirencester,
  Gloucestershire, 1846
St Peter's Church, Cheltenham, 1847–49
Colney Hatch Mental Hospital, Friern Barnet,
  Hertfordshire, 1847–51 (later Friern Hospital
  but now converted to flats) **89**
St Saviour's Church, Tetbury, Gloucestershire, 1848
Horsted Place, Sussex, 1850–52
Christ Church, Cannon Place, London, 1852
Witley Court, near Kidderminster,
  Worcestershire, 1855 (destroyed)

Davis, Henry David (1838–1915)
A partner of Ernest R Barrow Emmanuel (1868–
  1948).
Synagogue, Upper Berkeley Street, London,
  1870
City of London School for Boys, Victoria
  Embankment, London, 1879
63 St James's Street, London, 1887

Dawson, Joshua (*b. c.* 1812)
St Bartholomew R C church, Rainhill Stoops,
  Rainhill, Merseyside, 1838–40

Daws, William 72
Victoria Buildings, Victoria Street, Manchester,
  1874 (demolished) **72**

Deacon, Charles E (1844–1927)
A pupil of W Emerson and a partner of
  Aldridge.
St Benedict's Church, Everton, Liverpool,
  1886–87

St Dunstan's Church, Wavertree, Liverpool, 1886–89
City Education Offices, 14 St Thomas Street, Liverpool, 1898

Deane, Sir Thomas (Snr, 1792–1871) **75, 79, 92, 93**
A partner of Benjamin Woodward (1815–61), and of his son **Sir Thomas Newenham Deane**. He was made mayor of Cork, Ireland, and knighted in 1830.
Queen's College (*now* University College), Cork, 1845–49
with partners
Trinity College Museum, Dublin, 1854–60
Museum of Natural History (*now* University Museum), Oxford, 1855–60 **74, 75, 79, 79, 92, 93**
Crown Life Insurance Building, Bridge Street, London, 1855–58 (demolished) **27**
Llysdulas, near Llanwennlyfo, Anglesey, 1856 (house; demolished)
Oxford Union Society, Oxford, 1856–57
Kildare Street Club, Dublin, 1858–61
Kilkenny Castle, Ireland, 1858–62 (alterations)

Deane, Sir Thomas Newenham (Jnr, 1828–99)
The son and partner of **Sir Thomas Deane** Snr, he was knighted in 1890.
Church of Ireland Cathedral, Tuam, Galway, 1861–64
Meadow Building, Christ Church, Oxford, 1862–65
National Library and Museum, Dublin, 1885–90 (with his son, Thomas Manly Deane)

Deering, John Peter *see* **Gandy, John Peter**

Denison, Edmund *see* **Grimthorpe, Lord**

Derick, John Macduff (*d.* 1861)
St Saviour's Church, Leeds, 1839–45
St James' Church, Danes Road, Rusholme, Manchester, 1845
St Mark's Church, Pensnett, Staffordshire, 1846–49

de Soissons, Louis 12
Houses, Welwyn Garden City, Hertfordshire 1920 **12, 12**

Destailleur, Gabriel-Hippolyte (1822–93) **35**
Waddesdon Manor, Buckinghamshire, 1874–89 **35, 35**

de Trinqueti, Baron H 49
Albert Memorial Chapel, Windsor, Berkshire, *c.*1863 **49**

Devey, George (1820–86) **37–9, 41**
Cottages next to church, Penshurst, Kent, 1850
Betteshanger House, Kent, 1856–82 **37, 38**
Parish school, Benenden, Kent, 1861
Old Rectory, Wickwar, Gloucestershire, 1864
Akeley Wood, Buckinghamshire, 1867–78
Denne Hill, Kent, 1871–75
Hall Place, Kent, 1871–76
Goldings, Hertfordshire, 1871–77
St Alban's Court, Kent, 1874–78
Ascott, Buckinghamshire, 1874–88
Ashfold, Handcross, Sussex, 1875–78 (demolished)
Blakesware, Hertfordshire, 1876–79
Eythrope, Buckinghamshire, 1876–79
Gaunts House, Dorset, 1886
Minley Manor, Hampshire; additions, 1886

Dobson, John (1787–1865) **16**
Lilburn Tower, Northumberland, 1829–37 (interior mutilated)
Meldon Park, Northumberland, 1832
New Markets, Newcastle-upon-Tyne, 1835–36
Holme Eden Hall, Warwick, Cumbria, 1837
Beaufront Castle, Corbridge, Northumberland, 1837–41
Town Hall, North Shields, 1844
Central Station, Newcastle-upon-Tyne, 1846–65
St John's Church, Otterburn, Northumberland, 1858

Jesmond Parish Church, Newcastle-upon-Tyne, 1858
St Edward's Church, Sudbrooke, Lincolnshire, 1860
Grey Street, Newcastle-upon-Tyne, 1834–40 (east side, with Richard Grainger) **16**
with Robert Stephenson
High Level Bridge, Newcastle-upon-Tyne, 1847

Dockray, Robert B *see* **Stephenson, Robert**

Doll, Charles Fitzroy (1851–1929) **102, 103**
Trained at the Polyteknikum, Koblenz, he was articled in London to Charles Gritten and appointed surveyor to the Bedford Estates in Bloomsbury and Covent Garden in 1885.
Russell Hotel, Russell Square, London, 1898 **102, 103**
Imperial Hotel, Russell Square, London, 1905–11 (demolished)
Dillon's Bookshop block, Torrington Place, London, 1907

Donaldson, Thomas Leverton (1795–1885)
The son and pupil of James Donaldson, he studied at the Royal Academy Schools and travelled extensively in order to study classical architecture. He was a co-founder of the Institute of British Architects in 1835 and the first Professor of Architecture at University College, London, 1842–62. He was President of RIBA 1863–64 and was awarded the RIBA Medal in 1851.
Dr Williams' Library, Gordon Square, London, 1848
Great Hall (interior) and Library, University College, London, 1848
Leonards Lee, Sussex, 1853 (house)
German Hospital, Hackney, London, 1865

Donthorn, William John (1799–1859)
Upton Hall, Nottinghamshire, *c.* 1830
Highcliffe Castle, Hampshire, 1830–34 (remodelling; now a ruin)
Holkham Hall, Norfolk, 1844–50

Douglas, Campbell (1828–1910)
A pupil of **John Thomas Rochead**, he worked for **John Dobson** before becoming a partner of **John James Stevenson** and **James Sellars**.
Alloway Church, Ayr, 1858
Briggate Free Church, Glasgow, 1859 (demolished)
Hatfield House, Cove, Scotland, 1859 (demolished)

Douglas, John (1829–1911)
A pupil of **Edward Graham Paley** of Lancaster, he became a partner of D P Fordham in 1885, and of Minshill in 1898.
St John's Church, Aldford, Cheshire, 1866
Oakmere Hall, Sandiway, Cheshire, 1867
St Paul's Church, Helsby, Cheshire, 1868–70
Shotwick Park, Great Sughall, Cheshire, 1872
Broxton Old Hall, Cheshire, 1873
St Mary's Church, Whitegate, Cheshire, 1874
St Stephen's Church, Moulton, Cheshire, 1876
St Chad's Church, Hopwas, Staffordshire, 1879
St Mary's Church, Pulford, Cheshire, 1881–84
Flemish Gateway, Eaton Hall, Cheshire, 1882
The Paddocks, Eccleston, Cheshire, 1883
Abbeystead House, Over Wyresdale, Lancashire, 1886
St James' Church, Haydock, Lancashire, 1891
The Wern, Caernarfon, 1892 (house)
Glangwna, Caernarfon, 1893 (house)
Dee Banks, Chester; 1897 (own house)
St John the Evangelist church, Sandiway, Cheshire, 1902
St Paul's Church, Broughton, Chester, 1902
Port Sunlight model town, Cheshire, begun in 1888 (with other architects) **12, 21, 22, 24**

Doyle, John Francis (1840–1913)
Born in Liverpool; **Richard Norman Shaw** acted as consultant on his White Star Line offices (later the Pacific Steam Navigation Building), 30 James Street, Liverpool, 1895–98.

St Ambrose's Church, Widnes, Lancashire, 1879–93
Royal Insurance, Dale Street, Liverpool, 1896–1903
St Barnabas' Church, Allerton Road, Liverpool, 1900–1914

Drew, Sir Thomas (1838–1910)
He was born in Dublin and specialised in church restoration.
Ulster Bank, College Green, Dublin, 1887–91
Graduates Memorial Building, Library Square, Dublin, 1899–1902
St Anne's Cathedral, Belfast, 1899 (design only, completed by **William Henry Lynn**)
Church, Castle Archdale, Fermanagh, 1908

Du Cane, Sir Edmund Frederick (1830–1903) **89**
He joined the Royal Engineers in 1848 and rose to the rank of major-general. Appointed Inspector General of military prisons, he published *The Punishment and Prevention of Crime* in 1885.
Wormwood Scrubs Prison, Du Cane Road, London, 1873–85 **89**

Dudok, William Marinus (1884–1974)
He was trained as an engineer at the Royal Military Academy, Breda, the Netherlands, and in 1913 established his own practice in Leiden. Appointed director of the Municipal Works, Hilversum in 1915, he became Municipal Architect in 1927; from 1934 he was employed as a town planner for the Hague.
School, Geraniumstraat, Hilversum, 1917–18
Public Baths, Hilversum, 1920

Dunn, Archibald Matthias (1833–1917)
He trained in Bristol with **Charles Francis Hansom** before going into partnership with his son, Edward Joseph Hansom, from 1871–1900.
Downside Abbey, Stratton-on-the-Fosse, Somerset, 1872 (church transept)
Our Lady Help of Christians R C church, Bath, 1879–81
Our Lady and the English Myrtyrs R C church, Cambridge, 1887–90
Medical College (*now* Dental Hospital), Newcastle-upon-Tyne, 1887–95
St Michael's R C church, Newcastle-upon-Tyne, 1891

Dutert, Charles-Louis-Ferdinand *see* **Contamin, Victor**

Dyer, Charles (1794–1848)
Victoria Rooms (*now* part of Bristol University), Bristol, 1839–41 (later additions)

Dymond, George (*c.* 1797–1835)
and **Charles Fowler**
Higher Market, Queen Street, Exeter, Devon, 1835–38 (rebuilt)

Eads, James Buchanan (1820–87) **54, 55**
An engineer and inventor who invented a diving bell and made his fortune from sunken river steamboats. In 1861 he built eight ironclad Mississippi steamers in 100 days for the government.
Eads Bridge, St Louis, Missouri, USA 1874 **54**

Edgar, Robert (1837–73)
A partner of J L Kipling.
Wedgwood Memorial Institute, Burslem, Stoke-on-Trent, Staffordshire, 1863–69

Edge, Charles (*d.* 1867)
The Crescent, Filey, North Yorkshire, 1835–38

Edis, Col Sir Robert William (1839–1927) **100**
The author of *Decoration and Furniture of Town Houses*, 1881, he was knighted in 1919 and was a Colonel of the Artists' Corps of Volunteers.
Sandringham House, Norfolk, 1881, 1883 (additions including ballroom)

100 Piccadilly, London, 1883
Constitutional Club, Northumberland Avenue,
 London, 1884 **100**
Great Central Railway (*now* Landmark) Hotel,
 Marylebone Station, London, 1897–99

Eiffel, Alexandre Gustave (1832–1923) **54, 55, 62**
A civil engineer born at Dijon, France, noted for
 his Paris Exhibition tower and numerous bridges
 and viaducts. He also designed the framework
 for the Statue of Liberty, New York, and built
 the first Aerodynamics Laboratory, Paris.
Au Bon Marché store, Paris 1876, (with
 L C Boileau) **72**
Bridge over River Douro, Oporto, Portugal 1877
Garabit Viaduct, near Thonet, France, 1879 **55,** *55*
Eiffel Tower, *Exposition Universelle*, Paris, 1889 **62,** *62*

Ellet, Charles (1810–62) **55**
An American civil engineer, he studied bridge
 building in Paris, and built the first wire
 suspension bridge in America.
Bridge over River Ohio, Wheeling, West
 Virginia 1849–52 **55**

Ellis, Peter (1804–84) **28**
Oriel Chambers, Water Street, Liverpool, 1864
 28, *28*
16 Cook Street, Liverpool, 1866 **28**

Elmes, Harvey Lonsdale (1813–47) **77, 98**
The son and pupil of James Elmes; an assistant
 to **Henry Edmond Goodridge** in Bath.
Collegiate Institute, Shaw Street, Liverpool,
 1840–43
St George's Hall, Liverpool, 1841 **76,** *76,* **77, 98**
Lancashire County Lunatic Asylum, Rainhill, 1847
Allanhouse Towers, Woolton Road, Liverpool,
 1847 (house, demolished)

Elmslie, E W
A partner of F C Cope, C Eales, Franey and
 Haddon.
SS Thomas and Clement church, Winchester,
 1845–46
Imperial Hotel and Station, Great Malvern,
 Worcestershire, 1860–61 (hotel is now a girls'
 school)
Link Hotel, Great Malvern, Worcestershire,
 1860–62 (demolished)
Whitbourne Hall, near Bromyard,
 Herefordshire, 1860–62
Lloyds Bank, High Street, Worcester, 1861–62

Emden, Walter (1847–1913) **97**
Hotel Anglo-American, Livorno, Italy, 1875
Garrick Theatre, London, 1888 **97**
Grand Hotel and Brasserie de l'Europe, 10–15
 Leicester Square, London, 1899

Emerson, Sir William (1843–1924)
The son of a silk merchant, he was born at
 Whetstone, Middlesex, and educated at King's
 College, London. He became a pupil of **William
 Gillbee Habershon** and also of **Alfred Robert
 Pite** before working for **William Burges**. He
 was the winner of the first competition for
 Liverpool cathedral, 1886, President of RIBA,
 1899–1902, and was knighted in 1902.
Markets, Bombay, India, 1865–71
SS Mary and James church, Brighton, 1877–79
Hamilton House, Victoria Embankment,
 London, 1898–1901
Victoria Memorial, Calcutta, India, 1904–21

Emmett, John T (1828–98)
Congregational College, St John's Wood,
 London, 1849
New Independent Church, Bath Street,
 Blythwood, Glasgow, 1851

Espinasse, F (1880–1925)
A French exponent of *art nouveau.*
The Michelin Building, 61 Fulham Road,
 London, 1910–11 *right*

Fergusson, James (1808–86)
An architectural historian who had travelled to
 India as a merchant and wrote *Illustrated Handbook
 of Architecture*, 1859, *History of Architecture*, 1865,
 and *Indian and Eastern Architecture*, 1876. He was
 awarded the RIBA Gold Medal in 1871.
Marianne North Gallery, Royal Botanic
 Gardens, Kew, Richmond, Surrey, 1882

Ferrey, Benjamin (1810–80)
A pupil of **Augustus Charles Pugin**, he worked
 with **William Wilkins** and was awarded the
 RIBA Gold Medal in 1870.
All Saints' Church, Dorchester, Dorset, 1843–45
St Stephen's Church, Rochester Row, London,
 1847–50
St John's Church, Brixton, London, 1852–53
St Mary's Church, Buckland, Somerset, 1853–63
All Saints' Church, Blackheath, London, 1857–58
Huntsham Hall, Devon, 1869

Finch, Hill and **E L Paraire 96**
Oxford Theatre, St Giles Circus, London, 1861
 (demolished)
Holborn Theatre Royal, High Holborn,
 London, 1866 (destroyed) **96**
Horse Shoe Hotel, Tottenham Court Road,
 London, 1875

Fletcher, Sir Banister Flight (1866–1953) **15, 17**
The eldest son of Banister Fletcher (1833–99),
 educated at King's College and University College,
 London, he joined his father's practice in 1884,
 publishing *A History of Architecture on the Comparative
 Method for Students, Craftsmen and Amateurs* in 1896.
20 and 46 Harley Street, London, 1890s **17**
30 Wimpole Street, London, 1890s *15*
Goslett's, Charing Cross Road, London, 1897
 (demolished)

Flint, William (1801–62)
New Hall (*now* City Library), Wellington Street,
 Leicester, 1831

Flockton, Thomas James (1825–1900)
The son of **William Flockton** and a partner
 first of Abbot, then of Edward Mitchel Gibbs
 (1847–1935).
Williams Deacon's Bank, Church Street,
 Sheffield, 1866
Cutlers Hall, Sheffield; interior, 1867
Mappin Art Gallery, Sheffield, 1886–88
St John's Church, Ranmoor Park Road,
 Sheffield, 1887–89
with Edward Robert Robson
Firth College (later Central Schools), Sheffield,
 1877–79

Flockton, William (1804–64)
The Mount, Sheffield, South Yorkshire *c.* 1835
Wesley Grammar School (*now* King Edward VII
 School), Glossop Road, Sheffield, 1837–40
Savings Bank, Sheffield, 1858

Forbes, John
Pittville Pump Room, Cheltenham,
 Gloucestershire, 1825–30
Segrave Place, Pittville Central Drive,
 Cheltenham, Gloucestershire (thought to be by)
 c. 1825–30
St Paul's Church, St Paul's Road, Cheltenham,
 Gloucestershire, 1827–31

Fordham, D P *see* **Douglas, John**

Fothergill, Watson (1841–1928)
Worked with **Sir Arthur William Blomfield**,
 1862, and **John Middleton** (Cheltenham), 1864.
5–7 Lenton Road, Nottingham, 1873
Nottingham Express Offics, Parliament Street,
 Nottingham, 1876
Nottingham and Nottinghamshire Bank, Thurland
 Street, Nottingham, 1880–82 (later NatWest Bank)
Budworth Hall, Chipping Ongar, Essex, 1882
Baptist Church, Woodborough Road,
 Nottingham, 1884
15 George Street, Nottingham, 1895 (own office)
Jessop's Store, junction of King Street and Long
 Row, Nottingham, 1896–97

Fowke, Capt Francis (1823–65) **93, 94**
Commissioned in the Royal Engineers, 1842, he
 became an inspector of the Department of Science
 and Art in 1853, and was secretary to the British
 Commission at the Paris Exhibition, 1854.
Victoria and Albert Museum, Cromwell Road,
 London, 1856 onwards **93,** *93*
Raglan Barracks, Devonport, Plymouth, 1859–60
National Gallery, Dublin, 1859–60 (enlargements)
Royal Scottish Museum of Science and Art,
 Edinburgh, 1860–61
Royal Horticultural Society, South Kensington,
 London, 1861 (gardens and greenhouses,
 demolished)
Exhibition Building, London, 1862 (demolished)
Royal Albert Hall, London; design, 1864
 (construction by **Henry Young Darracott Scott**
 1867–71) **93,** *94*

Fowler, Charles (1791–1867) **55, 89**
He served his apprenticeship in Exeter, moving
 to London in 1814. Here he worked for D Laing,
 before setting up in practice on his own in
 1818. He was a co-founder of the Institute of
 British Architects; *see also* **Dymond, George**.
Syon House, Brentford, London, 1827–30
 (conservatory in the grounds) **55**
The Piazza, Covent Garden Market, London,
 c. 1828–30 **55,** *56*
Hungerford Market, London, 1831–33
 (demolished) **55**
St Paul's Church, Honiton, Devon, 1837–38
Higher Market, Exeter, Devon, 1837–38 **55**
Lodges, Maristow, Devon, 1839
County Lunatic Asylum, Exminster, Devon,
 1843–46 **89**
Powderham Castle, Devon; additions, 1848

Fowler, C Hodgson (1840–1910)
He was a pupil of **Sir George Gilbert Scott**, and
 specialised in restoration work.
Holy Innocents' Church, Tudhoe, Durham, 1866
St Edmund's Church, Bearpark, Durham, 1879
St Paul's Church, Grand Road, West Hartlepool,
 Durham, 1885
St Barnabas' Church, Middlesborough,
 Yorkshire, 1888
St Peter's Church, Norton, Yorkshire, 1894
Christ Church, Hepple, Northumberland, 1897
St Alban's Church, London Road, East Retford,
 Nottinghamshire, 1901
Rochester Cathedral, Kent; restoration, 1904–08

Fowler, James (1829–92)
The diocesan architect for Lincoln.
St Michael's Church, Louth, Lincolnshire, 1863
SS Mary and Peter church, Ludford Magna,
 Lincolnshire, 1864
St Nicholas' Church, Snitterby, Lincolnshire, 1866
Langton Hall, Langton-by-Partney, Lincolnshire,
 1866
St Swithun's Church, Lincoln, 1869–87
St Hilary's Church, Spridlington, Lincolnshire, 1875
Holy Trinity Church, Gedney Hill,
 Lincolnshire, 1875

Fowler, Sir John (1817–98) **55, 60**
A civil engineer on the London and Brighton

Railway, later the engineer and general manager of the Stockton and Hartlepool line. He was a member of the council of the Institution of Civil Engineers, 1849, and its president 1866–67. He took Benjamin Baker into partnership in 1875.
Pimlico Railway Bridge, 1860
Central Station, Manchester, 1876–79 **60**
Firth of Forth Bridge, 1882–90 (with partners, including Benjamin Baker) **11, 55, *55***

Francis, Frederick John (1818–96) and **Horace Francis** (1821–94)
St Paul's Church, Ringwood, Hampshire, 1853–55
School, Broomhouse Lane, Fulham, London, 1854–55
Christ Church, Lancaster Gate, London, 1854–55 (only the tower survives)
National Discount Offices, Cornhill, London, 1857
Westminster (*now* NatWest) Bank, High Street, Oxford, 1866
City Offices Company Building, 39–40 Lombard Street, London, 1868
Holborn Restaurant, London, 1873 (demolished)
Grand Hotel (*now* Grand Buildings), Charing Cross Road, London, 1878–80

Fraser, Patrick Allan (1813–90)
An amateur architect.
Hospital house, Arbroath, Angus, 1843–53
House with fortified bridge, Blackcraig, Perth, 1855–70
Mortuary Chapel, Arbroath, 1873–84

Freeman, R Knill (1838–1904)
He was born in Bolton.
Library and Museum, Derby, 1878

Galton, Sir Douglas Strutt (1822–99) **89**
He was made a First Captain in the Royal Engineers in 1855.
Herbert Royal Military Hospital, Woolwich, begun 1860 **89**
St Michael's Church, Lowfield Heath, Surrey, 1867
Cardiff Castle, 1868–81 **35, *36***

Gandy (later **Deering**), **John Peter** (1787–1850)
Pimlico Literary Institute, Ebury Street, London, 1830

Gane, Richard (1838–77) **66**
Abbey Cloth Mill, Bradford-upon-Avon, Wiltshire, 1875 **66**

Garner, Charles (1825–98) **97**
Théâtre de l'Opéra, Paris, France, 1875 ***96, 97***
Théâtre Marigny, Paris, France, 1883

Garner, Thomas (1839–1906)
A pupil of **Sir George Gilbert Scott**, he was in partnership with **George Frederick Bodley**, 1869–1897, then established his own practice.
Moreton House, Holly Walk, London, 1896
Downside Abbey, Stratton-on-the-Fosse, Somerset, 1901–05 (chancel of church)

Gaudí, Antoni (1852–1926) **106–8**
Born in Reus near Tarragona, Antoni Gaudí i Cornet studied architecture at the Escola Provincial d'Arquitectura, 1875–77. He worked in the offices of **Francisco de Paula de Villar**, whom he succeeded in 1883 in the building of the Sagrada Familia Cathedral, Barcelona. He established his own practice in Barcelona in 1878.
Street lights, Barcelona, 1879
Casa Vicens, Barcelona, 1883–85 **107**
Palacio Güell, Barcelona, 1885–89 (for friend and patron, the textile manufacturer Eusebi Güell)
Bishop's palace, Astorga, 1887–93 **107**
Colegio Teresiano, Barcelona, 1888–89 (completion)
Casa de los Botines, León, 1891–92
Casa Calvet, Barcelona, 1898–1900
Colonia Güell church, Barcelona, 1898 (begun)
Parque Güell, Barcelona, 1900–14 (two residences, entrance area and terracing) **108, *108***

Casa Batlló, Barcelona, 1904–06
Casa Milà, Barcelona, 1906–10
Sagrada Familia schoolhouse, Barcelona, completed 1909 **107**
Sagrada Familia cathedral, Barcelona, 1914 (building work still continues) ***106***

Geary, Stephen (1797–1854)
Highgate Cemetery, London, 1839 onwards

George, Sir Ernest (1839–1922) **19, 23**
Born in Southwark, London, the son of John George, a wholesale ironmonger; he entered the Royal Academy Schools in 1857 and won the Gold Medal in 1859. He was articled to Samuel Hewitt, before becoming a partner in turn of Thomas Vaughan, 1861–1875, **Harold Peto**, 1876 and Alfred B Yeates. He was awarded the RIBA Gold Medal in 1896, knighted in 1908 and became President of RIBA 1908–10.
St Pancras' Church, Rousdon, Devon, 1870
Rousdon House, Devon, 1870
Thomas Goode's, 17–21 South Audley Street, London, 1875–91
Bee-Hive Coffee House, Streatham High Road, London, 1878–79 (later Cow Rubber Works)
Woodhouse, Uplyme, Devon, 1879
Stoodleigh Court, Devon, 1881–83
20–26 and 35–45 Harrington Gardens, London, 1881–96 **19, *19***
1–18 Collingham Gardens, London, 1881–96 **23, *23***
Mount Street, London, c 1885–90 (houses)
St Andrew's Church, Guildersfield Road, London, 1886–87
Shiplake Court, Oxfordshire, 1889–90
Claridges Hotel, Brook Street, London, 1894–97
Golders Green Crematorium, Hoop Lane, London, 1905
Royal Exchange Buildings, London, 1907–08
Royal Academy of Music, Marylebone Road, London, 1910–11
Southwark Bridge, London, 1913–21

Gibson, Ernest (1864–1919)
A craftsman friend of William Morris, on whose advice he worked with **John Dando Sedding**, 1886–88.
The White House, North Avenue, Leicester, 1897
Stonywell Cottage, Charnwood Forest, Leicestershire, 1899
Lea Cottage, Charnwood Forest, Leicestershire, 1900
The Leasowes, Sapperton, Gloucestershire, 1901 (cottage)

Gibson, James Glen Sivewright (1861–1951)
A pupil of **Thomas Edward Collcutt** and a partner of Samuel Bridgman Russell (1864–1955) from 1890 to 1900.
West Riding County Offices, Wakefield, Yorkshire, 1894–98
Middlesex Guildhall, Storey's Gate, London, 1912–13

Gibson, John (1817–92) **26, 77**
A pupil of **Joseph Aloysius Hansom** in Birmingham, he later worked for **Sir Charles Barry** before setting up in practice in 1844. He was architect to the National Provincial Bank, 1864, and received the RIBA Gold Medal, 1890.
Central Baptist Chapel, Bloomsbury Street, London, 1845–48
Imperial Insurance Office, Threadneedle Street, London, 1846 (demolished)
National Bank (*now* Langside Hall), Queen's Park, Glasgow, 1847–49
St John the Baptist church, Shenstone, Staffordshire, 1853
St Margaret's Church, Bodelwyddan, Flint, 1856
Town Hall, Todmorden, Yorkshire, 1860–75 **77**
National Provincial Bank, 15 Bishopsgate, London, 1863–65 (later NatWest Bank)
Dodroyd Castle, Yorkshire, 1866–69
Unitarian Church, Todmorden, Yorkshire, 1869

SPCK Building, Northumberland Avenue, London, 1876–79
National Provincial Bank, Stockton, Durham, 1877 (later NatWest Bank)
Child's Bank, Fleet Street, London, 1879

Giles, John 102
Langham Hotel, Portland Place, London, 1865 **102**

Gill, Irving John (1870–1936)
Gill began working in 1890 in the offices of Dankmar Adler and Louis Sullivan in Chicago. He established his own practice in 1896 in San Diego, California, USA.
Christian Science Church, San Diego, 1904
Klauber House, San Diego, 1907–10
Wilson Acton Hotel, La Jolla, California, 1908
Lewis Courts development, Sierra Madre, 1910
Pacific Electric Railroad building, Torrance, 1912
Dodge House, Los Angeles, 1914–16 (demolished)
Horatio West Court, Santa Monica, 1919–21

Gingell, William Bruce (1818–1900) **26**
A partner of T R Lysaght.
Leeds and Yorkshire Assurance (*now* Leek and Westbourne Building Society), Commercial Street, Leeds, 1852
General Hospital, Guinea Street, Bristol, 1852–57
West of England and South Wales Bank, Corn Street, Bristol, 1854 (later Lloyds Bank) **26**
12 Temple Street, Bristol, 1865 (warehouse)

Goddard, Joseph (1839–1900)
A partner first of Paget then of Catlow.
St Andrew's Church, Tur Langton, Leicestershire, 1866
Clock Tower, Leicester, 1868
Leicestershire Bank, Granby Street, Leicester, 1870 (later HSBC Bank)
Caldecote Hall, Warwickshire, 1879
St Mary's Church, Radcliffe-on-Trent, Nottinghamshire, 1879

Godwin, Edward William (1833–86) **19, 29, 66, 81**
Born in Bristol, the son of a decorator, he was in partnership there with Henry Crisp, and a friend of **William Burges**. He went to London in 1865.
Town Hall, Northampton, 1860–64 **81**
Anderson's Warehouse, 104 Stokes Croft, Bristol, 1862
John Perry carriage factory, Bristol, 1862 **66**
Town Hall, Congleton, Cheshire, 1864–67
St Martin's Villas, 43–44 Billing Road, Northampton, 1865
Dromore Castle, Limerick, 1866–73
Gatehouse Lodge, Castle Ashby, Northamptonshire, 1867–68
Glenbergh Towers, Kerry, 1867–70 (demolished)
Guildhall, Plymouth, 1870–74
Beauvale House, Nottinghamshire, 1871–74
Fallows Green, Harpenden, Hertfordshire, 1872 (demolished)
The Manse, Greasley, Nottinghamshire, 1873
1 and 2 The Avenue, Bedford Park, London, 1875–77 **20, *20***
4, 5, and 6 Chelsea Embankment, London, 1875–77
The White House, 35 Tite Street, London, 1877–79 (demolished) **19, *19***
44 and 46 Tite Street, London, 1878 and 1884
34 Tite Street, London, 1882–84 (remodelling; since altered)

Godwin, George (1815–88)
Editor of *The Builder*, 1844–83.
St Mary's Church, The Boltons, London, 1850
St Jude's Church, Collingham Gardens, London, 1870
St Luke's Church, Redcliffe Square, London, 1872

Goldie, George (1828–87)
A pupil and partner of **Mathew Ellison Hadfield** and **John Grey Weightman**. He later worked with his son, Edward Goldie.
St Peter's R C church, Scarborough, Yorkshire, 1858

St Mary's R C church, Greenock, Renfrew, 1861
St Wilfrid's R C church, York, 1862–64
St Augustine's R C church, Stamford, Lincolnshire, 1864
Church of the Assumption (R C), Kensington Square, London, 1875

Goodridge, Henry Edmund (1800–63)
Prior Park, Bath, Avon, 1829–34 and 1836 (external staircase, wings and interiors)
Holy Trinity Church, Frome, Somerset, 1837–39
The Apostles R C cathedral, Bristol, 1839 (altered and continued by **Charles Francis Hansom** 1847–48)
Devizes Castle, Wiltshire, 1842
Lansdowne Cemetery, Bath, 1848 (entrance)
Percy Chapel, Charlotte Street, Bath, 1854 (with A S Goodridge)

Goodwin, Francis (1784–1835); *see also* **Lane, Richard**
St Mary's Church, Oxford Street, Bilston, West Midlands, 1829–30

Gough, Alexander Dick (1804–71)
A pupil of **Benjamin Dean Wyatt** and a partner to **Robert Lewis Roumieu**, 1836–48. He was joined in practice by two of his sons, Charles and **Hugh Roumieu Gough**.
St Matthew's Church, Essex Road, London, 1850 (demolished)
St Mark's Church, Tollington Park, London, 1853–54
St Paul's Church, Chatham, Kent, 1853–55
with Robert Lewis Roumieu
Milner Square, London, 1840

Gough, Hugh Roumieu (1843–1904)
St Cuthbert's Church, Philbeach Gardens, London, 1884–88
with John Pollard Seddon
St Paul's Church, Hammersmith, London, 1882–87

Gowans, Sir James (1821–90)
He was mostly employed as a railway and building contractor.
Rockville, 3 Napier Road, Edinburgh, 1858 (own house)
Lammerburn House, 10 Napier Road, Edinburgh, 1859
25–36 Castle Terrace, Edinburgh, 1866–70

Graham, James Gillespie (1777–1855)
Moray Place, Edinburgh, 1822–30
Town House / Assembly Rooms, Haddington, Lothian, 1831
Parish Church, Montrose, Tayside, 1832–34 (tower and spire)
St Margaret's Convent Chapel, Edinburgh, 1835
with Augustus Welby Northmore Pugin
Houses of Parliament, London (unexecuted designs)
St John's Tolbooth, Edinburgh, 1844

Green, Arthur (d. 1904) *as Archer and Green* 17
Cambridge Gate, Regent's Park, London, 1875
Whitehall Court, Victoria Embankment, London, 1884–87 17
Hyde Park Hotel, Knightsbridge, London, 1888
Hyde Park Court, Hyde Park, London, 1890

Green, Benjamin (c. 1811–58)
Theatre Royal, Grey Street, Newcastle-upon-Tyne, 1836–37; *see also* **Green, John**

Greene, Col Godfrey T (1807–86) 66
Director of Engineering and Architectural Works for the Admiralty.
Factory smithy, Sheerness, Kent, 1856
Foundry, including shipfitting shop and boatstore, Sheerness, Kent, 1857 66

Green, John (1787–1852) and **Benjamin Green**
Partners in Newcastle c. 1830–44.
Holy Trinity Church, Stockton-on-Tees, Cleveland, 1834–35

St Alban's Church, Earsdon, Northumberland, 1836–37
Tyne Master Mariners' Asylum, Tynemouth, 1837
Town Hall and Corn Market, Newcastle-upon-Tyne, 1837 (completed by John Johnston 1858–63)

Gregan, John Edgar (1813–55) 26
St John's Church, Longsight, Manchester, 1845–46
Heywood's Bank, St Ann's Square, Manchester, 1848–49 (later Williams Deacon's Bank) 26
Warehouse, junction of Portland Street and Parker Street, Manchester, 1850 (demolished)
Mechanics' Institute (*now* College of Commerce), Manchester, 1854

Grellier, William (1807–52)
St George's Sunday Schools, High Street, Macclesfield, Cheshire, 1835

Gribble, Herbert Augustus Keate (1847–94) 45, 46
London Oratory of St Philip Neri and the Church of the Immaculate Heart of Mary at Brompton, Kensington, London from 1878 45, *46*

Grimthorpe, Lord (1816–1905)
An amateur architect also known as **Edmund Beckett** and **Edmund Denison**, he was created **Baron Grimthorpe** in 1886.
St James' Church, Doncaster, Yorkshire, 1858
Abbey, St Albans, Hertfordshire, 1880–85 (restoration)
St Mary's Church, Doncaster, Yorkshire, 1885

Gropius, Walter (1883–1969) 70, 71
Educated at the Technische Hochschule in both Berlin and Munich, 1903–07; on graduating, he worked in the offices of **Peter Behrens**. He set up in practice with Adolf Meyer in 1910.
He was appointed director of the Großherzogliche Kunstgewerbeschule (Grand Ducal School of Applied Arts), Weimar, and to the Großherzogliche Hochschule für bildende Kunst (Grand Ducal Academy of Arts) and merged the two schools in 1919 into the State Bauhaus. He resigned in 1928 and moved to Berlin, where he became supervising architect of the Siemensstadt Estate, 1929–30.
He emigrated to England in 1934 and worked with Maxwell Fry until 1937. He was appointed professor of architecture at Harvard and collaborated in various schemes with Marcel Breuer and then Konrad Wachsmann on mass-produced houses. He founded The Architects Collaborative (TAC), which was a young artists' group, in 1946. His published works included *Internationale Architektur* in 1925 and *Bauhausbauten Dessau* in 1930.
Fagus factory, Hannoverschestrasse 58, Alfeld an der Leine, Germany, 1910–14
Model factory, Werkbund Exhibition, Köln, 1914 (both with Adolf Meyer) 70, 71

Guimard, Hector (1867–1942) 103, 109
Educated at the École des Arts Décoratifs and École des Beaux Arts, Paris, 1882–85; he met Victor Horta on a visit to Belgium in 1895. His later years were spent in New York.
Café, Quai d'Auteil, Paris, 1886
Castel Béranger, Paris, 1894–98 109, *109*
Canivet House, Paris
Castel Henriette, Sèvres, Paris
Maison Coilliot, Lille
Metro station entrances, Paris *104*, 109
Humbert de Romans building, Paris, 1902 (demolished) 109

Habershon
A family of partners 1849–58, comprising **Matthew** (father), **William Gillbee** and **Edward** (sons). They also worked in partnership with **Alfred Robert Pite**, J Follett Fawkner, W Yorke and E P L Brock.

St Thomas' Church, Kimberworth, Yorkshire, 1842
St James' Anglican Cathedral and mission buildings, Jerusalem, 1842–43
Stanhope Institute, St Marylebone Grammar School, London, 1856–57
Hannah Street Congregational Chapel, Cardiff, 1867
Park Hotel, Park Place, Cardiff, 1885

Hadfield, Mathew Ellison (1812–85); *see also* **Weightman, John Grey**
All Saints' R C church, Church Terrace, Glossop, Derbyshire, 1834–37
St Mary's R C church, Park Street, Worksop, Nottinghamshire, 1838–39

Hagley Son and **Hall** 88
Chorlton Union Workhouse, Cheshire 1856 *88*

Hakewill, Edward Charles (1812–72)
The son of architect Henry Hakewill and brother of John Henry Hakewill (1811–80); he studied as a pupil of **Philip Hardwick**, 1831–33.
St James' Church, Lower Clapton, London, 1840–41
St John of Jerusalem church, Lauriston Road, London 1845–48
St Peter's Church, Thurston, Suffolk, 1861–62

Hames, F J 82
Town Hall, Leicester 1874–76 *82*

Hamilton, David (1768–1843) 26, 77
Keir, Central Region, Scotland; enlargement, 1829–34
Dunlop House, Strathclyde, 1831–34
Lennox Castle, Lennoxtown, Central Region, 1837–41
with James Hamilton (*see below*)
Royal Exchange, Glasgow, 1829–30 (later Stirling's Library) 77
British Linen Bank, junction of Queen Street and Ingram Street, Glasgow, 1840 26
Western Club, Buchanan Street, Glasgow, 1841

Hamilton, James (c. 1807–62) 26, 100
Worked for **Alexander Kirkland** and later was joined by his own son **John**; formed a partnership with Irish architect Frank Stirrat which lasted until 1866; *see also* **Hamilton, David**.
Western Club, Buchanan Street, Glasgow, 1841 100
Ulster Bank, Belfast, 1858–60 26
Ulster Bank, Sligo, 1863
Henry Matier Mansion, Fort William, Belfast, 1871–73

Hamilton, Thomas (1784–1858)
Town Hall, Ayr, Strathclyde, 1828–30 (Wallace Tower added 1831–34)
Dean Orphanage, Edinburgh, 1833
Royal College of Physicians, 9 Queen Street, Edinburgh, 1845

Hansom, Charles Francis (1816–88)
The brother of **Joseph Aloysius Hansom**.
Clifton College, Bristol, 1860–80

Hansom, Joseph Aloysius (1803–82) 44, 45, 75
Founder of *The Builder*, 1842, and inventor of the Patent Safety Cab. A partner at various times of **Edward Welch, Edward Welby Pugin**, his own brother, **Charles Francis Hansom**, and sons Henry John Hansom and Joseph Stanislas Hansom.
Town Hall, Birmingham, 1832–60 75, *75*
Town Hall, Lutterworth, Leicestershire, 1836
Particular Baptist Chapel (*now* part of the Adult Education Centre), Belvoir Street, Leicester, 1845
St Walburga's R C church, Preston, Lancashire, 1850 45
SS Mary and Boniface R C cathedral, Plymouth, 1858
R C priory and nunnery, Abbotskerswell, Devon, 1863, 1871
Church of the Holy Name (R C), Manchester, 1869
St Philip Neri church (*now* R C cathedral), Arundel, Sussex, 1870–73

St Mary's R C priory, Fulham Road, London, 1876
St Cuthbert's College, Ushaw, Durham, 1885 (chapel by **Edward Welby Pugin**, 1842)
with Edward Welch (1806–88)
Victoria Terrace, Beaumaris, Anglesey, Gwynedd, 1830–35
Bodelwyddan Hall, Clwyd, *c.* 1830–40
Town Hall, Birmingham, West Midlands, 1832–34
Buckley Arms Hotel, Beaumaris, Anglesey, Gwynedd, 1835 (extended 1873)

Hardwick, Philip (1792–1870)
The son and pupil of Thomas Hardwick; he was awarded the RIBA Gold Medal in 1854.
Babraham Hall, Cambridgeshire, 1829–32
Goldsmiths' Hall, Foster Lane, London, 1829–35
City Club, Old Broad Street, London, 1832–33
Waterloo Crescent, Dover, Kent, 1834–38
Euston Station, London, 1835–39 (demolished)
Curzon Street Station, Birmingham, 1838
37 Belgrave Square (*now* Seaford House), London, 1842
with Philip Charles Hardwick
Great Hall, Euston Station, London, 1846–48 (demolished) *59*
Hall and Library, Lincoln's Inn, London, 1843–45

Hardwick, Philip Charles (1820–90) **50, 101, 102**
The son of **Philip Hardwick** (*see also* above), and a pupil of **Edward Blore**. He joined his father's practice in 1843, taking it over four years later.
Aldermaston Court, Berkshire, 1848–51
Great Western Royal Hotel, Paddington Station, Praed Street, London, 1851–53 **101**, *102*
St John's R C cathedral, Limerick, 1856–61
St Alphonsus' R C church, Limerick, 1858–62
St Leonard church, Newland, Worcestershire, 1862–64 **50**
Charterhouse School, Surrey, 1865–72
2 Palace Gate, London, 1873–76

Hare, Henry Thomas (1861–1921) **81, 86**
Born in Scarborough, Yorkshire, he was a student at the École des Beaux Arts, Paris, was articled to C A Bury and became President of RIBA, 1917–19.
County Hall, Stafford, 1893–95
Town Hall, Oxford, 1893–97 **81**
Passmore Edwards Library and Baths, Shoreditch, London, 1897
Westminster College, Cambridge, 1899 **86**
Town Hall, Henley, Oxfordshire, 1900
Municipal buildings, Harrogate, Yorkshire, 1902
Public Library, Islington, London, 1905
Public Library, Fulham, London, 1908–09

Harper, John (1809–42)
St Peter's School, Clifton, York, 1838 onwards

Harris, Thomas (1830–1900)
The author of *Victorian Architecture*, 1860.
Milner Field, Bingley, Yorkshire, 1873–77
Bedstone Court, Shropshire, 1884
Stokesay Court, Shropshire, 1889

Hartley, Jesse (1780–1860) **64**
Trained as a stonemason and bridgemaster; engineer for the Bolton and Manchester Railway and Canal, he was later the surveyor and engineer of Liverpool docks and harbour walls, 1824–60.
Brunswick Dock, Liverpool, 1832 (except tower)
Waterloo Dock, Liverpool, 1834
Albert Dock, Liverpool, 1841–45 **64**, *64*
Railway Dock and Castle Street Warehouse, Hull, 1846 (demolished)
Victoria Tower, near Stanley Dock, Liverpool, 1848
Stanley Dock, Liverpool, 1850–57 **64**
Wapping Dock, Liverpool, 1855
West Canada Dock, Liverpool, 1858

Hawkins, Major Rhode (1820–84)
A pupil of **Edward Blore**; appointed architect to the committee of the Council of Education, and accompanied Sir Charles Fellows' (1799–1860) expedition to Constantinople in 1841.

Royal Victoria Patriotic School, Wandsworth, London, 1857
St Michael's Church, Exeter, 1867–68
St John's Church, North Holmwood, Holmwood, Surrey, 1875

Hay
Brothers **John** and **William Hardie Hay** (1813–1901) and **James Murdoch** (1823–1915).
Holy Trinity Church, Breck Road, Liverpool, 1847
Academy, Greenock, 1855 (demolished)
East Free (*now* Baptist) Church, Brechin, Angus, 1856
Chalmers Church, Bridge of Allan, Stirling, 1856
Buccleuch and Greyfriars Free Church, East Cross Causeway, Edinburgh, 1857
Holy Trinity Church, Traverse Street, St Helens, Lancashire, 1857
Augustine-Bristo Congregational Church, George IV Bridge, Edinburgh, 1859–61
Liverpool Cathedral, 1886 (unexecuted project)

Hay, William (1818–80)
The son of **John Hay** and a pupil of **John Henderson**, he worked for **Sir George Gilbert Scott**, 1847–50, before moving to Canada, 1853–60, and to Australia, 1868–78. He was a partner of G Henderson, 1846–1905.
St John's Longside church, Peterhead, 1853
St Giles's Cathedral, Edinburgh, 1871–84 (restoration)
Old St Paul's Episcopal Church, Edinburgh, 1881–1906
Government House, Hamilton, Bermuda, 1885
Holy Trinity Cathedral, Hamilton, Bermuda, 1885–1905
Craiglockhart Church, Edinburgh, 1889–1901 (with G Henderson)

Haycock, Edward (1790–1870)
A family practice in Shrewsbury headed by **John Hiram Haycock**, with son **Edward Haycock** Snr, and grandson **Edward Haycock** Jnr.
Shire Hall, Monmouth, Monmouthshire, 1829–30
St George's Church, Drinkwater Street, Frankwell, Shropshire, 1829–32
St David's Church, Barmouth, Gwynedd, 1830
Clytha Park, near Abergavenny, Monmouthshire, *c.* 1830
Millichope Park, Shropshire, 1835–40 (modified 1970)
St Catherine's Church, Dodington, Whitchurch, Shropshire, 1836–40
Glynllifon Park, Llandwrog, Gwynedd, 1836–40 (thought to be by)
Music Hall, The Square, Shrewsbury, Shropshire, 1839–40
Christ Church, Cressage, Shropshire, 1841
St Edward's Church, Dorrington, Shropshire, 1845
Netley Hall, near Longnor, Shropshire, 1854–58

Hayward, John (1808–91)
In practice with his son and partner Pearson Barry Hayward (1838–88).
SS Philip and James church, Ilfracombe, Devon, 1856
Albert Memorial Museum, Exeter, 1865–66

Hayward, Charles Forster (1830–1905)
Harrow School, Peterborough Road, Grove Hill, Middlesex, 1864–74 (gymnasium, laboratories and boarding houses)
Harrow Village Public Hall, Harrow-on-the-Hill, Middlesex, 1864

Heiton, Andrew (1823–94)
A pupil of his father and of **David Bryce**.
St Mary's Monastery, Perth, 1867
Castleroy, Broughty Ferry, Dundee, 1867 (demolished)
Victoria Buildings, 36–44 Tay Street, Perth, 1872
Atholl Palace, Pitlochry, Perth, 1878 (hydropathic)

Henderson, John (1804–62)
A pupil of **Thomas Hamilton**.

3 George IV Bridge, Edinburgh, 1836
Natural History Museum, Montrose, 1837
St Mary's Church, Dumfries, 1838
Trinity College, Glenalmond, Perth, 1843–51
St Mary's Episcopal Church, Arbroath, 1854

Hennébique, François (1842–1921) **69**
A French-born civil engineer who introduced the use of reinforced concrete in the building industry, patenting his system in 1892. He built the first reinforced-concrete bridge at Viggen, Switzerland, 1894, and the first grain elevator at Roubaix, 1895.
Charles Six Spinning Mill, Tourcoing, France, 1895 **69**
Weaver & Co flour mill, Swansea, 1897–98 (with Napoleon le Brun) **69**, *69*

Hering, Frederick 19
2 Palace Green, Kensington, London, 1860–62 **19**

Heywood, William
As surveyor for the City of London, he was responsible for the design of Holborn Viaduct *below*. The bridge across the Fleet valley connects Holborn with Newgate. It was opened by Queen Victoria in 1869, having taken six years to build.

Hibbert, James (1833–1903)
Fishergate Baptist Church, Preston, 1857
Harris Museum and Library, Preston, 1882–93

Hill, William (1827–89) **77**
Methodist College, Ranmoor, Sheffield, 1863–64
Town Hall, Bolton, Lancashire, 1866–73 **77**
Guildhall, Portsmouth, 1886–90 **77**

Hine, Thomas Chambers (1813–99)
Joined in practice in 1867 by his son, **George Thomas Hine**.
Bentinck Memorial, Mansfield, Nottinghamshire, 1849
Corn Exchange, Thurland Street, Nottingham, 1850
Park Estate, Nottingham, 1850
Flintham Hall, Nottinghamshire, 1851–54
Thomas Adams Warehouse, Stoney Street, Nottingham, 1854–55
Christ Church, Basford, Nottingham, 1856
Cranfield Court, Bedfordshire, 1862–64 (demolished)
St Matthias' Church, Sneinton, Nottingham, 1867–68
Nottingham Castle, 1875–78 (conversion to museum)
Nottingham Station, 1898

Hoff, Robert van't (1887–1979)
He was educated at the School of Art, Birmingham, 1906–11, and the Architectural Association School, London, 1911–14. During a short stay in the USA he worked for **Frank Lloyd Wright**, and when back in the Netherlands he became involved in the De Stijl movement, working with Pieter J C Klaarhammer, but left the group after a difference of opinion with Theo van Doesburg.
Henny Villa, Huis ter Heide, near Utrecht, 1915–19

Hoffmann, Josef (1870–1956) **110–112**
Educated at the Staatsgewerbeschule, Brno, Bohemia, he worked for the Militärbauamt, Würzburg,

Germany, moving to Vienna in 1892. There he studied under Carl von Hasenauer and **Otto Kolomon Wagner** (1841–1918) at the Academy of Arts, and won the Rome Prize. He worked in the offices of Otto Wagner and with a group of artists in 1895 formed first the Siebener Club (Club 7) then, in 1897, the Vienna Sezession which he left in 1905 with the Klimt Group.
   He taught at the Vienna Kunstgewerbeschule from 1899, and concentrated on designing interiors until forming the Wiener Werkstätte (Vienna Workshop) with Koloman Moser in 1903. In 1912 he was involved in the foundation of the Austrian Werkbund.
Purkersdorf Sanatorium, 1904–06
Palais Stoclet, Brussels, 1905–11 (mosaics by Gustav Klimt) 112, *112*
Primavesi House, Vienna, 1915
Werkbund Exhibition; four houses, Vienna, 1932

Holding, **Matthew Henry** (*d.* 1910)
81–87 St Giles' Street, Northampton, 1880s
St Mary's Church, Towcester Road, Northampton, 1885
St Paul's Church, Semilong Road, Northampton, 1890
St Matthew's Church, Kettering Road, Northampton, 1891–94
Holy Trinity Church, Balmoral Road, Northampton, 1909 (with E de W Holding)
Town Hall, Northampton, 1889–92 (with A W Jeffery; extensions)

Holme, **F** and **G** 76
Sessions House, Liverpool, 1882 76

Honeyman and Keppie
A partnership, established in 1885, between **John Honeyman** (1831–1914) and **John Keppie** (1863–1945). They were joined by the draughtsman **Charles Rennie Mackintosh** in 1889, who later became a partner.
Lansdowne Church, Great Western Road, Woodside, Glasgow, 1862
Museum, Paisley, Glasgow, 1866
Ca' d'Oro Warehouse, 41–55 Gordon Street, Glasgow, 1872 (altered)
Westbourne Church, Kelvinside, Glasgow, 1880
by **Keppie**
Fairfield Offices, Govan, Glasgow, 1890
by **Mackintosh**
Glasgow Herald Building, 60–76 Mitchell Street, Glasgow, 1893

Hopper, **Thomas** (1776–1856)
Penrhyn Castle, near Bangor, Gwynedd, 1825–44
Margam Abbey, West Glamorgan, 1830–35 (gutted)
Danbury Place, Essex, 1832
Amesbury House, Amesbury, Wiltshire, 1834–40 (Webb's house of *c.* 1660, rebuilt along lines of original)

Horne, **Herbert Percy** *see* **Mackmurdo**, **Arthur Heygate**

Horsley, **Gerald Callcott** (1862–1917)
The second son of Callcott Horsley (1817–1903), who was the artist credited with designing the first Christmas card in 1843. Gerald was articled to **Richard Norman Shaw** in 1879 and was among his pupils who founded the Art Workers' Guild. He entered the Royal Academy Schools in 1881, and was the first winner of the Owen Jones prize and travelling studentship.
Bron y Nant House, Colwyn Bay, North Wales, 1889
St Chad's Church, Longsdon, Staffordshire, 1903–04

Horta, **Victor** (1861–1947) 11, 73, 107–9
Educated at the Académies des Beaux-Arts, Ghent and Brussels, he worked in the offices of Alphonse Balat from 1880. He is thought to have introduced the use of iron in the construction of private houses, at the Hôtel Tassel. He taught at the Free University, Brussels, from 1897 and

in 1912 was appointed professor at the Académie des Beaux-Arts, becoming director in 1927.
Hôtel Tassel, Brussels, 1892–93 *108*
Maison Autrique, Brussels, 1893
Maison Winssinger, Brussels, 1895–96
Hôtel van Eetvelde, Brussels, 1895–97 *10*
Hôtel Deprez, Brussels, 1895–97 *108*
Hôtel Solvay, Brussels, 1895–1900
Maison du Peuple (Belgian Socialist Party HQ), Brussels, 1896–99 (demolished) 109, *109*
Hôtel Horta (now Horta Museum), Brussels, 1898–1901 *below* **108**

À l'Innovation department store, rue Neuve, Brussels, 1901 (demolished) *73*

Hoskins, **G O** 81
Town Hall, Middlesborough, 1883–89 **81**

Howard, **Sir Ebenezer** (1850–1928) 12, 24, *24*, 25
Born in London, he emigrated to Nebraska in 1872, but returned in 1877. He published *Tomorrow: A Peaceful Path to Real Reform*, 1989, in which he envisaged self-contained communities with both rural and urban amenities, and green belts. This led to the formation of the Garden City Association. He was knighted in 1927.

Humbert, **Albert Jenkins** (1822–77)
St Mildred's Church, Whippingham, Isle of Wight, 1854–62
Mausoleum for Prince Albert, Frogmore, Windsor, Berkshire, 1862–68
Sandringham House, Norfolk, 1870 (for Edward, Prince of Wales)

Hutchens, **Charles** (*c.* 1781–1834)
St Mary's Church, Penzance, Cornwall, 1832–36

Hutchinson, **Henry** *see* **Rickman and Hutchinson**

I'Anson, **Edward** (1812–88) 27
Educated at Merchant Taylors' School; Surveyor to Merchant Taylors' Co and to St Bartholomew's Hospital, London, and President of RIBA, 1886.
Royal Exchange Buildings, Freeman's Place, London, 1842–44 (demolished) 27
British and Foreign Bible Society, 146 Queen Victoria Street, London, 1866–67
65 Cornhill, London, 1871
School of Medicine for St Bartholomew's Hospital, Giltspur Street, London, 1878–79
Corn Exchange Chambers, 2 Seething Lane, London, 1879
Corn Exchange, Seething Lane, London, 1881
Central Library, Walworth Road, London, 1893

Jackson, **Sir Thomas Graham** (1835–1924) **86**
Educated at Wadham College, Oxford, articled to **Sir George Gilbert Scott**, 1858, he set up in practice on his own in 1862, was awarded RIBA's Gold Medal 1910 and his baronetcy in 1913.
Ellesmere Memorial, Walkden, Lancashire, 1868
St Peter's Church, Hornblotton, Somerset, 1872–74
Examination Schools, Oxford, 1876–82 86, *86*

Thorne House, Somerset, 1877–82
Girls' High School (*now* part of the University), Banbury Road, Oxford, 1879
Boys' High School, George Street, Oxford, 1880–81
2–3 Hare Court, Temple, London, 1897
School chapel, Giggleswick, Yorkshire, 1897
New Buildings, Brasenose College, Oxford, 1909–11

James, **Joseph** (1828–75)
A pupil of **Samuel Whitfield Daukes**.
Congregational Church, Barnsley, Yorkshire, 1854–56
Square Congregational Church, Halifax, Yorkshire, 1855–57 (partly demolished)
Congregational Chapel, Cemetery Road, Sheffield, 1859 (demolished)
Arundel Square Congregational Church, Barnsbury, London, 1862

James, **Seward and Thomas** *see* **Seward**, **Edwin**

Jeanneret-Gris, *see* **Le Corbusier**

Jearrad, **Robert William** (*d.* 1846) and **C Jearrad**
Queen's Hotel, Cheltenham, Gloucestershire, 1836–39
Christ Church, Malvern Road, Cheltenham, Gloucestershire, 1838–40 (interior 1883)
Lansdown Parade, Cheltenham, Gloucestershire, 1838–41

Jebb, **Sir Joshua** (1793–1863) **89**
Surveyor-general of convict prisons, and from 1844 inspector-general of military prisons.
Pentonville Prison, London, 1840–42 **89**

Jeckyll (**Jeckell**), **Thomas** (1827–81)
St Andrew's Church, Thorpe, Norwich, 1866
St Peter's Church, Lilley, Hertfordshire, 1870–71
49 Princes Gate, London, 1876 ('Peacock Room', painted by Whistler, now in Freer Gallery of Art, Washington DC)
Chapel Field Gardens 'Pagoda', Norwich, 1880 (cast-iron music pavilion; demolished)

Jenney, **William Le Baron** (1832–1907) **66, 69**
An American civil engineer and architect whose technical innovations were of vital importance in the development of the skyscraper. He studied in Paris, 1859–61, before serving in the American Civil War. He later taught architecture at the University of Michigan, Ann Arbor, 1876–80.
Leiter Building, Chicago, 1879 (demolished)
Home Insurance Building, Chicago, 1883–85 (demolished 1929) 66
Manhattan Building, Chicago, 1889–90 *68*, 69
Second Leiter Building (later Sears, Roebuck & Co's Loop Store), Chicago, 1889–90 (with W B Mundie) *below* 66

Joass, **John James** (1868–1952)
Born at Dingwall, Scotland, the son of an architect; he joined the office of Sir Rowland Anderson, Edinburgh, and studied there at the College of Art. He won the RIBA Pugin Prize, and travelling studentship in 1892, entering the office of Sir Ernest George, London the following year. In 1895 he was awarded the RIBA Owen Jones Prize, and

the following year joined the office of John Belcher, becoming a partner to Belcher in 1905; *see* **Belcher, John**

Jones, Sir Horace (1819–87) **54**, **72**, **98**, **99**
Architect and surveyor to the City of London Corporation, he was president of RIBA, 1882–83, and knighted in 1886.
St Michael's Church, Cherry Burton, Yorkshire, 1852–53
'Old' Town Hall, Cardiff, 1853
Surrey Zoological Gardens, Southwark, London, 1856 **98**, *99*
Smithfield Market, London, 1866
Marshall and Snelgrove Store, London, 1870 (demolished) **72**
Billingsgate Market, London, 1875–77 (destroyed)
Temple Bar Memorial, London, 1880
Leadenhall Market, London, 1881
Tower Bridge, London, 1886–94 **54**

Jones, Owen (1809–74)
A pupil of **Lewis Vulliamy** and the author of *The Grammar of Ornament*, 1856. He was the joint director of decoration of the Crystal Palace; awarded the RIBA Gold Medal in 1857.
24 Kensington Palace Gardens, London, *c.* 1845
Crystal Palace, London, 1851 (interior decoration)
Crystal Palace after removal to Sydenham, 1852–54 (courts; destroyed by fire)
St James' Concert Hall, Piccadilly, London, 1856 (demolished)
Osler's Gallery, Oxford Street, London, 1856–60 (demolished)
Abbottsfield House, Somerset, 1872

Kahn, Albert (1869–1942) **70**, **71**
Established in practice in 1896 with George W Nettleton and Alexander Trowbridge; later he was a partner of George D Mason, in whose offices he had previously been employed. His reputation was made through his designs of numerous factory buildings in north America, especially for the automotive industry. This led to the commissioning of over 500 factories within the Soviet Union, for which he enlisted the services of his brother, **Moritz**. Later he was to concentrate on aircraft-assembly plants for Second World War aircraft production. His brother, **Louis**, took over as director of **Albert Kahn Associates** upon his death.
Childrens' hospital, Detroit, 1896 (with George W Nettleton and Alexander Trowbridge)
Palms Apartment House, Detroit, 1901–02 (with George D Mason)
University of Michigan, Detroit, 1903 (with Louis Kahn)
Glass plant, Ford Motor Company, Dearborn, Michigan, 1924 **70**, **71**

Kay, Joseph (1775–1847)
College Approach, Nelson Road and King William Walk, Greenwich, London, *c.* 1829–30

Keane, John B (*d.* 1859)
Court House, Nenagh, Tipperary, 1833
Queen's College (*now* University College), Galway, 1847–49
Court House, Waterford, 1849

Keeling, Enoch Bassett (1837–86)
St Mark's Church, Notting Hill, London, 1862–63
Strand Music Hall, London, 1864 (demolished)
St Andrew's Church, Glengall Road, London, 1864

Kendall, Henry Edward (Snr, 1776–1875)
A pupil of Thomas Leverton and a founder of RIBA.
24 Belgrave Square (*now* Downshire House), London, 1830
Sessions House, Market Place, Sleaford, Lincolnshire, 1830
Carr's Hospital, Eastgate, Sleaford, Lincolnshire, 1830 and 1841–46
Knebworth House, Hertfordshire, 1844 (remodelling)

Kendall, Henry Edward (Jnr, 1805–85)
Son and pupil of **Henry Edward Kendall** Snr, and a partner to Frederick Mew
St John's Church, Kensal Green, London, 1843–44
Lunatic Asylum, Brentwood, Essex, 1853
St Patrick's Church, Hove, Sussex, 1858
St Francis' Hospital, Haywards Heath, Sussex, 1859

Kennedy, Henry (*d.* 1897)
Church, ffestiniog, Gwynedd, 1844–45
St James' Church, Bangor, Gwynedd, 1864–66

Keppie, John *see* **Honeyman and Keppie**

Kerr, Robert (1823–1904)
A founder and the first President of the Architectural Association, 1847–48. He was Professor of the Arts of Construction, King's College, London, and author of *The Gentleman's House*, 1864.
Bear Wood, Berkshire, 1865–74
Ford Manor, Surrey, 1868
Ascot Heath House, Berkshire, 1868

Kinnear, Charles George Hood *see* **Peddie and Kinnear**

Kirkland, Alexander (1824–92)
55 St Vincent Crescent, Glasgow, 1850
Suspension Bridge, Glasgow, 1851
37–51 Miller Street, Glasgow, 1854 (demolished)

Knightley, Thomas Edward (1823–1905)
Birkbeck Bank, Holborn, London, 1895–96 (later Westminster Bank; demolished)
with Charles John Phipps
Queen's Hall, Langham Place, London, 1891 (demolished)

Knowles, James Thomas (Snr, 1806–84) **100**, **101**
191–92 Fleet Street, London, 1854–55
Cedar Terrace and Thorton Terrace, London, 1860
Hedsor House, Buckinghamshire, 1865–68
with Sir James Thomas Knowles Jnr
Grosvenor Hotel, Victoria Station, London, 1860–62 **100**, *101*

Knowles, Sir James Thomas (Jnr, 1831–1908) **17**
Son and pupil of **James Thomas Knowles** Snr (*see also above*), he was the founder and editor of *The Nineteenth Century* review, and the founder of the Metaphysical Society, 1869. He was knighted in 1903.
Cedars Estate, Clapham, London, 1860 **17**
Thatched House Club, 76 St James's Street, London, 1862–64
Park Town Estate, Battersea, London, 1863–66
St Philip's Church, Queenstown Road, London, 1867–68
Aldworth, Blackdown, Sussex, 1868–69

Laloux, Victor (1850–1937) **58**
Gare d'Orsay, Paris, France, 1900 *59*
Birkbeck Bank, Holborn, London, 1895–96 (later Westminster Bank; demolished)

Lamb, Edward Buckton (1806–69)
A pupil of Lewis NockallsCottingham (1787–1847) and contributor of illustrations to *The Builder*, he published *Etchings of Gothic Ornament*, 1830, and *Studies of Ancient Domestic Architecture*, 1846.
Elkington Hall, Lincolnshire, 1841
All Saints' Church, Thirkleby, Yorkshire, 1845–50
Christ Church, West Hartlepool, Durham, 1854
Episcopal Church, Castle Douglas, Dumfries, 1856
SS Simon and Jude church, Englefield Green, Surrey, 1856–59
Town Hall, Eye, Suffolk, 1857
St Mary's Church, Braisworth, Suffolk, 1857–58
Town Hall, Berkhampstead, Hertfordshire, 1858
Hughenden Manor, Buckinghamshire, 1863–66 (alterations)
St Martin's Church, Vicar's Road, London, 1865–66

St Mary Magdalene Church, Canning Road, Addiscombe, Surrey, 1868

Lanchester, Henry Vaughan (1863–1953) **82**
The son and pupil in London of H J Lanchester (1834–1914) who entered the Royal Academy Schools in 1886, from 1894 practiced with James Stewart and Edward Alfred Rickards (1872–1920), and won the RIBA Gold Medal in 1934.
Civic Centre, Cardiff, 1897 (designs)
Town Hall, Deptford, London, 1900–03
City Hall and Law Courts, Cardiff, 1906 **82**, **83**

Lane, Richard
St Mary's Church, Church Street, Oldham, Greater Manchester, 1827–30
Blue Coat School, Horsedge Street, Oldham, Greater Manchester, 1829–34
Regional College of Art, Grosvenor Square, Chorlton-on-Medlock, Manchester, 1830
Infirmary, Wellington Road South, Stockport, Greater Manchester, 1832–33
Grammar School, Northgate, Wakefield, West Yorkshire, 1833–34
with Francis Goodwin
St Thomas' Church, Broad Street, Pendleton, 1829–31

Lanyon, Sir Charles (1813–89)
A civil engineer who was appointed surveyor of Co Antrim, Ireland, 1836–60. He was a partner of **William Henry Lynn** until 1872, and then of his own son, John Lanyon, becoming president of the Royal Institute of Architects of Ireland, 1862–68, MP for Belfast 1866, a knight in 1868 and High Sheriff of Co Antrim 1876.
Palm House, Botanic Gardens, Belfast, 1839
Queen's College (University), Belfast, 1849
Killyleagh Castle, Down, 1849–51
Sinclair Seamen's Church, Belfast, 1857
Richardson Sons and Owden Warehouse, Belfast, 1869 (later Water Offices)
Carlisle Memorial Church, Belfast, 1872–75

Lapidge, Edward (1779–1860)
St John the Baptist church, St John's Road, Hampton Wick, Richmond-upon-Thames, 1829–31

Latham, John (*b. c.* 1805)
Christ Church, Bow Lane, Preston, Lancashire, 1836
St Mary's Church, St Mary's Street, Preston, Lancashire, 1836–38
St Thomas' Church, Lancaster Road, Preston, Lancashire, 1837

Lavirotte, Jules Aimé (1864–1928) **7**, **108**
29 Avenue Rapp, Paris, France, 1901 *6*, **7**, *109*
Hôtel Céramique, Paris, France, 1904

le Brun, Napoleon (1821–1901) see **Hennébique, François**

Le Corbusier (1887–1965)
Charles-Edouard Jeanneret-Gris was educated at the School of Applied Arts, La Chaux-de-Fonds, Switzerland, then employed in the offices of **Peter Behrens**, 1910–11. When he moved to Paris in 1917, he changed his name to Le Corbusier; in 1918 he published *Après le Cubisme* with Amédée Ozenfant and was appointed editor of the journal *L'Esprit Nouveau* in 1920, entering into partnership with his cousin Pierre Jeanneret in 1922. In 1923 he published *Vers une Architecture*, a collection of his articles from *L'Esprit Nouveau*.
He was a founder member of the Congrès Internationaux d'Architecture Moderne (CIAM) in 1928 . He published *Charta of Athens* in 1944, the set of reflections and demands compiled by CIAM in 1933, further developed by Le Corbusier in 1941, promoting a contemporary functional city.
Vallet Villa, La Chaux-de-Fonds, Switzerland, 1905 (his first home)
Schwob Villa, La Chaux-de-Fonds, Switzerland, 1916

Leeming and Leeming
A partnership between brothers **John** and **Joseph**,
  established in Halifax, Yorkshire, in 1872.
Admiralty, Whitehall, London, 1894–95
Borough Market, Halifax, Yorkshire, 1895
City Markets, Leeds, Yorkshire, 1903 (front block)

Leeson, Richard John *see* **Oliver and Leeson**

Leiper, William (1839–1916) **65**
A pupil of **James Boucher** and **James Cousland**,
  he was later employed by Cousland in London.
Dowanhill Church, Glasgow, 1865
Camphill Church, Glasgow, 1878
Templeton's Factory, Glasgow Green, Glasgow,
  1889 **65**
147–51 West George Street, Glasgow, 1892

Leslie, James (1801–89)
and **John Taylor** (*d. c.* 1841)
Custom House, Dundee, Tayside, 1839–40

Lethaby, William Richard (1857–1931) **41, 51**
Born in Barnstable, Devon, the son of a carver
  and gilder; in 1879 he won the Soane
  Medallion and travelling scholarship. After
  returning from France he became a pupil of
  Richard Norman Shaw, entering the Royal
  Academy Schools in 1880. He later became the
  chief assistant to Shaw before setting up in
  practice on his own in 1891. He was the first
  Principal of the Central School of Arts and
  Crafts, London, founded in 1894, and the
  author of *Architecture, Mysticism and Myth*,
  published in 1892.
Avon Tyrrell, Hampshire, 1891
Melsetter House, Isle of Hoy, Orkney, 1898
High Coxlease, Lyndhurst, Hampshire, 1898
Eagle Insurance Co, Colmore Row,
  Birmingham, 1900
All Saints' Church, Brockhampton,
  Herefordshire, 1901–02 **51**

Lewis, T Hayter 98
The Alhambra, Leicester Square, London, 1854 **98**

Livesay, Augustus Frederick (1807–79)
Holy Trinity Church, Trowbridge, Wiltshire, 1838
St Mary's Church, Andover, Hampshire
  (completed by **Sydney Smirke**), 1840–46

Locke, Joseph (1805–60) **57**
A civil engineer, he aided George Stephenson in
  the construction of the Manchester–Liverpool
  railway, before constructing various lines on his
  own throughout Europe. He was appointed
  president of the Institute of Civil Engineers in
  1850 and 1859. He designed the Crewe
  locomotive engine.
Lime Street Station, Liverpool, 1949–50 (with
  Richard Turner) **57**

Lockwood, Henry Francis (1811–78) **21, 66, 81**
A partner to Richard (1834–1904) and William
  Mawson in Bradford, Yorkshire, 1849–74,
  before moving to London.
Warehouses, Drake Street, Bradford, 1850
St George's Hall, Bradford, 1851–52
Mills and model town, Saltaire, Yorkshire,
  1851–76 **21, *21*, 66**
Wool Exchange, Bradford, 1864–67 **81**
Kirkgate Markets, Bradford, 1869–72
  (demolished)
Town Hall, Bradford, 1869–73 **81**
62 and 65 Vicar Lane, Bradford, 1871, 1873
  (warehouses)
with Thomas Allom
Great Thornton St Chapel, Hull, 1843

Lockwood, Thomas Meakin (1830–1900)
Town Hall, Newport, Wales, 1885
Grosvenor Museum and Schools, Chester,
  1885–86
Corner of Bridge Street and Eastgate Street,
  Chester, 1888

Loos, Adolf (1870–1933) **13**
Educated at the Technische Hochschule,
  Dresden, Loos settled in Vienna in 1896. He
  made his reputation as an author of articles
  which first appeared in the *Neue Freie Presse* and
  were later published as a collection entitled *Ins
  Leere Gesprochen* in 1921 and *Trotzdam* in 1931.
   In 1903 he edited the short-lived *Das andere –
  ein blatt zur einführung abendländischer kultur in
  österreich* and published his famous *Ornament und
  Verbrechen* (*Ornament and Crime*) in 1908. He formed,
  and taught at, a free school of architecture in
  1912. He became chief architect of the Vienna
  Siedlungsamt in 1920, leaving in 1922 for
  Paris, where he lectured at the Sorbonne.
Café Museum, Vienna, 1907 (rebuilding)
Kärntner Bar (Carinthia Bar), Vienna, 1907
Michaelerplatz, Vienna, 1909–11 (house)
Goldman & Salatsch Building, Vienna, 1909–11
Steiner House, Vienna, 1910 **13**

Lorimer, Sir Robert Stodart (1864–1929)
Born in Edinburgh, he was educated at Edinburgh
  Academy and Edinburgh University. He was
  articled to **Sir Rowand Anderson** and **James
  Maitland Wardrop** before working with
  George Frederick Bodley. In 1893 he set up in
  practice on his own in Edinburgh.
Miss Guthrie Wright's House, Colinton,
  Edinburgh, 1893
Briglands House, Kinross, 1898
Rowallan House, Ayr, 1903–06
House, Ardkinglas, Argyll, 1906
St Peter's R C church, Morningside, Edinburgh,
  1906
University Library, St Andrews, Fife, 1907
Order of the Thistle chapel, St Giles' Cathedral,
  Edinburgh, 1909–11

Loudon, John Claudius (1783–1843) **16**
A landscape gardener and horticultural writer,
  he began to compile the *Encyclopaedia of Cottage,
  Farm and Villa Architecture*, 1823, established the
  Architectural Magazine, 1834, and published *Suburban
  Gardener and Villa Companion*, 1836. He was
  responsible for the mass introduction of the plane
  tree in London's streets and parks, and invented
  the system for curving glass that was used by
  Sir Joseph Paxton for the Crystal Palace.
3 Porchester Terrace, London, 1823 (own house) **16**

Lutyens, Sir Edwin Landseer (1869–1944) **12,
25, 38–40, 51**
He entered South Kensington Schools to study
  architecture in 1885, but left before completing
  the course to join the offices of **Sir Ernest
  George** and **Harold Peto**, setting up in practice
  on his own in 1888. He was a consultant
  architect for Hampstead Garden Suburb,
  1908–09; joint architect, with Sir Herbert Baker
  (1862–1946), for New Delhi, 1913–30;
  appointed to the War Graves Commission,
  1917; knighted in 1918; awarded the RIBA
  Gold Medal in 1921 and made President of the
  Royal Academy in 1938.
Crooksbury Lodge, Farnham, Surrey, 1890
Chinthurst Hill, Surrey, 1894
Munstead Wood, Surrey, 1896 **39, *39***
Le Bois des Moutiers, Varengeville, France, 1897–98
Goddards, Abinger, Surrey, 1898
Orchards, Godalming, Surrey, 1898–99
Deanery Garden, Sonning, Berkshire, 1899 **39**
Tigbourne Court, near Witley, Surrey, 1899 **39, *40***
British Pavilion, Paris Exhibition, 1900
Grey Walls, Gullane, East Lothian, 1900–01
British Pavilion, International Exhibition, Rome,
  1909–11
St Jude's Church, Hampstead Garden Suburb,
  London, 1909–13 **51**
Cenotaph, Whitehall, London, 1919 *right*

Lynn, William Henry (1829–1915)
A partner of **Sir Charles Lanyon** until 1872.
Town Hall, Chester, 1864
St Patrick's Church, Jordanstown, Antrim, 1866

Town Hall, Barrow-in-Furness, Lancashire, 1878–87
St Anne's Cathedral, Belfast, 1899 (supervision
  of completion; designed by **Sir Thomas Drew**)

Macartney, Sir Mervyn Edmund (1853–1932)
Educated at Lincoln College, Oxford, 1873–77,
  he entered the offices of **Richard Norman
  Shaw**, before establishing his own practice in
  1882. He was a founder of the Art Workers'
  Guild, and knighted in 1930.
167 Queen's Gate, London, 1889
Sandhills, Bletchingley, Surrey, 1893
Guinness Trust Flats, Vauxhall Walk, Lambeth,
  London, 1893
Frithwood House, Northwood, Middlesex, 1900

Mackenzie, Dr Alexander Marshall, (1848–1933)
He was educated at Elgin Academy and trained
  with **James Matthews** and **David Bryce**,
  returning to partner Matthews in 1877 in
  Aberdeen.
Northern Assurance Buildings, 146 Union
  Street, Aberdeen, 1885
Art Gallery, Museum, War Memorial and Art
  School, Aberdeen, 1885
Free Scottish Church, Rosemount Viaduct,
  Aberdeen, 1892
Marischal College (Broad Street front),
  Aberdeen, 1896–1906
Waldorf Hotel, Aldwych, London, 1907–08

Mackenzie, Thomas (1814–54)
The father of **Dr Alexander Marshall Mackenzie**,
  he was a pupil of **William M Mackenzie**, and
  worked for **Archibold Simpson** and **William
  Robertson** in Elgin, Moray
Museum, Elgin, Moray, 1842
Milne's School, Fochabers, Moray, 1845
Bank of Scotland, 9–11 High Street, Inverness, 1847
Ballindalloch, Stirling; reconstruction, 1847
Town Hall, Fraserburgh, Aberdeen, 1853

Mackintosh, Charles Rennie (1868–1928) **9,
10, 40, 41, 86, 87, 112**
The second son of the eleven children of a Glasgow
  police superintendent, he was articled to John
  Hutchinson and attended evening classes at the
  Glasgow School of Art. In 1889 he became an
  assistant to **John Honeyman** and **John Keppie**,
  and in the same year won the Alexander 'Greek'
  Thomson travelling scholarship, which enabled
  him to visit France, Belgium and Italy.
   In 1897 he won the first prize in a competition
  for the new building for the Glasgow School of
  Art, which was subsequently built in two stages,
  1897–99 and 1907–09. By the time Honeyman
  retired in 1904 Mackintosh was a full partner,

but it is his furniture and interior designs on which his high esteem rests. He resigned and moved to London in 1913, thereafter only designing furniture and textiles until he retired to Port Vendres, France, in 1923.
Martyrs School, 11 Barony Street, Glasgow, 1895
Buchanan Street Tea Rooms, Glasgow, 1896 *113*
School of Art, Glasgow, 1896–1909 **86**, **87**, *112*, **113**
St Cuthbert and Queen's Cross Church, Woodside, Glasgow, 1897
Windyhill House, Kilmacolm, Strathclyde, 1901
Ingram Street Tea Rooms, Glasgow, 1901–02
Hill House, Helensburgh, Argyll and Bute, 1902 **40**
Willow Tea Rooms, Sauchiehall Street, Glasgow, 1903 **113**

Mackison, William (1833–1906)
A pupil and partner of Francis Mackison in Stirling, he moved to Dundee in 1868.
5–17 Clarendon Place, Stirling, 1863 (large villas)
Whitehall Street and Crescent, Dundee, 1885–99
73–97 and 68–110 Commercial Street, Dundee, 1871–92 (with J Lessels)

Mackmurdo, Arthur Heygate (1851–1942) **41**, **109**, **112**
A pupil of **James Brooks**, he travelled to Italy with John Ruskin in 1874, establishing his own practice in 1875, and founding the Century Guild in 1882. He wrote *Wren's City Churches* in 1883 and was editor of *The Hobby Horse*.
6 Private Road, Enfield, Middlesex, 1883
25 Cadogan Gardens, London, 1893–94
12 Hans Road, London, 1894
Brooklyn, 8 Private Road, Enfield, Middlesex, 1886–87 (with Herbert Percy Horne [1864–1916])

MacLaren, James (1829–93) **41**
A pupil of **David Bryce** and a partner to G S Aitken (1836–1921).
Clement Park, Lochee, Dundee, 1854
Cox's Stack, Camperdown Works, Lochee, Dundee, 1865
Balthayock House, Kinnoull, Perth, 1870
Ahsludie House, Monifieth, Angus, 1870
Calcutta Buildings, Commercial Street, Dundee, 1877
Cox Bros, Meadow Place, Dundee, 1886 (later Sidlaw Industries)

MacLaren, James Marjoribanks (1843–90) **66**
A pupil in Glasgow of **James Salmon**, **Campbell Douglas** and **John James Stevenson**.
Camperdown linen works, Lochee, Dundee, 1865–66 **66**
High School, Stirling, 1887–88 (new wing)
22 Avonmore Road, Kensington, London, 1888–89
Glenlyon House, Fortingall, Perth, 1889 (farm buildings and cottages)
10–12 Palace Court, Bayswater, London, 1889–90

Maddox, George Vaughan (1802–64)
Methodist Chapel and Masonic Hall, Monmouth, Monmouthshire, 1837
Priory Street, Monmouth, Monmouthshire, 1837–39
Market Hall (*now* post office and museum), Priory Street, Monmouth, Monmouthshire, 1839

Mair, George James John (*c.* 1809–69)
Northwood House, West Cowes, IoW, 1838 onwards

Marrable, Frederick (1818–72)
Superintending architect to Metropolitan Board of Works, 1856–62.
Old County Hall, Spring Gardens, Trafalgar Square, London, 1860 (demolished)
Garrick Club, Garrick Street, London, 1864 *right*
St Peter's Church, Wickham Road, Deptford, 1866–70 (tower by **Sir Arthur William Blomfield**)

Martin, William (*d.* 1899)
A partner of **John Henry Chamberlain** 1864–83; after Chamberlain's death, he worked under the name of **Martin and Chamberlain**.
St John the Evangelist church, Sparkhill, Birmingham, 1888
Library, Spring Hill, Birmingham, 1893
Library and baths, Green Lane, Small Heath, Birmingham, 1893
19 Newhall Street, Birmingham, 1896

Matcham, Frank (1854–1920) **98**
He was the nephew of T Robinson, architect and surveyor to the Lord Chamberlain, and was born in Newton Abbot, South Devon. Matcham designed and improved more than 100 places of entertainment, to become the leading theatre and music-hall architect of 1880–1912.
Empire Palace, Newgate Street, Newcastle-upon-Tyne, 1879 **98**
Grand Theatre, Blackpool, 1894
Grand Opera House, Belfast, 1895
Empire Theatre, Leeds, 1898
County and Cross Arcades, Leeds, 1898–1900
Hippodrome, London, 1899–1900 **98**
Theatre Royal, Portsmouth, 1900
Hackney Empire, London, 1900
Opera House, Buxton, Derbyshire, 1903
Kursaal, Harrogate, 1903
Coliseum Theatre, London, 1904 **98**

Matheson, Robert (1808–77)
A pupil of W Nixon who later became a government architect.
Palm House, Botanic Gardens, Edinburgh, 1855
New Register House, Edinburgh, 1856–62
Post Office, Edinburgh, 1861–65

Matthews, James (1820–98)
A pupil of **Archibald Simpson**, he worked for **Sir George Gilbert Scott** before becoming a partner to **Thomas Mackenzie** and later his son, **Dr Alexander Marshall Mackenzie**.
Grammar School, Aberdeen, 1861
Town and County Bank, Union Street, Aberdeen, 1862 (later Clydesdale Bank)
Ardo, Deeside, Aberdeen, 1877
St Brycedale, Kirkcaldy, Fife, 1878
Town Hall, Inverness, 1878–82 (with Lawrie)

Mawson, R *see* Lockwood, Henry Francis

May, E J 20

McCarthy, James J (1817–82)
R C Chapel, Maynooth College, Kildare, 1852–82
Armagh Cathedral, 1853–82 (completion)
St Saviour R C church, Dublin, 1858
St Macarthan's Cathedral, Monaghan, 1861–82
Cathedral, Thurles, Tipperary, 1862–72
Cahermoyle House, Limerick, 1871
St Patrick's R C church, Dungannon, Tyrone, 1876
SS Peter and Paul R C church, Kilmallock, Co Limerick, Ireland, 1879

McGibbon, William F (1857–1923) **66**
Paint warehouse, Tradeston Street, Glasgow, 1900 **66**

McKim, Mead and **White** 58
This was an American practice, formed by **Charles Follen McKim** (1847–1909), **William Rutherford Mead** and **Stanford White** (1853–1906).
Low House, Bristol, Rhode Island, 1887 (demolished 1962)
Boston Public Library, Massachusetts, 1887–95
State Capitol, Rhode Island, 1891–93
Columbia University, New York City, 1894–98
Pennsylvania Station, New York City, 1902–11 (demolished 1963) *59*

Medland, James (1808–94) and **John** (1840–1913)
James Medland was an assistant to **Samuel Whitfield Daukes** before becoming a partner of **James Hamilton** and then of A W Maberly.
Eastgate Street Market, Gloucester; entrance, 1856
Cemetery Chapels, Cemetery Road, Gloucester, 1857
Corn Hall, Cirencester, Gloucestershire; entrance, 1862

Mengoni, Giuseppe 72
Galleria Vittorio Emanuele II, Milan, 1877 *72*

Mewès and **Davis** 66
Ritz Hotel, London, 1903–06 **66**

Micklethwaite, John Thomas (1843–1906)
A pupil of **Sir George Gilbert Scott**, and a partner first with fellow-pupil **George Somers Clarke** Jnr, then Sir Charles Nicholson (1867–1949) between 1893–94, before setting up in his own practice in 1896. He was architect to St George's Chapel, Windsor, 1900, and surveyor to the dean and chapter of Westminster Abbey, 1898. He published *Ornaments of the Rubric*, 1897.
St Paul's Church, Augustus Road, Putney, London, 1886–96
St Peter's Church, Bocking, Essex, 1896

Middleton, John (*d.* 1885)
A partner of H A Prothero.
St John's Church, Neasham, Darlington, 1847–48
St Mark's Church, Lansdown, Cheltenham, 1862–67
Abbey Holme, Cheltenham, 1865 (own house; demolished, ceiling at Bowes Museum, Barnard Castle)
St Peter's Church, Clearwell, Gloucestershire, 1866
All Saints' Church, Pittville, Cheltenham, 1868
St Stephen's Church, Tivoli, Cheltenham, 1873
Christ Church, Cheltenham, 1883 (interior, with others)

Mills and **Murgatroyd** 81
Alexander William Mills (*d.* 1905) in partnership with **James Murgatroyd** (*d.* 1887).
Royal Exchange, Manchester, 1869–74 (now with theatre built inside) 81
Assembly Rooms, Strangeways, Manchester, 1857–59 (with J G Crace)

Mitchell, Arthur George Sydney (1856–1930)
A pupil of **Sir Robert Rowand Anderson**.
3 Rothesay Place, Edinburgh, 1883
Well Court, Edinburgh, 1884
Craig House, Edinburgh, 1889 (asylum)
Ramsay Gardens, Edinburgh, 1893 (the greater part of)

Moffatt, W B *see* Scott, Sir George Gilbert

Moore, Temple Lushington (1856–1920)
The son of Major-General G F Moore, he entered the Royal Academy Schools in 1877, and was a pupil of, and later an assistant to, **George Gilbert Scott** Jnr. He later entered into partnership with his son, Richard Moore, and his nephew-in-law, Leslie Moore, and was responsible for the design of 17 new churches between 1885 and 1917.

All Saints' Church, Peterborough, 1886–94
Good Shepherd church, Lake, Isle of White,
 1892
St Cuthbert's Church, Middlesborough,
 Yorkshire, 1900
Manor House, Bilbrough, Yorkshire, 1901
Hexham Abbey, 1902–08 (nave)
St Wilfrid's Church, Harrogate, Yorkshire,
 1904–14
Anglican Cathedral, Nairobi, Kenya, 1914

Moreing, Charles (*d.* 1825)
Ingress Abbey, Greenhithe, Kent, *c.* 1832–34

Morris, William (1834–96) **8, 9, 20, 37, 50, 112**
Craftsman, poet and political activist, he was
 born in Walthamstow, London, and educated
 at Marlborough College, before studying for
 holy orders at Oxford. He renounced the
 Church and studied architecture. He founded
 the Kelmscott Press, Hammersmith in 1890,
 issuing his own works and reprints of classics.

Morrison, William Vitruvius (1794–1838)
Court house, Carlow, Co Carlow, Ireland, 1830

Moseley, William (1799–1880) and **Andrew
 Moseley**
City Bank, Threadneedle Street, London, 1856

Mountain, Charles the Younger (1773–1839)
Whitefriars Gate, Kingston-upon-Hull,
 Humberside, 1829–30 (south side terrace)
Guildhall, Register Square, Beverley,
 Humberside, 1832 (portico)
with Richard Hey Sharp
Assembly Rooms (*now* New Theatre), Kingston
 Square, Kingston-upon-Hull, Humberside, 1830

Mountford, Edward William (1855–1908) **76,
 81, 82**
Born at Shipston-on-Stow, Warwickshire, he
 went to school in Somerset and was articled to
 William Gillbee Habershon and **Alfred
 Robert Pite** in 1871; he set up his own practice
 in 1881.
Battersea Public Library, Lavender Hill,
 London, 1888–89
St Andrew's Church, Garratt Lane, London,
 1888–91
Battersea Polytechnic, London, 1890–94
Town Hall, Sheffield, 1890–97 (won in open
 competition) **81**
Town Hall, Battersea, London, 1892 **82**
Northampton Institute, Finsbury, London,
 1893–96
College of Technology, Liverpool, 1896–1902 **76**
Central Criminal Court, Old Bailey, London,
 1900–07 *below*

Mundie, W B (1863–1939) *see* **Jenney, William
 Le Baron**

Murdoch, James *see* **Hay**

Murgatroyd, James *see* **Mills** and **Murgatroyd**

Murray, James *see* **Pugin, Edward Welby**

Nash, John (1752–1835) **35**
Buckingham Palace, St James's Park, London,
 1825–30 (remodelling of earlier house;
 entrance front is of 1913)
Aroid House No 1, Royal Botanic Gardens,
 Kew, Richmond, Surrey, *c.* 1825–30
St Mary Haggerston, Shoreditch, London,
 1826–27 (destroyed) **44**
Carlton House Terrace, London, 1827–33
St Martin's School, St Martin's Place, Trafalgar
 Square, London, *c.* 1830

Nesfield, William Eden (1834–88) **21, 37, 38, 41**
The son of the landscape gardener William
 Andrews Nesfield (1835–88), he was a pupil of
 William Burn 1851–53, then of his uncle,
 Anthony Salvin, 1853–56. He established his
 own practice in 1858 and shared offices with
 Richard Norman Shaw, with whom he
 entered into partnership in 1866.
Shipley Hall, Derbyshire, 1860–61 (farm buildings)
Combe Abbey, Warwickshire, 1863–65 (demolished)
Lodge, Regents Park, London, 1864 (demolished)
Crewe Hall, Cheshire; estate cottages, 1865 **21**
Cloverley Hall, Shropshire, 1866–68 (partly
 demolished)
Temperate House Lodge, Royal Botanic
 Gardens, Kew, Richmond, Surrey, 1866
Kinmel Park, near Abergele, Conwy, 1868 **38**, *38*
Southampton Lodge, Broadlands, Hampshire,
 1870
Holy Trinity Church, Calverhall, Shropshire,
 1872–78
Plas Dinan house, Montgomery, 1873–74
Loughton Hall, Essex, 1878
Grammar School, Newport, Essex, 1878

Newton, Ernest (1856–1922)
Born in London, he was articled to **Richard
 Norman Shaw** in 1873, remaining with him as
 an assistant before leaving to set up in practice
 in 1879. He became RIBA President 1914–17,
 and was awarded the RIBA Gold Medal in 1918.
House of Retreat, Lloyd Square, Clerkenwell,
 London, 1880
Fremlington House, Devon, 1881
St Barnabas' vicarage, Beckenham, Kent, 1888
Bullers Wood, Chislehurst, 1889
Red Court, Haslemere, Surrey, 1894 (house)
Glebeland, Wokingham, Berkshire, 1897 (house)

Nicholl, Samuel J (1826–95)
A pupil of **Joseph John Scoles**
St Charles' R C church, Ogle Street, London, 1862
St Wilfrid's Church, Preston, Lancashire, 1879
 (with Ignatius Scoles)

Nicholson, William Adams (1803–53)
Town Hall, Market Place, Mansfield,
 Nottinghamshire, 1836

Norton, John (1823–1904)
A pupil of **Benjamin Ferrey**.
St John the Evangelist church, Marton Road,
 Middlesbrough, Yorkshire, 1864–66
Elveden Hall, Suffolk, 1870–71
Southwestern Hotel, Southampton, 1872

Olbrich, Joseph Maria (1867–1908) **110, 111**
Graduated from the Staatsgewerbeschule,
 Vienna, in 1886, whereupon he worked in the
 offices of the August Bartel construction
 company, Troppan, Austria. He went on to
 study architecture at the Academy of Fine Arts,
 Vienna, in 1890, where he won the Rome Prize
 in 1893. He found work in the offices of **Otto**

Koloman Wagner and helped to found the
 Vienna Sezession in 1897. When invited by
 Grand Duke Ernst Ludwig to join the Artists'
 Colony, he moved to Darmstadt in 1899. He
 remained there for eight years as the
 construction manager on the Mathildenhöhe.
Exhibition hall for the Vienna Sezession,
 Vienna, 1897–98 *110*, 111, *111*
Vienna Interior, World's Fair, Vienna, 1900
Habich House, Mathildenhöhe, Darmstadt,
 1900–1901
Ernst Ludwig Haus, Darmstadt, 1901 **111**
Wedding Tower and Exhibition Hall,
 Darmstadt, completed 1908
Tietz Department Store, Düsseldorf, begun 1908

Oliver and **Leeson 98**
Thomas Oliver in partnership with **Richard
 John Leeson**.
St Luke's Church, Wallsend, Northumberland,
 1886
Empire Music Hall, Newcastle-upon-Tyne, 1891 **98**
Co-operative Wholesale Society, West Blandford
 Street, Newcastle-upon-Tyne, 1899
Cathedral Buildings, Dean Street, Newcastle-
 upon-Tyne, 1900

Oud, Jacobus Johannes Pieter (1890–1963)
Educated at the Quellinus School of Applied
 Arts, Amsterdam, he worked in the offices of
 Petrus J H Cuypers, Amsterdam, before
 completing his education at the State School of
 Design, Amsterdam, and the Technical
 University, Delft. He worked as a freelance
 architect in Purmerend and Leiden, founding
 the Association de Sphinx in 1916 with Theo
 Van Doesburg and forming the De Stijl group
 of artists with Piet Mondrian, Vilmos Huszar
 and Antony Kok in 1917. He was appointed
 City Planner, Rotterdam, in 1918 and received
 an honorary doctorate at the Technical
 University, Delft, in 1954.
Café de Unie, Scheveningen, 1917
Terrace housing, Scheveningen, 1917 (as De Stijl)

Owen, Jacob (1778–1870)
Architect and engineer to the Irish Board of
 Works, 1832–56
Mountjoy Prison, Dublin, 1850

Owen, Thomas Ellis (1804–62)
Portland Terrace, Southsea, 1845–46
The Vale, Southsea; houses, 1850
with Jacob Owen, his father
Holy Trinity Church, Fareham, Portsmouth,
 1835–37

Paley, Edward Graham (1823–95) **51**
Initially a partner to **Edmund Sharpe**, he was
 joined in 1868 by Hubert James Austin and
 later by his son Henry Austin, the firm
 continuing as Austin and Paley.
R C cathedral, Lancaster, 1857–59
St Chad's Church, Kirkby, Lancashire, 1869–71
Leighton Hall, Yealand Conyers, Lancashire, 1870
SS Matthew and James church, Mossley Hill,
 Liverpool, 1870–75
Holker Hall, Lancashire, 1871
St Thomas' Church, Halliwell, Bolton,
 Lancashire, 1875
St James' Church, Daisy Hill, Lancashire, 1879–81
All Souls' church, Astley Bridge, Bolton,
 Lancashire, 1880–81
St Peter's Church, Leigh, Lancashire, 1880–81
St Mary's Church, Dalton-in-Furness,
 Lancashire, 1882–85
St John's Church, Pilling, Lancashire, 1883–87
Christ Church, Waterloo, Lancashire, 1891–94
St Peter's Church, Broughton East, Lancashire,
 1892–94
St George's Church, Buston Road, Stockport,
 Cheshire, 1893–97 **51**, *51*
St Matthew's Church, Highfield, Wigan,
 Lancashire, 1894
School chapel, Sedbergh, Yorkshire, 1897

Papworth, John Buonarotti (1775–1847) **36**
St James' Church, Suffolk Square, Cheltenham,
 Gloucestershire, 1826–32 (completion)
Park Hill (*now* St Michael's Convent), off
 Streatham Common North, Streatham,
 London, *c.* 1830 onwards
Lansdown Terrace, Cheltenham,
 Gloucestershire, *c.* 1830 (thought to be by)
Cranbury Park, near Eastleigh, Hampshire,
 1830s (additions)

Parker, Charles (1799–1881) **36**
A pupil of **Sir Jeffry Wyatville**, he set up in
 practice in 1830 and published *Villa Rustica*, an
 important work on domestic dwellings near
 Rome and Florence, in 1832.
Hoare's Bank, Fleet Street, City of London,
 1830–32
St Raphael's R C church, Kingston, Surrey,
 1846–47
Christ Church, St Albans, Hertfordshire, 1850–51
Parker, Richard Barry (1867–1947) **13, 24, 24**
Trained in the design of domestic interiors, he
 was a disciple of **William Morris**, and articled
 to George Faulkner Armitage. He opened his
 own office at Buxton in 1894, and was joined
 by **Raymond Unwin**; together they published
 The Art of Building a Home, 1901; *see* **Unwin,
 Raymond**.

Parnell, Charles Octavius (*d.* 1865) **100**
Westminster Bank, Lombard Street, London, 1861
Whitehall Club, 47 Parliament Street, London,
 1864–66
Army and Navy Club, Pall Mall, London,
 1848–51 (with A Smith; demolished) **100**

Paull, Henry John (*d.* 1888)
In partnership at various times with Aycliffe,
 Bickerdike, Bonella and Robinson.
West Hill Park Estate, Halifax, 1863–68 and
Philips Park cemetery, Beswick, Manchester,
 1866 (both with Aycliffe)
Christ Church Congregational church,
 Westminster Bridge Road, London, 1873–75
 (with Bickerdike; demolished)
Islington Chapel, Upper Street, London, 1888
 (with Bonella)
Public Baths, Henry Square, Ashton-under-
 Lyne, Lancashire, 1870 (demolished) and
Promenade Hospital, Southport, Lancashire,
 1882–83 (both with Robinson)

Paxton, Sir Joseph (1801–65) **10, 21, 55–57**
A gardener and architect, from 1826 he was
 superintendent of the gardens at Chatsworth.
 He was knighted for his design work for the
 Industrial Exhibition of 1850, the building
 which became known generally as the Crystal
 Palace.
Great Stove, Chatsworth, Derbyshire, 1836–40
 (greenhouse; demolished) **55,** *56, 58*
Model village, Edensor, Derbyshire, 1838 **21**
Princes Park, Liverpool, 1842–44
Birkenhead Park, Birkenhead, Cheshire, 1843
Victoria Regia lily house, Chatsworth,
 Derbyshire, 1849–50
Crystal Palace, London, 1850–51 (re-erected at
 Sydenham 1853–54; demolished) **7,** *7,* **10,** *56,
 57, 57, 58*
Ferrières, near Paris, France, 1853–59
 (Rothschild house)
Mentmore Towers, Buckinghamshire, 1851–54
 (with G H Stokes)

Peachy, William *see* **Prosser, Thomas**

Peacock, Joseph (1821–93)
St Simon Zelotes church, Milner Street, London,
 1858–59
St Stephen's Church, Gloucester Road, London,
 1864
St Andrew's Church, Perth, 1869
Church of the Holy Cross, Cromer Street,
 London, 1887–88

Pearce, J B (1843–1903)
Town Hall, Great Yarmouth, 1882

Pearson, John Loughborough (1817–97) **49, 50**
He practised with **Anthony Salvin** and **Philip
 Hardwick** in London before establishing his
 own practice in 1843. He worked on
 restorations at Lincoln Cathedral, 1870,
 Westminster Hall, *c.* 1885, and the north
 transept of Westminster Abbey; he was
 awarded the RIBA Gold Medal in 1880.
St Mary's Church, Ellerton, Yorkshire, 1846–48
Treberfydd House and church, Brecon,
 1848–50
St Matthew's Church, Landscove, Devon,
 1849–50
Quar Wood House, near Stow-on-the-Wold,
 Gloucestershire, 1857 (much altered)
St Mary's Church, Dalton Holme, Yorkshire,
 1858–61
St Peter's Church, Daylesford, Gloucestershire,
 1860
St Peter's Church, Kennington Lane, London,
 1863–65 (designed 1860) **50**
Christ Church, Appleton-le-Moors, Yorkshire,
 1863–65
St John the Evangelist church, Sutton Veny,
 Wiltshire, 1866–68
Roundwick House, Sussex, 1868
St Mary's Church, including vicarage and
 school, Freeland, Oxfordshire, 1868–73 **49,** *49*
St Augustine with St John's Church, Kilburn
 Park Road, London, 1871–98 **49, 50,** *50*
St John the Divine church, Sylvan Hill, London,
 1875–87
St Alban's Church, Bordesley, Birmingham,
 1879–81
St Michael's Church, Croydon, Surrey, 1880–85
Cathedral, Truro, Cornwall, 1880–1910 **50,** *50*
St George's Church, Culercoats,
 Northumberland, 1882–84
St Agnes' Church, Sefton Park, Liverpool,
 1883–85
St Bartholomew's Church, Thurstaston,
 Cheshire, 1884–85
St Theodore's Church, Port Talbot, Glamorgan,
 1895–97
Cathedral, Brisbane, Australia, 1901
Catholic Apostolic Church, Maida Avenue,
 London, 1891–93
Astor Estate Office, Victoria Embankment,
 London, 1892–95

Peck, F *see* **Coe, Henry Edward**

Peddie and **Kinnear**
John Dick Peddie (1824–91), in partnership
 with **Charles George Hood Kinnear**
 (1830–94).
Cockburn Street, Edinburgh, 1860
Town Hall, Aberdeen, 1861–66
Morgan Academy, Dundee, 1863–66
Glenmayne, Peebles, Scottish Borders, 1869
Hydropathic hotel, Dunblane, Perth, 1877
Hotel and arcade complex, 91–115 Hope Street,
 Glasgow, 1877
Craiglockhart Hydropathic hotel (*now*
 R C college), Edinburgh, 1878–80

Peddie, John More Dick (1853–1921)
The son of **John Dick Peddie**, he attended the
 Edinburgh Academy, studied in Germany and
 became an assistant in the office of **Sir George
 Gilbert Scott** in London. He later joined his
 father's practice, becoming a partner in 1879.
Bank of Scotland, 101–03 George Street,
 Edinburgh, 1884
Standard Life building, 3 George Street,
 Edinburgh, 1898–1900
Scottish Provident building, 17–29 St Vincent
 Place, Glasgow, 1905–06
with Sir George Washington Browne
National Bank, Buchanan Street / St Vincent
 Street, Glasgow, 1899 (later Royal Bank)

Pennethorne, Sir James (1801–71) **29, 78**
A pupil of **John Nash** and **Augustus Charles
 Pugin**. He was awarded the RIBA Gold Medal
 in 1865 and knighted in 1870.
Swithland Hall, Leicestershire, 1834
Public Record Office, Chancery Lane, London,
 1850–51 **29, 78**
Somerset House, Lancaster Place, London,
 1852–56 (west façade)
Buckingham Palace, London, 1853–55
 (ballroom wing)
Duchy of Cornwall Offices, 10 Buckingham
 Gate, London, 1854
Marlborough House, The Mall, London,
 1861–63 (stables, outbuildings and attic storey)
London University buildings, Burlington
 Gardens, London, 1866–69

Penrose, Francis Cranmer (1817–1903)
Educated at Winchester and Magdalene College,
 Cambridge, he was also an archaeologist and
 astronomer but studied architecture in Europe,
 1842–45, making careful measurements of
 Greek classical buildings; these were published
 in *Principles of Athenian Architecture*, 1851. He was
 the Surveyor of St Paul's Cathedral from 1852,
 and president of RIBA 1894–96.
Market House, Castle Cary, Somerset, 1855
St Paul's Cathedral, London, 1860 (pulpit)
Rectory (*now* manor house), Hornblotton,
 Somerset, 1867
British School, Athens, 1882

Penson, Richard Kyrke (1816–86)
A partner to **A Ritchie** (Chester and Swansea).
College, Ruthin, Denbigh, 1855–56
St Mark's Church, Hope Road, Wrecsam,
 1856–58 (demolished)

Penson, Thomas (Jnr, 1791–1859)
St Agatha's Church, Llanymynech, Shropshire,
 1842
Market, Wrecsam, 1848
Shrewsbury Station, 1848 (altered)

Penson, Thomas Mainwaring (1818–64)
The son of **Thomas Penson** Jnr.
Old Cemetery, Grosvenor Road, Chester,
 1848–50
34 and 36 Eastgate Street, Chester, 1856
Browns Crypt Buildings, Eastgate Street,
 Chester, 1858

Perret, Auguste (1874–1954)
Educated at the École des Beaux-Arts, Paris, he
 established a construction firm in 1905 with his
 brothers Gustave and Claude. After the Second
 World War he was very involved with the
 reconstruction of Le Havre, 1945–54.
House, Rue Franklin, Paris, 1903
Garage, Rue Ponthieu, Paris, 1905
Théâtre des Champs-Elysées, Paris, 1911–13
 (from a conception of **Henry-Clément van de
 Velde**)
Esders clothing workshop, 1919

Petit, Revd John Louis (1801–68)
A highly-regarded architectural writer, educated
 at Trinity College, Cambridge. He published
 Remarks on Architectural Character, 1846, and
 Architectural Studies in France, 1854.
Church, Caerdeon, near Newport, Wales,
 1862–63

Peto, Harold Ainsworth (1854–1933) **19, 23**
Articled in 1871 to a Lowestoft architect, J
 Clements, later he joined the offices of Harold
 Peto, becoming a partner in 1876. He retired
 through ill-health to Italy in 1895, to study
 gardens. He returned to England later and
 continued to design gardens and interiors; *see*
 George, Ernest.

Phipps, Charles John (1835–97) **96–99, 103**
Articled in Bath, where he began to practise in

1858 and reconstructed the Bath Theatre, 1862–63. Then he moved to London and became recognised as the authority on theatre construction. He worked on the construction and alteration of more than twenty theatres in London, in addition to those in many provincial towns.
Theatre Royal, Upper Parliament Street, Nottingham, 1865 **96**, **99**
Theatre Royal, Exeter, 1868 (destroyed) **96**
Star and Garter Hotel, Richmond, Surrey, 1874 (demolished)
Haymarket Theatre, London, 1879 **97**
Savoy Theatre, London, 1881 **97**, **99**
Lyric Theatre, Shaftsbury Avenue, London, 1888 **97**
Tivoli Music Hall, London, 1888–90 **98**
Daly's, Cranbourn Street, London, 1891–93 **98**
Her Majesty's Theatre, Haymarket, London, 1891–97 **98**
Carlton Hotel, London, 1897–99 (designed 1891; demolished) **103**
with Thomas Edward Knightley
Queen's Hall, Langham Place, London, 1891 (demolished)

Picton, Sir James Allanson (1805–89) **27**
A respected historian, he was partner to his son, William Henry Picton (1836–1900); he originated the Liverpool Public Library and Museum, and published *Memorials of Liverpool*, 1873. He was knighted in 1881.
Holy Trinity Church, Hoylake, Cheshire, 1834
Richmond Buildings, 26 Chapel Street, Liverpool, 1857 (demolished) **27**
Hargreaves Building, 5 Chapel Street, Liverpool, 1861
The Temple, Dale Street, Liverpool, 1864–65
Victoria Wesleyan chapel (*now* Juvenile Court), Crosshall Street, Liverpool, 1878–80

Pilkington, Frederick Thomas (1832–98)
Trained with his father, Thomas Pilkington.
Trinity Church, Irvine, Ayr, 1861–63
Children's Asylum, Larbert, Stirling, 1861–70
Barclay Church, Edinburgh, 1862–63
St John's Church, Edenside, Kelso, 1867
Hydropathic hotel, Moffat, Dumfries, 1875–77 (demolished)
Windsor Hotel, Victoria Street, London, 1881–83 (demolished)

Pirie, John Bridgeford (1851–92)
A pupil of A Ellis, he worked for **David Bryce** and **James Matthews**.
Queen's Cross Church, Aberdeen, 1880
Town Hall, Macduff, Banff, 1884
Hamilton Place, Aberdeen, 1884 (demolished)
St Palladiua's Church, Drumtochty, Kincardine, 1885
50 Queen's Road, Aberdeen, 1886

Pite, Alfred Robert (1832–1911)
Articled to **Matthew Habershon** before working in the office of John Belcher Snr, 1851, he returned to partner **William Gillbee Habershon**, 1860–78.

Pite, Arthur Beresford (1861–1934) **15**
The younger of the two sons of **Alfred Robert Pite**, he was renowned for his architectural drawings. He was educated at King's College School and at University College, London, entering the South Kensington Schools of Design in 1876. In the same year he was articled to the practice of **Habershon** and J Follett Fawckner, and then, in 1881, to his own father. He won the Donaldson Medal in 1879, the Grissell Medal in 1880 and the Soane Medal in 1882, the same year in which he entered the office of **John Belcher** Jnr. He was Professor of Architecture at the Royal College of Art, 1900–23.
82 Mortimer Street, Marylebone, London, 1896
Christchurch, north Brixton, London, 1898–1903
37 Harley Street, London, 1899 **14**

Playfair, William Henry (1789–1857) **91**
The nephew of John Playfair, he trained under W Stark and **Sir Robert Smirke**, and practised in Edinburgh, where he laid out part of the New Town between 1815 and 1820.
Preston Grange, Prestonpans, Lothian, 1830 (remodelling)
Dugald Stewart Monument, Calton Hill, Edinburgh, *c.* 1830
Surgeon's Hall, Nicholson Street, Edinburgh, 1832
Royal Scottish Institution, The Mount, Edinburgh, 1832–35 (extensions) **91**
Craigcrook Castle, Cramond, Edinburgh, 1835
Bonaly Tower, Edinburgh, 1836–38 (wings added 1870s)
Floors Castle, Kelso; remodelling, 1838
Donaldson's Hospital, Edinburgh, 1842–45
Free Church College, Edinburgh, 1846–50
National Gallery of Scotland, Edinburgh, 1850–54 **91**

Plumbe, Sir Rowland (1838–1919)
Bryant and May Match Tax Testimonial Fountain, Bow Road, Poplar, London, 1872
Noel Park Estate, Wood Green, London, 1881
St John's Church, Loxwood, Sussex, 1896
Nile Street, Shoreditch, London, 1896 (council flats)
YMCA, Great Russell Street, London, 1911 (demolished)

Poelzig, Hans (1869–1936)
Having graduated in 1899 from the Technische Hochschule, Berlin-Charlottenburg, he worked for the Preußisches Staatsbaumt. In 1900 he was appointed professor at the Kunst-und Gewerbeschule, Breslau, where he was promoted to principal, 1903–16. After this he became professor and municipal architect of Dresden, taught at the Prussian Academy of Arts from 1920, and from 1924 also at the Technische Hochschule, Berlin-Charlottenburg.
Chemical factory, Luban, Poland, 1911 (formerly Germany)
Exhibition structure, Century Exhibition, Breslau, Germany, 1913

Ponton, Archibald (*d.* 1880) **53**, **66**
Worked first as an associate of **John Foster** than as a partner to W V Gough (1842–1918).
Museum and Library (*now* University), Bristol, 1866–71
Chemist shop, High Street, Bristol, 1869 (demolished)
Granary Warehouse, Welsh Back, Bristol, 1871 **52**, **66**
Holy Nativity church, Knowle, Bristol, 1871–73

Pope, Richard Shackleton (1791–1854) **81**
Vyvyan Terrace, Clifton, Bristol, 1835
St Mary on the Quay R C church, Bristol, 1839
Guildhall, Broad Street, Bristol, 1843 **80**, **81**
with Isambard Kingdom Brunel
Royal Western Hotel (*now* offices), Bristol 1837

Pope, T S 83
Assize Courts, Small Street, Bristol, 1867 (with J Bindon) **83**

Potter, Joseph (*c.* 1756–1842)
St Mary's R C College, New Oscott, Perry Bar, Birmingham, West Midlands, 1835–38

Potter, Robert (*c.* 1795–1854)
Savings Bank, Surrey Street, Sheffield, South Yorkshire, 1831 (enlarged 1860)

Poulton and **Woodman**
W F Poulton in partnership with **W H Woodman** (1822–79).
French Congregational Church, Halkett Place, St Helier, Channel Islands, 1854
Congregational Church, South Street, Dorchester, Dorset, 1856–57

Town Hall, Wokingham, Surrey, 1860
St Mary's Church, Batsford, Gloucestershire, 1861–62

Pownall, Frederick Hyde (*b.* 1825)
2–4 Brook Street, London, 1860
St Peter's Church, London Docks, Wapping Lane, London, 1865–66
Corpus Christi R C church, Maiden Lane, London, 1873–74
Highgate Police Court, Archway Road, London, 1897

Prichard, John (1817–86)
He was Llandaff Diocesan Architect, 1846–86; and a partner of **John Pollard Seddon**, 1853–63.
Llandaff Cathedral; additions, 1843–82
St Mary's Church, Aberavon, near Port Talbot, Glamorgan, 1857–58
Ettington Park, Warwickshire, 1858–63
House, Jerez de la Frontera, Spain, 1864

Prior, Edward Schroeder (1852–1932) **41**, **51**
Born at Greenwich, London, the son of barrister John Venn Prior; he was educated at Harrow and Caius College, Cambridge, where he was later made a Fellow. He was articled to **Richard Norman Shaw** in 1874 and was one of Shaw's pupils and assistants who formed the St George's Art Society, the forerunner of the Art Workers' Guild. Prior was a founder member of the Guild, and Master in 1906. He was also secretary of the Arts and Crafts Exhibition Society, 1902–17.
Red House, Byron Hill, Harrow, Middlesex, 1883
Henry Martyn Memorial Hall, Cambridge, 1884–86
The Barn, Exmouth, Devon, 1897 (house)
Iychgate, Brantham, Suffolk, 1897
Zoological Laboratory, Cambridge, 1901–04
St Andrew's Church, Roker, Tyne and Wear, 1906–07 **51**

Pritchett, James Pigott (Snr, 1789–1868)
In partnership in York, first with Watson and later with his son James Pigott Pritchett (Jnr, 1830–91).
St James' Church, Meltham Mills, Yorkshire, 1845
Huddersfield Station, 1845–50
St Nicholas' Church, Durham, 1857–58

Prosser, Thomas with Peachy, William
Central Station, York, 1871–77 **59**

Prynne, George Halford Fellowes (1853–1927)
Educated at Chard College, Somerset, and Haileybury; in 1871 he went to Canada, becoming a pupil of R C Windyer of Toronto. On his return to London he was employed in the offices of **George Edmund Street** and worked in the site office of the Royal Courts of Justice, in the Strand. He entered the Royal Academy Schools in 1876.
St Peter's Church, Budleigh Salterton, Devon, 1893
St John the Baptist church, Horrabridge, Devon, 1893
Hadlow Grange, Kent, 1895
Holy Trinity Church, Roehampton, London, 1895

Pugin, Augustus Welby Northmore (1812–52) **9**, **33**, **36**, **44**, **45**, **47**, **50**, **63**, **64**, **78**, **84**, **85**
The son of Augustus Charles Pugin, he was educated at Christ's Hospital, London, and trained by his father. He inherited a remarkable facility in draughtsmanship, and obtained a regular practice, partly through the patronage of the Earl of Shrewsbury. He published *Gothic Furniture*, 1835, and *Contrasts*, 1836, the latter being an attack on the 'pagan' method of architecture. These were followed by *True*

Principles of Pointed or Christian Architecture, 1841, after which his ecclesiastical practice became very extensive.
King Edward VI School, Birmingham; decorative detailing for Sir Charles Barry, 1833–37 (demolished)
Catholic Chapel, Oxburgh Hall, Norfolk, 1835 (thought to be by, or by **John Chessell Buckler**)
House, Alderbury, Wiltshire, 1835 (own house, altered 1870)
St Marie's Grange, Alderbury, Wiltshire, 1835–36 **36**
New Palace of Westminster (Houses of Parliament), London, 1835–60 (decorative detailing for **Sir Charles Barry**) *3*, *77*, *78*, *78*, *79*, *79*
St Mary's R C church, Derby, 1837–39 **50**
St James' R C church, Forbury Road, Reading, Berkshire, 1837–40
Scarisbrick Hall, Lancashire, 1837–45 **33**, *33*
St Alban's R C church, Chester Road, Macclesfield, Cheshire, 1838–41 **50**
St Michael's R C church, Gorey, Wexford, 1839
St Chad's Cathedral, Birmingham, 1839–41
St Wilfrid's R C church, Hulme, Manchester, 1839–42
Mount St Bernard Abbey, Leicestershire, 1839–44
St John's Hospital, Alton, Staffordshire, 1840
St Oswald's R C church, Old Swan, Liverpool, 1840–42
St George's Cathedral, Southwark, London, 1841 (mostly destroyed)
School, Spetchley, Worcestershire, 1841 **85**
St Barnabas' Cathedral, Nottingham, 1841–44
St Giles' R C church, Cheadle, Staffordshire, 1841–46
St Mary's Cathedral, Killarney, 1842
St Peter's R C church, Woolwich New Road, London, 1842–50 (incomplete)
Radcliffe College, Leicestershire, 1843 **85**
Magdalen College, Oxford, 1843–44 (gateway; demolished)
The Grange, Ramsgate, Kent, 1843–44
St Mary's R C cathedral, Newcastle-upon-Tyne, 1844 **44**
St Alphonsus' R C church, Barntown, Wexford, 1844
Glebe Farm, Rampisham, Dorset, 1845–46
St Peter's R C church, Marlow, Buckinghamshire, 1845–48
St Augustine's R C church, Ramsgate, Kent, 1845–51
R C Chapel, St Edmund's College, Old Hall Green, Hertfordshire, 1845–53
St Osmund's R C church, Salisbury, 1847–49
St Thomas of Canterbury R C church, Rylston Road, London, 1847–49
Rolle Mortuary Chapel, Bicton, Devon, 1850
with James Gillespie Graham
Houses of Parliament, London, 1836 (designs, unexecuted)

Pugin, Edward Welby (1834–75) **45**
The son of **Augustus Welby Northmore Pugin**, he took over his father's large firm in 1852 and practised for 14 years.
with James Murray
Our Lady of Help cathedral, Shrewsbury, 1853
Bishop Eton Monastery, Childwall, Liverpool, 1858
Our Lady of Reconciliation R C church, Vauxhall Road, Liverpool, 1859
St Francis' R C church, Gorton, Manchester, 1864 **45**
Carlton Towers, Carlton-in-Balne, Yorkshire, 1874
with George Coppinger Ashlin, his brother-in-law
SS Augustine and John R C church, St Thomas Street, Dublin, 1862
Sacred Heart R C church, Donnybrook, Dublin, 1866
Queenstown (*now* Cobh) Cathedral, 1868–1919

Radford, William and **Francis 17**
Holland Park Estate, London, 1860–79 **17**

Railton, William (1801–77)
A pupil of William Inwood (1771–1843) and architect to the Ecclesiastical Commissioners, 1838–40.
House and R C chapel, Grace-Dieu, Leicestershire, 1833–34
Nelson's Column, Trafalgar Square, London, 1840–43
Holy Trinity Church, Hoxton, London, 1848

Rampling, Clark (*d.* 1875)
Medical Institution, Hope Street, Liverpool, 1836–37

Redmayne, George Tunstall (1840–1912)
Scottish Widows Fund offices, Albert Square, Manchester, 1874
College of Art, Chorlton-on-Medlock, Manchester, 1880–81

Rennie, Sir John (1794–1874)
Royal William Victualling Yard, Plymouth, Devon, 1826–32

Repton, George Stanley (1786–1858)
Widworthy Court, near Honiton, Devon, 1830
Dumbleton Hall, near Evesham, Gloucestershire, *c.* 1830
Camerton Court, Somerset, 1838–40
Headmaster's House, Winchester College, Winchester, 1839–41

Repton, John Adey (1775–1860)
The son of Humphry Repton (1775–1860).
Buckhurst Park, Withyham, East Sussex, *c.* 1830–35

Rhind, David (1808–83)
Commercial Bank of Scotland, George Street, Edinburgh, 1844–46
Daniel Stewarts College, Edinburgh, 1849–53
Commercial Bank, Gordon Street, Glasgow, 1854
Life Assurance of Scotland offices, Princes Street, Edinburgh, 1855–59 (demolished)

Ricardo, Halsey Ralph (1854–1928)
Born in Bath, he was articled to Cheltenham architect **John Middleton**; later he worked with **Basil Champneys** and after 1888 with William De Morgan and his Arts and Crafts Exhibition Society.
Offices, Great George Street, London, 1887 (demolished)
Town Hall, Oxford, 1892 (competition design, unexecuted)
15–17 Melbury Road, Kensington, London, 1893–94
Howrah Station, Calcutta, 1898
8 Addison Road, London, 1906–07

Richardson, Charles James (1806–71)
A pupil of Sir John Soane (1753–1837), he wrote several books on villas.
13 Kensington Palace Gardens, London

Rickman, Thomas (1776–1841)
Bank, English Street, Carlisle, Cumbria, 1830
St Mary's Church, Lower Hardres, Kent, 1831–32
Matfen Hall, Northumberland, 1832–35
All Saints' Church, Stretton-on-Dunsmore, Warwickshire, 1835–37
St James' Church, Hartlebury, Worcestershire, 1836–37 (nave)
Holy Ascension church, Settle, North Yorkshire, 1836–38
Christ Church, Chapel Hill, Clevedon, Avon, 1838–39
with Henry Hutchinson (1800–31).
St John's College New Court, Cambridge, Cambridgeshire, 1825–31
Holy Trinity Church, Wigton Road, Carlisle, Cumbria, 1828–30

Midland Bank, Waterloo Street, Birmingham, West Midlands, 1830
St David's Church, Haigh, Lancashire, 1830
with Hussey
Holy Cross church, Goodnestone, Kent, 1838–41 (addition of nave and chancel)

Ritchie, A *see* **Penson, Richard Kyrke**

Roberts, Henry (1803–76) **22**
A pupil of **Charles Fowler**, he worked in the offices of **Sir Robert Smirke** and was architect to the Society for Improving the Conditions of the Labouring Classes.
Fishmongers' Hall, William Street, London, 1831–34
Escott House, Ottery St Mary, Devon, 1837
Escott Church, Devon, 1839–40
London Bridge Station, London, 1844–46 (demolished)
'Model Houses', Streatham Street, Bloomsbury, London, 1849–50 **22**
Model cottage for Great Exhibition, London, 1851 (now in Kennington Park)

Robertson, John of Derby **21**
Model village, Edensor, Derbyshire, 1838 **21**

Robertson, John Murray (1844–1901)
A pupil of **Andrew Heiton**.
India Buildings, Dundee, 1874
Beach Tower, Broughty Ferry, Dundee, 1874
Caledonian Insurance offices, Albert Square, Dundee, 1879–80
The Cottage, Lochee, Dundee, 1880 (later Landsdowne; demolished)
The Bughties, Broughty Ferry, Dundee, 1882
Technical Institute, Dundee, 1886 (former)
Free Library and Baths, Lochee, Dundee, 1895
Fyffe's Building, 89 Nethergate, Dundee, 1895
Royal Victoria Hospital, Dundee, 1899

Robertson, William (*c.* 1786–1841)
Court House and Public Offices, Elgin, Grampian, 1837 (rebuilt *c.* 1930)

Robinson, George Thomas (1828–97)
Old Town Hall, Burslem, Stoke-on-Trent, Staffordshire, 1852–57
St Patrick's Church tower, Earlswood, Warwickshire, 1860

Robson, Edward Robert (1835–1917) **17**, **81**, **84**, **86**
An assistant to **John Dobson** and **Sir George Gilbert Scott**; Robson was the partner of **John James Stevenson**, 1870–75, and architect to the School Board for London, 1872–84; *see also* **Flockton, Thomas James**.
St Cuthbert's Church, North Road, Durham, 1858
St Mary's Church, West Rainton, Durham, 1864
West Street School, London Fields, London, *c.* 1870 **86**, **87**
Queen Anne's Mansions, Broadway, London, 1876–88 (demolished) **17**
Town Hall, Loftus, Yorkshire, 1878
The People's Palace (*now* Queen Mary College, London University), Mile End Road, London, 1885–90
Grammar School, Dunstable, Bedfordshire, 1887–94
Institute of Painters in Watercolour, 193 Piccadilly, London, 1881
Princess Hall, Cheltenham Ladies College, Cheltenham, 1896–98
Municipal Offices, Liverpool, 1864–68 (with John Weightman) **81**
with John James Stevenson
Bonner Street Primary School, Hackney, London, 1875

Rochead, John Thomas (1814–78)
A pupil of **David Bryce**, he later worked for **David Hamilton**, practising in Glasgow between 1841 and 1870.

Grosvenor Terrace, Glasgow, 1855
John Street Church, Cochrane, Glasgow, 1859
Wallace Monument, Abbey Craig, Stirling, 1859–69
St Mary's Free Church, Albany Street, Edinburgh, 1860–61
Bank of Scotland, 2 St Vincent Place, Glasgow, 1869

Roebling, John Augustus (1806–69) **54**
A German-born civil engineer, he emigrated to the USA in 1831, and developed the first machinery to produce metal ropes.
Brooklyn Suspension Bridge, New York City, completed 1883 **54**, *55*
Rolfe, Clapton Crabb (1845–1907)
The nephew of **William Wilkinson**.
Church, Hailey, Oxfordshire, 1866–69
Artisans' houses, Kingston Road, Oxford, 1870
St Thomas' Vicarage, Oxford, 1893

Ross, Alexander (1834–1925)
St Andrew's Cathedral, Inverness, 1866–68
Queensgate, Inverness, 1870, 1889, 1898 (market, arcade and offices)
Ardross Street and Terrace, Inverness, 1873–88
St Margaret's Episcopal Church, Aberlour, Banff, 1875–79

Roumieu, Robert Lewis (1814–77) **66**
A pupil of **Benjamin Dean Wyatt** and later a partner of **Alexander Dick Gough**, 1836–48.
Literary Institute, Almeida Street, London, 1837
Milner Square, Islington, London, 1841
Tollington Park Estate, Hornsey, London, 1860–70
French Hospital, Victoria Park Road, London, 1865
The Priory, Roehampton, Middlesex, 1866
33–35 Eastcheap, London, 1868 **66**, *66*

Rowland, Samuel (*d. c.* 1845)
St Bride's Church, Percy Street, Liverpool, 1830–31
Royal Bank, Dale Street, Liverpool, 1837–38

Rushforth, Thomas Henry
St Aubyn's Church, James Piers, 1815–95
St Agnes' Church, St Agnes, Cornwall, 1848
St Michael's Mount, Cornwall, 1850–78 (additions)
St Margaret's Church, Welsh Bicknor, Hereford, 1859
St Thomas' Church, Greetland, Yorkshire, 1859
All Saints' Church, Reading, Berkshire, 1865
Garden Court Building, Middle Temple, London, 1884–85

Ruskin, John (1819–1900) **8, 9, 17, 64, 65, 112**
This London-born writer and art critic studied at Oxford, where he became Professor of Fine Art in 1870. He published *The Seven Lamps of Architecture*, 1848, and *The Stones of Venice*, 1851–53.

Salmon, James (1805–88)
A pupil of John Brash.
St Matthew's Church, Bath Street, Glasgow, 1849 (demolished)

Salmon, James (1873–1924) **113**
Hatrack, 142–4 St Vincent Street, Glasgow, 1899–1902 **113**
Anderston Savings Bank, Argyle Street, Glasgow, 1899

Salomons, Edward (1827–1906) **96, 100**
A pupil of **John Edgar Gregan**.
Crystal Palace, Trafford Park, Manchester, 1856–57 (art treasures exhibition, demolished)
Synagogue, Cheetham Hill Road, Manchester, 1858
Prince's Theatre, Manchester, *c.* 1864 **96**
Prince of Wales Theatre, Liverpool, 1866 **96**
Agnew's, 43 Old Bond Street, London, 1877
Reform Club, King Street, Manchester, 1870–71 (with Jones) **100**

Salvin, Anthony (1799–1881) **34**
He worked for **John Nash** before setting up in practice in London in 1828. He executed restorations at the Tower of London, Windsor Castle and other castles and country seats. He was Vice President of RIBA in 1839 and Gold Medallist in 1863.
Mamhead House, near Topsham, Devon, 1828–30
Moreby Hall, near York, North Yorkshire, 1828–33
Leven Grove (later Skutterskelfe House), Rugby-in-Cleveland, Cleveland, 1831
Harlaxton Manor, Lincolnshire, 1831–37
Scotney Castle, Lamberhurst, Kent, 1837–44
Christ Church, Kilndown, Kent, 1840 (alterations)
Peckforton Castle, Cheshire, 1844–50 **32, 33**, *34*
Penoyre, Brecon, 1846–48
St Stephen's Church, Hammersmith, London, 1849–50
Gurney Bank, Great Yarmouth, Norfolk, 1854 (later Barclays Bank)
Keele Hall, Staffordshire, 1854–65
St Mark's Church, Torquay, Devon, 1856–57
Thoresby Hall, Nottinghamshire, 1864–75
Paddockhurst (*now* Worth Priory), Sussex, 1869–72

Sambell, Philip (1798–1874)
Doric Column, Lemon Street, Truro, Cornwall, 1835
Baptist Chapel, Clarence Street, Penzance, Cornwall, 1835–36

Sanderson, James (*c.* 1791–1835)
Town Hall, Lind Street, Ryde, Isle of Wight, 1830

Saulnier, Jules (1817–81) **66**
Chocolat Menier factory, Noisel-sur-Marne, France, 1871–72 **66**

Savage, James (1779–1852)
Holy Trinity Church, Tottenham Green, Tottenham, London, 1828–30
St Mary's Church, High Road, Ilford, London, 1829–31

Schuchov, Vladimir Grigorevich (1853–1939)
He studied engineering, 1871–76, at the Polytechnic of Moscow and worked in St Petersburg, planning locomotive sheds. Between 1878–80 he worked on pipelines in Baku, commissioned by Alexander V Bovi. On his return to Moscow he became chief engineer in Bovi's office, developing a new water supply system for the city in 1886. He was involved in bridge construction for the railways and developed large-roof construction, publishing *The Roofing Bond* in 1897.
Petrovskij Arcade, Moscow, 1893
Adziogol Lighthouse, near Chersson, Ukraine, 1911 (demolished)
Central Post Office, Moscow, 1912 (with glass roof)
Kiev Railway Station, Moscow, 1912–17
Transmitting tower, Comintern Radio Station Shabolovka, Moscow, 1919–22

Schwedler, Johann Wilhelm 60
Furnace house, Imperial Continental Gas Association, Berlin, 1863 **60**

Scoles, Joseph John (1798–1863)
A pupil of Joseph Ireland, 1812. He set up in practice in London in 1826.
Catholic church, Holywell, Clwyd, 1833 (extended 1895)
St Ignatius R C church, Meadow Street, Preston, Lancashire, 1833–36
St Peter's R C church, Stonyhurst, Lancashire, 1834–35
Our Lady R C church, Lisson Grove, London, 1835
St Mary's R C church, Newport, Wales, 1839–40
St John the Evangelist R C church, Duncan Terrace, London, 1843

Prior Park, Bath, Avon (chapel), 1844
Church of the Immaculate Conception (R C), Farm Street, London, 1844–50
St Paul's R C church, Prior Park, Bath, 1844–63
St Mary's R C church, Regent Road, Great Yarmouth, Norfolk, 1848–50
Oratorians' House, Brompton Oratory, London, 1853

Scott, Abraham Henthorn 65, 67
T Houldsworth & Co Mills, Reddish, Lancashire, 1865 **65**

Scott, Daniel 66
Robinson's Emporium, West Hartlepool, Durham, 1896 **66**

Scott, Sir George Gilbert (1811–78) **34, 35, 50, 64, 79–81, 86, 89, 101, 107**
A pupil of **Sir Robert Smirke** 1832–34, he practised independently and, 1835–1846, with W B Moffatt (1812–87). He was appointed restoring architect for Ely Cathedral in 1847 and later to the cathedrals of Hereford, Lichfield, Salisbury and Rippon. In 1849 he was made architect to the dean and chapter of Westminster Abbey, and architect for the India Office in 1861. He was professor of architecture at the Royal Academy from 1868, knighted in 1872 and President of RIBA 1873–76.
Workhouse (*now* hospital), Old Windsor, Berkshire, 1835
Workhouse, Great Dunmow, Essex, 1840 **89**
Martyrs' Memorial, Oxford, 1841–44
Gaol, Reading, Berkshire, 1842–44 **89**
St John the Baptist church, Westwood Heath, near Coventry, 1842–45
St John the Evangelist church, West Meon, Hampshire, 1843–45
Cathedral, St Johns, Newfoundland, 1846
St Andrew's Church, Bradfield, Berkshire, 1847–48
St Ann's Church, Alderney, Channel Isles, 1847–50
Cottages, Llam, Staffordshire, 1854
St George's Church, Doncaster, 1854
Dean's Yard Buildings, Westminster, London, 1854
Harrow School Chapel and Vaughan Library, Harrow-on-the-Hill, Middlesex, 1854–57
All Souls' church, Haley Hill, Halifax, 1855–59 **50**
Government Offices, London, 1856–57 (competition design, unexecuted)
St Matthias' Church, Richmond, Surrey, 1856–58
Chapel, Exeter College, Oxford, 1856–60 **86**
Literary Institute, Sandbach, Cheshire, 1857
Cathedral, Lichfield, Staffordshire, 1857 (restoration)
St Michael's Church, Crewe Green, Cheshire, 1857–58
St Michael's Church, Cornhill, London, 1857–60 (porch)
St Michael's Church, Leafield, Oxfordshire, 1858–60 **50**
Kelham Hall, Nottinghamshire, 1858–61 *34, 35*
Walton Hall, Warwickshire, 1858–62
St Bartholomew's Church, Ranmore Common, Surrey, 1859
Hafodunos House, Denbigh, 1861–66
Town Hall, Preston, Lancashire, 1862 (demolished) **81**
Government offices, Parliament Street, Downing Street, St James's Park and King Charles Street, London, 1863–74 **79–81**
Chapel, St John's College, Cambridge, 1863–69 **86**
Albert Memorial, Kensington Gore, London, 1864–75 **80**, *80*, **93, 94**
Infirmary, Leeds, 1864–68 **89**
Sudeley Almshouses, Winchcombe, Gloucestershire, 1865
Glasgow University, 1865 *and* 1868–71 **86**
Midland Grand Hotel, St Pancras Station, Euston Road, London, 1865–77 **80**, *80*, **101**
Brill's Baths, Brighton, 1866 (demolished)

St Mary Abbots church, Kensington High Street, London, 1869–79
Lincoln's Inn, London, 1871–73 (addition to Library)
Episcopal Cathedral, Edinburgh, 1874–79
with W B Moffatt
St Giles' Church, Camberwell Church Street, London, 1842–44
Infant Orphans' Asylum (*now* Royal Wanstead School), Hollybush Hill, London, 1843–45

Scott, George Gilbert (Jnr, 1839–97) **86**
The eldest son and pupil of **Sir George Gilbert Scott**, and father of **Sir Giles Gilbert Scott** (1880–1960).
Peterhouse Hall, Cambridge 1870 (remodelling and redecoration)
St Mark's vicarage, Leamington, Warwickshire, 1875
Rectory, Woolton Hill, Hampshire, 1875–77
St Mark's Church, Leamington, Warwickshire, 1876
3 and 5 Salisbury Street, Hull, 1877–79
Holy Trinity and St Andrew church, Ashe, Hampshire, 1877–79
New Building, Pembroke College, Cambridge, 1879 **86**
St John the Baptist R C church, Norwich, 1891–1910 (continued by his brother **John Oldrid Scott**)

Scott, Lieut-Col, later **Major-Gen Henry Young Darracott** (1822–83) **93**
Educated at the Military Academy, Woolwich, he joined the Royal Engineers and was appointed senior instructor in field works at Woolwich, 1851, and first captain and instructor in surveying at Brompton, Chatham, 1855. He was made architect of the Department of Science and Art in 1865, after **Capt Francis Fowke**, and retired in 1871.
Royal Albert Hall, Kensington Gore, London, 1867–71 **93, 94**
with James William Wild
Science Schools, Huxley Building (*now* part of Victoria and Albert Museum), Exhibition Road, London, 1867–71

Scott, John Oldrid (1841–1913)
The second son of **Sir George Gilbert Scott**, he joined his father's offices in 1860 and succeeded to his practice.
Greek Orthodox Cathedral of Aghia Sophia, Moscow Road, London, 1874–82
St Mary's Church, Slough, Buckinghamshire, 1875–1913
St Mary's Church, Chailey, Sussex, 1876
St Paul's Church, New Cross, Oldham Road, Manchester, 1876
Chapel, Bradfield College, Berkshire, 1890–1901

Scott, Mackay Hugh Baillie (1865–1945) **41**
Born in Ramsgate, Kent, he was the eldest of 14 children. He was educated at the Royal Agricultural College, Cirencester, and was articled to the Bath City Architect, Charles E Davis, 1886–89.
Oakleigh, Douglas, Isle of Man, 1892–93
Bexton Croft, Knutsford, Cheshire, 1896
White Lodge, Wantage, Berkshire, 1898–99
Blackwell House, Bowness-on-Windermere, Cumbria, 1898–99
White House, Helensburgh, Argyll and Bute, 1899–1900

Sedding, John Dando (1838–91)
A pupil of **George Edmund Street**, 1858–65. He was a partner in Cornwall of his brother, Edmund Sedding (1836–68), before going to London in 1875; he was assisted by **Henry Wilson**.
St Clement's Church, Boscombe, Bournemouth, Dorset, 1871–73 (completed by Wilson)
Lodge, Flete, Devon, 1887

All Saints' vicarage, Plymouth, 1887
Church of the Holy Redeemer, Exmouth Market, London, 1887–98 (with tower by Henry Wilson)
All Saints' Church, Falmouth, Cornwall, 1887–90
Holy Trinity Church, Sloane Street, London, 1888 onwards **51**
Industrial Schools, Knowle, Bristol, 1890

Seddon, John Pollard (1827–1906)
A pupil of **Thomas Leverton Donaldson** and partner to **John Prichard**, 1853–63.
Hotel, Southerndown, Glamorgan, 1852–62
Hotel (*now* University College), Aberystwyth, 1864–90
Powell Almshouses, Fulham, London, 1869
Spencer Road, Birchington-on-Sea, Kent, 1869 (bungalows including Westcliff Bungalow for Dante Gabriel Rossetti)
St Peter's Church, Ayot St Peter, Hertfordshire, 1875
St Catherine's Church, Hoarwithy, Herefordshire, 1880–85 (remodelling)
with Hugh Roumieu Gough
St Paul's Church, Hammersmith, London, 1880–88

Sellars, James (1843–88) **77**
A pupil of **Hugh Barclay**, and a partner to **Campbell Douglas**, 1872–88.
St Andrew's Halls, Glasgow, 1873 **77**
Belmont and Hillhead Parish Church, Glasgow, 1875
Belhaven Church (*now* St Luke's Greek Orthodox Church), Glasgow, 1877
Kelvinside Academy, Glasgow, 1877
Finnieston Church (*now* Kelvingrove Church), Glasgow, 1878
144–46 West George Street, Glasgow, 1879
Wylie and Lochead's Department Store, Buchanan Street, Glasgow, 1884

Seward, Edwin (1853–1924)
Central (*now* Morgan) Arcade, Cardiff, 1896
as **James, Seward and Thomas**
Central Library, Cardiff, 1882
Coal Exchange, Mount Stuart Square, Cardiff, 1883–86

Sharp, Richard Hey (*c.* 1793–1853)
Assembly Rooms (*now* New Theatre), Kingston Square, Hull, Humberside, 1830–34
with Samuel Sharp
The Crescent, Scarborough, Yorkshire *c.* 1835

Sharp, Samuel (1808–74)
St James' Church, Thornes, Wakefield, Yorkshire, 1829–31

Sharpe, Edmund (1809–77)
Educated at St John's College, Cambridge, he studied architecture in France and Germany. He was articled to **Thomas Rickman**, and practised in Lancaster as a partner of **Edward Graham Paley**, 1836–51. He abandoned architecture for engineering and engaged in railway construction from 1851.
St Mark's Church, Buncer Lane, Blackburn, Lancashire, 1836–38
St Stephen's Church, Lever Bridge, Bolton, Lancashire, 1842–45
St Mary's Church, Knowsley, Lancashire, 1843–44 (additions by Paley 1860)
Carpernwray Hall, Lancashire, 1844
Holy Trinity Church, Fallowfield, Manchester, 1845–46

Shaw, John (Snr, 1776–1832)
St Dunstan-in-the-West Church, Fleet Street, City of London, 1829–33

Shaw, John (Jnr, 1803–70) **85, 87**
The son and pupil of **John Shaw** Snr, he was Surveyor of Christ's Hospital, London, and Eton College.
Christ Church, Watney Street, Stepney, London, 1841 (demolished)

Goldsmiths' College, Deptford, London, 1843–44
New Buildings, Eton College, Buckinghamshire, 1844–46
Wellington College, Berkshire, 1856–59 **85, 87**

Shaw, Richard Norman (1831–1912) **9, 11, 12, 17, 19, 20, 37, 38, 41, 44, 85, 107**
He was born in Edinburgh but his father died just two years after his birth, leaving the family in debt. In 1846 they moved to London, where Shaw was articled to **William Burn**. A travelling scholarship took him abroad in 1854–55 to France, Belgium, Italy and Germany. He published *Architectural Sketches from the Continent*, 1858, and the following year became the chief assistant to **George Edmund Street**, setting up in practice in London with **William Eden Nesfield** in 1862. By the end of the 1870s he had become the most celebrated domestic architect in England.
Holy Trinity Church, Bingley, Yorkshire, 1866–68 (demolished)
Glen Andred, Groombridge, Sussex, 1866–68
English Church, Lyons, France, 1867–69 (demolished)
Leyswood, Groombridge, Sussex, 1868–69 (partly demolished) **38, 38**
School, Church Preen, Shropshire, 1870 **85**
Grims Dyke, Harrow Weald, Stanmore, Middlesex, 1870–72
Cragside, Rothbury, Northumberland, 1870–*c.* 85 **38, 38**
New Zealand Chambers, Leadenhall Street, London 1871–73 (demolished)
Lowther Lodge, Kensington Gore, London, 1873–75 **19**
196 Queen's Gate, London, 1874–76
8 and 11 Melbury Road, London, 1875–76
6 Ellerdale Road, London, 1875–76
Old Swan House, 17 Chelsea Embankment, London, 1875–77 **19**
Pierrepoint, Frensham, Surrey, 1876–78
Adcote, Shropshire, 1876–81
Farnley House, 15 Chelsea Embankment, London, 1877–79
Bedford Park Estate (including St Michael and All Angels Church, the Tabard public house, and 24–34 Woodstock Road), Turnham Green, London, 1875–81 **9, 9, 16, 20, 20**
St Margaret's Church, Ilkley, Yorkshire, 1878–79
Clock House, 8 Chelsea Embankment, London, 1878–80
Flete, Devon, 1878–83
St Michael and All Angels church, Bedford Park, Middlesex, 1879–82
Albert Hall Mansions, Kensington Gore, London, 1879–86 **17, 17**
Alliance Assurance Offices, 1–2 St James's Street, London, 1882–83
39 Frognal, London, 1884–85
Cragside, Rothbury, Northumberland, 1885
Holy Trinity Church, Latimer Road, London, 1887–89 (altered)
Metropolitan Police Central Offices, New Scotland Yard, Victoria Embankment, London, 1887–91 and 1898–1907
170 Queen's Gate, London, 1888–90
Bryanston, Dorset, 1889–94
All Saints' Church, Richards Castle, Herefordshire, 1890–93
All Saints' Church, Galley Hill, Swanscombe, Kent, 1894–95
Piccadilly Hotel, Piccadilly, London, 1905
with Ernest Newton
Alliance Assurance Offices, 88 St James's Street, London, 1901–95

Sherlock, Cornelius 76
Picton Reading Room, Liverpool, 1874 **76**
Walker Art Gallery, Liverpool, 1875 **76**

Simmonds, G H 96
Royal Pavilion Theatre, Whitechapel Road, London, 1858 **96**

Simpson, Archibald (1790–1847)
A pupil of David Laing (1774–1856) and Robert
 Lugar (c. 1773–1855) in London.
Anderson Institution, Elgin, Grampian, 1830–33
Old Infirmary, Woolmanhill, Aberdeen, 1833–40
St Nicholas East Church, Aberdeen, 1835–37
New Market, Aberdeen, 1840–42 (demolished)
Marischel College, Aberdeen, 1842
Triple Kirks, Aberdeen, 1843
Simpson, James (d. 1864)
Centenary Methodist Church, St Saviourgate,
 York, 1839–40

Skipper, George John (1854–1948)
Crispin Hill, Street, Somerset, 1894–95 (with
 other buildings)
Hotel de Paris, Cromer, Norfolk, 1894–96
7 London Street, Norwich, 1896 (own office)
Royal Arcade, Norwich, 1898
Norwich Union Insurance offices, Norwich,
 1901–06
Norfolk and Suffolk Yacht Club House,
 Lowestoft, 1902
Norwich Union branch office, 30 St Andrew's
 Street, Cambridge, 1904 (demolished)
Norwich and London Accident Insurance
 offices, St Giles Street, Norwich, 1904 (later
 Telephone House)
Sennowe Park, Guist, Norfolk, 1904–11

Slater, William (1819–72) *81, 85*
A pupil of **Richard Cromwell Carpenter**,
 whom he succeeded in business, later taking
 his son, **Richard Herbert Carpenter**, into
 partnership 1863–72.
Town Hall, Loughborough, Leicestershire,
 1854–55 *81*
SS Simon and Jude church, Earl Shilton,
 Leicestershire, 1856
Christ Church, Bray, near Dublin, 1859
Church, Basseterre, St Kit's, West Indies, 1860
with Richard Herbert Carpenter
Ardingly College, Sussex, 1864

Smalman, John (c. 1783–1852)
Quatford Castle, Shropshire, 1829–30

Smirke, Sir Robert (1781–1867) *91*
The second son of the artist Robert Smirke, he
 worked briefly in the offices of Sir John Soane
 (1753–1837). He was knighted in 1832 and
 awarded the RIBA Gold Medal in 1853.
Drayton Manor, Staffordshire, 1820–35
British Museum, Great Russell Street,
 Bloomsbury, London, 1823–46 (including
 portico, not begun until 1842) *91, 91, 94*
Assize Courts, Lincoln Castle, Lincoln, 1823–30
Normanby Park, near Scunthorpe, Humberside,
 1825–30 (additions and alterations 1906)
King's College (east wing of Somerset House),
 Strand, London, 1829–35
Church and mausoleum, Markham Clinton,
 Nottinghamshire, 1831–32
12 Belgrave Square, London, c. 1833
with Sydney Smirke
Oxford and Cambridge University Club, Pall
 Mall, London, 1835–38

Smirke, Sydney (1798–1877)
The fifth son of Robert Smirke, the brother of
 Sir Robert Smirke and the latter's pupil. He
 was awarded the RIBA Gold Medal in 1860,
 appointed Professor of Architecture at the
 Royal Academy 1861–65, and founded the
 Architects' Benevolent Society in 1852.
Bazaar, Oxford Street, London, 1834 (demolished)
Royal Bethlem Hospital, Lambeth Road,
 London, 1838–46 (additions to portico and
 dome; later Imperial War Museum)
Paper Buildings, King's Bench Walk, London,
 1838–48
Carlton Club, Pall Mall, London, 1845–56
 (demolished) *44*
St John the Baptist church, Loughton, Essex,
 1846

Athenaeum, Bury, Lancashire, 1846–47
British Museum Reading Room, Great Russell
 Street, London, 1854–57
Burlington House, Piccadilly, London, 1867–74
 (additions)
Inner Temple (hall and library), London,
 1868–70 *44*
with Sir Robert Smirke
Oxford and Cambridge University Club, Pall
 Mall, London, 1835–38
with George Basevi
Conservative Club, St James's Street, London,
 1843–45 *100*
with Sir William Tite
Brookwood Cemetery, near Woking, Surrey,
 1854–56

Smith, Charles S (b. c. 1790)
Grove Park, Hampton-on-the-Hill,
 Warwickshire, 1833–38

Smith, George (1793–1877)
Exchange Coffee Room, junction of Castle
 Street and Exchange Street, Dundee, Tayside,
 1828–30

Smith, John (1781–1852)
He was from Aberdeen, but trained in London.
North Church, King Street, Aberdeen, 1830
South Church, King Street, Aberdeen, 1830–31
Cluny Castle, Aberdeen, 1836
Forglen House, Banff, 1839

Smith, Samuel Pountney (1812–83)
Holy Trinity Church, Leaton, Shropshire, 1859–72

Smith, William (1817–91)
Trained with **Thomas Leverton Donaldson**
 and followed his father, **John Smith**, as City
 Architect of Aberdeen.
Balmoral Castle, near Ballater, Aberdeen,
 1853–55
Boys' and Girls' Hospital, 352 King Street,
 Aberdeen, 1869–71 (later Institute of
 Technology School of Navigation)

Snell, Henry Saxon (1830–1904)
A pupil of **Sir James Pennethorne**, and later an
 assistant to **Sir Joseph Paxton** and
 Sir William Tite.
Archway Hospital, London, 1869–79
St Charles' Hospital, North Kensington,
 London, 1879
Victoria Hospital for Children, Chelsea,
 London, 1885

Spence, T R *51*
St George's Church, Osborne Road, Newcastle-
 upon-Tyne, 1888–98 *51*

Sprague, W G R (1865–1933) *98*
A specialist in the design of theatres, being
 responsible for more than 30 during his career.
 His version of renaissance, which was both rich
 and delicate, was ideal for the theatres of his
 age, and a style well understood by the joiners,
 carvers, plaster modellers and upholsterers who
 brought his designs speedily to fruition.
Shakespeare Theatre and Opera House,
 Lavender Hill, Battersea, London, 1896
Broadway, New Cross, London, 1897
Grand, Fulham, London, 1897
The Coronet, Notting Hill Gate, London, 1898;
 converted into a cinema *98*
Kennington Theatre, London, 1898
Balham Hippodrome, London, 1899
Rotherhithe Hippodrome, London, 1899
Wyndham's, Charing Cross Road, London,
 1899 *98*
Camden, Camden Town, London, 1901 *98*
King's Theatre, Hammersmith, London, 1902
New Theatre (now the Albery Theatre), St
 Martin's Lane, London, 1903 *98*
The Waldorf (later the Strand), Aldwych,
 London, 1905 *98*

Aldwych Theatre, Aldwych, London, 1905; a
 twin of the Strand theatre with an identical
 façade *98*
Globe, Shaftesbury Avenue, London, 1906;
 twinned with the Queen's *98*
Queen's, Shaftesbury Avenue, London, 1907;
 the frontage was damaged during the Second
 World War and replaced in 1958 *98*
Ambassadors, West Street, London, 1913 *98*
St Martin's, West Street, London, 1916 *98*
with Bertie Crewe
Camberwell Empire, London, 1894

Starforth, John (1823–98)
A pupil of **William Burn** and **David Bryce**.
Greyfriars Church, Dumfries, 1867
Royal Infirmary, Dumfries, 1869
Hydropathic hotel, Peebles, 1878 (demolished)
Parish church, Moffat, Dumfries, 1882

Stephenson, Robert (1803–59) *54, 60*
The son of **George Stephenson**, he was
 educated at Edinburgh University and began
 work in Newcastle Locomotive factory in 1823.
 He was the civil engineer responsible for the
 construction of the London and Birmingham
 Railway line, 1835–39; see also **Dobson, John**.
Euston Station train shed, London, 1835–39 *60*
Derby Tri-junct Station, Derbyshire, 1839–41
 (with Francis Thompson) *60*
Britannia Bridge, Menai Straits, 1845–50; 1,000
 men worked on the building of the bridge,
 which used 2 million rivets. The bridge was
 constructed of tubular sections which were
 ferried along the Straits and then jacked up into
 position. To test the bridge on the day it was
 opened, three locomotives hauling coal wagons
 and weighing a total of 300 tons remained on
 the bridge for three hours before proceeding to
 the other side, to rapturous applause. On
 23 May 1970 a fire in the structure caused the
 bridge to expand, causing irreparable damage.
 The bridge was restored as a double-deck
 structure on steel arches, with a road deck
 above and railway below *54*
Royal Border Bridge, Berwick-upon-Tweed,
 Northumberland, opened 1850 *54, 54*
Victoria Bridge, Montreal, Canada, 1854–59
Roundhouse engine house and terminus, Chalk
 Farm Road, London, 1847 (with R B Dockray
 and Normandy; converted to a theatre with
 seating for 600 in 1967) *59, 60*

Stevens see **Coe, Henry Edward**

Stevens and **Hunt** *72*
Harrods Department Store, Knightsbridge,
 London, 1897–1905 *72*

Stevenson, John James (1831–1908) *18, 19, 39*
Educated at Glasgow University, he worked in
 the offices of **David Bryce** in 1856, then for
 Sir George Gilbert Scott between 1858–60.
 He was the partner of **Campbell Douglas** and
 Edward Robert Robson, 1870–75, and in 1880
 published *House Architecture*, in two volumes.
Parish church, Kelvinside, Glasgow, 1862
Red House, 140 Bayswater Road, London, 1871
 (demolished) *18, 19, 19*
8 Palace Gate, London, 1873–75
42–48 Pont Street, London, 1876–78
1–2 Lowther Gardens, London, 1877–78
80 Ken Hill, Snettisham, Norfolk, 1879–80
63–73 Cadogan Square, London, 1881–86
1 Fitzjohn's Avenue, London, 1883
Kensington Court, London, 1883–90 (houses)
with Edward Robert Robson
Primary School, Bonner Street, Hackney,
 London, 1872–75

Stirling, William (1772–1838)
Garden House, Central Region, Scotland, 1830

Stokes, Leonard Aloysius Scott (1858–1925)
Though he was born in Southport, Lancashire,

the family moved to London where he was articled to the church architect, **Samuel J Nicholl**, of Kentish Town, 1871–74. He then worked for James Gandy, acting for a time as clerk of works for **George Edmund Street** during the restoration of Christ Church Cathedral, Dublin. He also worked for a time for **Thomas Edward Collcutt** and **George Frederick Bodley**, was appointed President of RIBA 1910–12, and awarded the RIBA Gold Medal in 1919.
Sacred Heart R C church, Exeter, 1883–84
St Clare's R C church, Sefton Park, Liverpool, 1888
Church of the Sacred Heart and St Michael's Convent and Girls' School, Waterlooville, Hampshire, 1885–95
Our Lady Help of Christians R C church, Folkestone, Kent, 1889
All Souls' R C church, Peterborough, 1896
Shooters Hill House, Pangbourne, Berkshire, 1898
All Saints' R C convent, London Colney, Hertfordshire, 1899–1903
Minterne House, Dorset, 1903–05

Street, George Edmund (1824–81) 36, 37, 50, 64, 82, 83, 85
A pupil of **Owen Browne Carter** in Winchester, 1841–44, he worked for **Sir George Gilbert Scott**, 1844–49, before setting up in practice on his own in London in 1849. He moved to Wantage and then to Oxford before returning to London in 1856. He received the RIBA Gold Medal in 1874 and was made President of RIBA in 1881, when he was also professor of architecture at the Royal Academy. Among much restoration work was that carried out at York Minster and Salisbury and Carlisle cathedrals. After his death his son, Arthur Edmund Street, (1855–1938), continued with the practice.
St Mary's Church, Par, Cornwall, 1847
Vicarage, Wantage, Berkshire, 1849–50
Schools, Inkpen, Berkshire, 1850 85
Vicarage, Colnbrook, Buckinghamshire, 1853
All Saints' vicarage, school and cottages, Boyne Hill, Berkshire, 1854–55 85
Lille Cathedral, France, 1855 (unexecuted design)
St James the Less church, East Hanney, Berkshire, 1856
St Thomas' Church, Watchfield, Berkshire, 1857–58
St James' Church, vicarage and school, New Bradwell, Wolverton, Buckinghamshire, 1857–60 37
St Paul's Church, Herne Hill, London, 1858
St John's Church, Howsham, Yorkshire, 1859
St James the Less church, Lillington Gardens, Vauxhall Bridge Road, London, 1859–61
SS Philip and James church, Oxford, 1859–65
All Saints' vicarage and school, Denstone, Staffordshire, 1860–62
St John's Church, Torquay, Devon, 1861
Crimea Memorial Church, Constantinople, 1863–68
St Mary's Church, Fawley, Berkshire, 1864–66
St Saviour's Church, Eastbourne, Sussex, 1865–72
Convent, East Grinstead, Sussex, 1865–90
Chapel of former workhouse, Shipmeadow, Suffolk, 1866
St Mary's Church and school, Westcott, Buckinghamshire, 1866–70
St Mary Magdalene church, Woodchester Square, London, 1867–78 50
St John the Divine church, Vassall Road, London, 1871–74 and 1887–88
American Episcopal Church, Rome, 1872–76
All Saints' Church, Lower Common, London, 1873–74
Holmedale, Holmbury St Mary, Surrey, 1873–76
St James' Church, Kingston, Dorset, 1873–80
Royal Courts of Justice, Strand, London, 1874–82 82, 82

St Mary's Church, Holmbury St Mary, Surrey, 1877–79
English Church, Mürren, Switzerland, 1878
4 Cadogan Square, London, 1879
All Saints' English Church, Rome, 1880–87
American Church, Paris, 1880–1906
St James' Church, Sussex Gardens, London, 1881–82 (except tower and entrance)

Street, Thomas Edward 103
Cavendish Hotel, Eastbourne, Sussex, *c.* 1866
below **103**

Sugden, William (1820–92)
In 1881 he was joined in partnership in Leek, Staffordshire, by his son, W Larner Sugden (*d.* 1901).
District Bank, Derby Street, Leek, Staffordshire, 1882
Nicholson Institute, Stockwell Street, Leek, Staffordshire, 1882–84
Model houses, Aintree, near Liverpool, 1888

Sullivan, Louis Henry (1856–1924) 73, 105, 106
He was educated at the Massachusetts Institute of Technology, Cambridge, and at the École des Beaux-Arts, Paris. He was employed in the offices of the engineer Dankmar Adler, becoming joint director of the office in 1879; in 1881 the practice was renamed **Allen and Sullivan**. He published *The Tall Office Building Artistically Considered* in 1896.
Auditorium Building, Chicago, 1886–1893 105, *105*
Walker Warehouse, Chicago, 1888–89
Wainwright Building, St Louis, 1890–91
Guaranty Building, Buffalo, 1894–96 105, *105*
Bayard Building, New York, 1897–98
Gage Building, Chicago, 1898–99
Schlesinger & Mayer Store (*now* Carson Pirie Scott & Co.), Chicago, 1899–1904 73
Farmers' National Bank, Owatonna, Minnesota, 1907–08
Van Allen Store, Clinton, Iowa, 1913–15

Tanner, Sir Henry (1848–1935) 75
Post office, Birmingham, 1891 75

Tarver, Edward John (1842–91)
A pupil of **Benjamin Ferrey**.
Rectory, Holy Trinity, Broadstairs, Kent, 1870
St Peter's Church, Tyringham, Buckinghamshire, 1871
All Souls' Church, High Street, Harlesden, Greater London, 1875–79 and 1890
St Mary's R C church, Hooton, Cheshire, 1879

Tattersall, Richard (*c.* 1803–44)
Cumberland Infirmary, Newton Road, Carlisle, 1830–32 (remodelled 1870s)
Dixon's Mills, Junction Street, Carlisle, 1836
Cotton Mill, Golborne, Lancashire, 1839

Taut, Bruno (1880–1938) 60
Educated at the Baugewerksschule (school for master builders), Königsberg, he worked in various architectural offices in Germany before establishing his own practice with Franz Hoffman in 1909. He was appointed architectural advisor to the German Garden

City Promotion Society. After the First World War he published *Alpine Architektur* in 1918 and *Die Stadtkrane* in 1919, as well as articles in the journal *Frühlicht*, of which he later became co-editor. He was a co-founder and a director of Arbeitsrat für Kunst (Council for Art) in 1918 and in the following year became a founder member of the group of artists and architects known as the *Gläserne Kette* (glass chain). In 1921 he was appointed City Architect of Magdeburg, leaving in 1923 to become involved in large-scale housing. He joined *der Ring* group of architects in 1926, taking part in the Werkbund Exhibition, Stuttgart, the following year. He taught at the University of Berlin-Charlottenburg between 1930 and 1932, moved to Moscow in 1933 and then to Japan. In 1936 he became professor at the Academy of Art, Istanbul.
Convalescent Home, Bad Harzburg, 1909 (for the Siemens company)
Federation of German Steel Manufacturers' Pavilion, Building Trade Exhibition, Leipzig, 1913
Monument to Steel, Federation of German Bridge and Railway Manufacturers' Pavilion, Building Trade Exhibition, Leipzig, 1913
am Falkenberg, Berlin-Grünau, 1913–14 (garden suburb)
Reform, Magdeburg, 1913–21 (garden suburb)
Glass Industry building, Werkbund Exhibition, Köln, 1914 60, *60*

Taylor, James Medland (1833–1909)
A partner of Henry Taylor.
St Peter's Church, Parr, St Helens, Lancashire, 1864–65
Christ Church, Blackpool, 1865–66
St Thomas' Church, Hyde, Cheshire, 1867–68
St Mary's Church, Haughton Green, Lancashire, 1874–76
St George's Church, Daubhill, Bolton, Lancashire, 1880
St Agnes' Church, Levenshulme, Manchester, 1884–85

Taylor, John *see* **Leslie, James**

Telford, Thomas (1757–1834) 7, 53
Menai Straits Bridge, 1826 53, *54*
Bridge, Morpeth, Northumberland, 1831
Bridge, Chirk, Wrecsam, 1831

Teulon, Samuel Sanders (1812–73)
A brother of W Milford Teulon (1823–1900), and a pupil of George Legg; he set up in practice in 1840.
Tortworth Court, Gloucestershire, 1849–52
St Margaret's Church, Angmering, Sussex, 1852–53
St Andrew's Church, Lambeth, London, 1854 (demolished)
Cottages, Layton's Gate, Windsor, Berkshire, 1854 (for Crown labourers)
Chapel School, Curridge, Berkshire, 1854
St John the Baptist church, Burringham, Lincolnshire, 1856
St Thomas' vicarage and schools, Wells, Somerset, 1856
Shadwell Park, Norfolk, 1856–60 (additions)
Christ Church, Wimbledon, London, 1857–60
St James' Church, Leckhampstead, Berkshire, 1858–60
St Mark's Church, Silvertown, London, 1859
Elvetham Hall, Hampshire, 1859–62
St John the Baptist church, Huntley, Gloucestershire, 1861–63
Bestwood Lodge, Nottinghamshire, 1862–64
Ealing Parish Church, St Mary's Road, London, 1866–73 (restoration)
St Stephen's Church, Rosslyn Hill, London, 1869–76

Thomas, Sir Alfred Brumwell (1868–1928) 28
He was articled to W Seckham and studied

under Farrow at the Architectural Association school, beginning to practise in 1894. He was knighted in 1906.
Belfast City Hall, Belfast, Ireland, 1898–1906 **28**
Stockport Town Hall, Cheshire, 1903–08
Plumstead (*now* Woolwich) Town Hall, London, 1905

Thomas, John (1813–62)
A sculptor and architectural draughtsman who was employed by **Sir Charles Barry** on the decorations of the Houses of Parliament.
Model village (including school, St Mary's Church and Hall) Somerleyton, Suffolk, 1844
Royal Hotel and houses, Marine Parade, Lowestoft, 1847
Preston Hall, Aylesford, Kent, 1850 (later a chest hospital)

Thomas; James, Seward and *see* **Seward, Edwin**

Thomas, Walter Aubrey 29
Royal Liver Building, Pier Head, Liverpool, 1908–11 **29**, *29*

Thomason, Yeoville (1826–1901) **75, 100**
Union Club, Newell Street, Birmingham, 1869 **100**
Council House, Chamberlain Place, Birmingham, begun in 1874 **75**, *76*
City Museum and Art Gallery, Congreve Street, Birmingham 1880s **75**, *76*

Thompson, Francis
Appointed architect for the North Midland Railway, 1835.
26 stations on Derby to Leeds railway line, 1840 (some demolished)
Trijunct Station and North Midland Hotel, Derby, 1840
General Station, Chester, 1847–48
Cambridge station, 1852
with Robert Stephenson
Chester to Holyhead railway line and stations, 1850
Britannia Bridge, Menai Straits, 1845–50 (with Robert Stephenson and W Fairbairn)

Thomson, Alexander 'Greek' (1817–75)
Worked with **John Baird** (*see* above entry), 1836–49, before becoming a partner to another John Baird (no relation) of Glasgow, 1849–57. He later entered partnership with his brother, G Thomson, and R Turnbull.
3–11 Dunlop Street, Glasgow, 1849 (warehouses; demolished)
Free Church, junction of Hutchesontown and Caledonia Road, Glasgow, 1856 (destroyed)
Langside House, 25 Mansionhouse Road, Glasgow, 1856
Holmwood House, Netherlee Road, Cathcart, Glasgow, 1856
Walmer Crescent, Paisley Road, West Ibrox, Glasgow, 1857
St Vincent Street U P Church, Glasgow, 1858
1–10 Moray Place, Strathbungo, Glasgow, 1859
Grosvenor Buildings, 68–80 Gordon Street, Glasgow, 1859–64
Cairney Warehouses, Bath Street, Glasgow, 1860 (demolished)
Buck's Head warehouse, 63 Argyle Street, Glasgow, 1863
Queen's Park U P Church, Glasgow, 1867 (demolished)
Great Western Terrace, Kelvinside, Glasgow, 1867
Egyptian Halls, 84–100 Union Street, Glasgow, 1871
200 and 202 Nitsdale Road, Pollokshields, Glasgow, 1871

Thomson, James (1835–1905)
A pupil of James Brown who became an assistant to **John Baird** before succeeding him.

Crown Circus, Dowanhill, Glasgow, 1858–75
217–21 Argyle Street, Glasgow, 1863
Belhaven Terrace, Glasgow, 1866
202–12 Sauchiehall Street, Glasgow, 1895
Liverpool and Globe Building, junction of Hope Street and West George Street, London, 1898

Tite, Sir William (1798–1873)
Elected as MP for Bath 1855–73, he was awarded the RIBA Gold Medal in 1856, knighted in 1869 and made President of RIBA 1861–63.
Chapels at the South Metropolitan Cemetery, West Norwood, London, 1837
Nine Elms Station, London, 1838 (demolished)
Royal Exchange, City of London, 1841–44
Perth Station, 1848
Windsor Station, Windsor, Berkshire, 1851
St James' Church, Gerrards Cross, Buckinghamshire, 1859
with Sydney Smirke
Brookwood Cemetery, near Woking, Surrey, 1854–56

Townsend, Charles Harrison (1851–1928) **51, 95**
Born in Birkenhead, he was articled to Walter Scott in Liverpool, but the family moved to London *c.* 1880, where he joined the offices of Lewis Banks. He became a partner in 1884, and later set up in practice, *c.* 1888. He was Master of the Art Workers' Guild.
All Saints' Church, Ennismore Gardens, London, 1892 (west front only)
Bishopsgate Institute, 230 Bishopsgate, London, 1892–94
Blatchfield, Blackheath, London, 1894
St Martin's Church, Blackheath, London, 1895
Whitechapel Art Gallery, 80–82 Whitechapel High Street, London, 1897–99
Horniman Museum, London Road, Forest Hill, London, 1898–1901 **95**, *95*
St Mary the Virgin church, Great Warley, Essex, 1902–04 **51**

Trubshaw, C (*d.* 1917) **102**
Midland Hotel, Manchester, 1898 **102**

Trubshaw, Thomas (1802–42)
Fernleigh Workhouse, Marston Road, Stafford, 1837–38 (later a hospital)

Truefitt, George (1824–1902)
He worked for **Sancton Wood**, was appointed surveyor to the Tufnell Park Estate, London, and published *Designs for Country Churches*, 1850.
1 Middleton Grove, London, 1859 (own house)
St George's Church (*now* St George's Theatre), Tufnell Park Road, London, 1866–68
Royal Exchange Assurance Offices, Chancery Lane / Brown Street, Manchester, 1868
St George's Church, Worthing, Sussex, 1868
Lloyds Bank, Altrincham, Cheshire, 1870
St John's Church, Bromley, Kent, 1880
St Mary's Church, Davyhulme, Lancashire, 1889–90

Turner, Richard 11, 56, 57, 60
Palm House, Glasnevin, near Dublin, Ireland, 1843–38 **60**
Winter Gardens, Regent's Park, London, 1845–46 (demolished) **60**
with Decimus Burton
Palm House, Royal Botanic Gardens, Kew, Richmond, Surrey, 1844–48 *11*, **56**
with Joseph Locke
Lime Street Station, Liverpool, 1849–50 **57**, *76*

Underwood, Henry Jones (1804–52)
A pupil of **Sir Robert Smirke**.
SS Mary and Nicholas church, Littlemore, Oxfordshire, 1835
Botanical Gardens Library and Lecture Room (*now* Magdalen College Bursary), Oxford, 1835
St Paul's Church, Walton Street, Oxford, Oxfordshire, 1836 (later an arts centre)

Holy Trinity Church, Sibford Gower, Oxfordshire, 1840

Unsworth, William Frederick (1850–1912) **96**
An assistant to **George Edmund Street** and **William Burges** who entered into partnership with Inigo Triggs and Dodgshun.
Shakespeare Theatre, Stratford-on-Avon, 1876–79 (demolished) **96**
Art Gallery and Library, Stratford-on-Avon, 1881
Christ Church, Woking, Surrey, 1887–79
All Saints' Church, Woodham, Surrey, 1893

Unwin, Raymond (1863–1940) **13, 24, *24*, 25**
Born near Rotherham, he was educated at Magdalen College, Oxford, and trained as an engineer before entering into partnership with his cousin, **Barry Parker**, and marrying Parker's sister. He was appointed chief planning inspector of the local government board in 1914, was President of RIBA, 1931–33, knighted in 1932, appointed professor of town planning, Columbia University, USA, and received the RIBA gold medal in 1937.
New Earswick garden village, New York, 1903
Letchworth Garden City (plans), Hertfordshire, 1904 **12, 24**
Hampstead Garden Suburb (plans), London, 1907–14 **12**, *12*, **13, 24, *25***

van de Velde, Henry-Clément (1863–1957) **87, 109**
He studied painting at the Académie des Beaux-Arts, Antwerp, 1880–83, and in Paris 1884–85. In 1887 he was involved in the formation of *L'Art indépendant* and in 1889 joined the Brussels avant-garde group *Les XX*. His furniture designs are considered to have made an important contribution to the development of *art nouveau*; he formed his own furniture production company in 1898, and was appointed art counsellor to the court of Grand Duke Wilhelm Ernst in 1904. He was director of the Kunstgewerbeschule, 1904–14, and director of the Institut Supérieure d'Architecture et des Arts Décoratifs, Brussels, until 1935. He taught at the University of Ghent, 1925–36.
Bloemenwerf, Uccle, near Brussels, 1895 (own house)
Habana Company tobacco shop, Berlin, 1899
Folkwang Museum, Hagen, 1900–1902 (interior decoration)
Haby hairdressing salon, Berlin, 1901
Kunstgewerbeschule, Weimer, 1904
Saxon School of Arts and Crafts, Weimar, 1906 **87**
Theatre, Werkbund Exhibition, Köln, 1914

Verity, Francis (Frank) Thomas (1867–1937) **23, 98**
The son of **Thomas Verity**, he studied at University College, London, and at the Architectural Association. In 1887 he entered the Royal Academy Schools, and in 1889 he won its Tite Prize.
96–97 Piccadilly, London, 1891
Imperial Theatre, Tothill Street, Westminster, London, 1901 (rebuilding of interior for Lillie Langtry who was then the manager; in 1907 it was removed to a cinema in Canning Town, which burnt down in 1931) **98**
Apartment block, Cleveland Row, London, 1905 **23**
25–26 Berkeley Square, London, 1906 **23**
Scala Theatre and restaurant, Charlotte Street, London, 1908 (demolished 1970)
11a and 11b Portland Place, London, 1908
12 Hyde Park Place, London, 1908 **23**
St George's House (façade), Regent Street, London, 1911

Verity, Thomas (1837–91) **97**
An associate of G H Hunt, and later a partner to his own son, **Francis (Frank) Thomas Verity**,

from 1889. He was the surveyor of theatres for the Lord Chamberlain from 1878 until his death.
Criterion Theatre and Restaurant, Piccadilly Circus, London, 1870–74 (later remodelled inside, not by him) **97**
Baths, Scarborough, Yorkshire, 1877–80
Comedy Theatre, Pantin Street, London, 1881 **97**
Empire Theatre, Leicester Square, London, 1882 **97**
Guildhall, Nottingham, 1884–88 (with G H Hunt)

Voysey, Charles Francis Annesley (1857–1941) **11, 39–41**
Born near Hull, this son of a clergyman was articled to **John Pollard Seddon** in 1874 and worked for **Henry Saxon Snell** and **George Devey**, 1880. He established his own practice in London in 1882, and was awarded the RIBA Gold Medal in 1940.
The Cottage, Bishops Itchington, Warwickshire, 1888 **39**
Bannut Tree Farm, Castlemorton, Worcestershire, 1890
Forster House, Bedford Park, Middlesex, 1890
Wentworth Arms and Wortley Cottages, Elmesthorpe, Leicestershire, 1890
Broadleys and Moor Crag, Lake Windermere, Cartmel Fell, Lancashire, 1898–1900 **39**
Winsford Cottage Hospital, Halwill, Devon, 1900
Tower House, Bognor, Sussex, 1900 **40**
The Orchard, Chorleywood, Hertfordshire, 1900–01 **40**
The Pastures, North Luffenham, Rutland, 1901

Vulliamy, George John (1817–86)
The second son of clockmaker Benjamin Lewis Vulliamy (1780–1854), he was a pupil of **Sir Charles Barry**, 1836–41, settled in London in 1843 to work with his uncle **Lewis Vulliamy**, and was appointed architect to the Metropolitan Board of Works, 1861–86.

Vulliamy, Lewis (1791–1871)
A pupil of **Sir Robert Smirke**, he settled in London in 1822 and worked until 1861 with his nephew, **George John Vulliamy** (1817–86).
St Bartholomew's Church, Westwood Hill, Sydenham, London, 1827–32
Law Society, 113 Chancery Lane, London, 1831; situated on the west side of Chancery Lane at its southern end, the Society is a voluntary organisation of solicitors, originally known as the Law Institute; it dates from 1825 *below*

Hickey's Almshouses, Richmond, Surrey, 1834
Royal Institute, Albemarle Street, London, 1838 (façade)
All Saints' Church, Ennismore Gardens, London, 1846–49
Dorchester House, Park Lane, London, 1848–63 (demolished)

Wagner, Otto Koloman (1841–1918) **110–112**
Educated at the Vienna Polytechnic, the Royal Building Academy, Berlin, and the Vienna Academy of Fine Arts, he worked in the offices of Ludwig von Förster. In 1890 he was commissioned to redevelop Vienna where he was the city planner from 1894, at the same time taking the chair of architecture at the Academy of Fine Arts. In 1895 he published *Moderne Architektur* and in 1899 he joined the Vienna Sezession group of artists.
am Schottenring, Vienna, 1877 (house)
Majolika House, Vienna, 1898–1899; glazed earthenware slabs covered the entire façade of this wildly Sezessionist building, which has also been described as tattooed architecture *below*

Linke Wienzeile, Vienna, 1899 (apartment buildings)
Stadtbahn, Vienna, completion 1901 (municipal railway system including 34 stations, together with bridges and viaducts)
am Steinhof, Vienna, 1902–07 (church)
Imperial and Royal Post Office Savings Bank, Vienna, 1904–12
Neustiftgasse, Vienna, 1910 (apartment buildings)
Lupus Sanatorium, Vienna, 1910–13
Döblergasse, Vienna, 1912 (apartment buildings)
Villa Wagner, Vienna, 1920 (designed 1912–13) *111*

Walker, George
Worked with John Wardle for Richard Grainger.
Clayton Street, Grainger Street and west side of Grey Street, Central Exchange, Newcastle-upon-Tyne, 1834–40

Walker, James Campbell (1822–88)
A pupil of **William Burn** and **David Bryce**.
Blair Drummond, Kincardine, Perth, 1868
Municipal Buildings, Dunfermline, 1875

Walters, Edward (1808–72) **27**
He worked in Constantinople, 1832–37, and then in Manchester, 1839–65.
Cobden Warehouse, 15 Mosley Street, Manchester, 1839
Silas Schwabe Warehouse, Manchester, 1845 (demolished)
Cavendish Street Independent Chapel, Manchester, 1847–48
Brown and Son Warehouse, 9 Portland Street, Manchester, 1851–52 (demolished) **27**
Free Trade Hall, Manchester, 1853 **27, 27**
34, 10 and 12 Charlotte Street, Manchester, 1855, 1857, and 1860 (warehouses)
Manchester and Salford Bank, Mosley Street, Manchester, 1860 (later Williams Deacon's Bank)
Stations at Bakewell, Miller's Dale and Matlock, Derbyshire, 1860

Ward, F J 66
Albert Buildings, 39–49 Queen Victoria Street, London, 1871 **66**

Wardell, William Wilkinson (1823–99)
A friend of **Augustus Welby Northmore Pugin**, he went to Australia in 1857 and was appointed Inspector-General of Public Works and Buildings, Victoria, 1869–78.
St Birinus' R C church, Dorchester, Oxfordshire, 1849
Our Lady of Victories R C church, Clapham, London, 1849–51
Our Lady Star of the Sea R C church, Greenwich, London, 1851
St Patrick's R C cathedral, Melbourne, Australia, 1858–97
St John's College, Sydney University, Sydney, 1859
St Mary's R C cathedral, Sydney, 1865

Wardrop, **James Maitland** (1824–82)
Worked for **David Bryce**, before becoming a
partner of Thomas Brown.
County buildings, Wigtown, Dumfries and
Galloway, 1862
Lochinch House, near Castle Kennedy,
Wigtown, 1864
Callander Park, Falkirk, 1869–77 (remodelling)
Beaufort Castle, Beauly, Inverness, 1880

Waring and **Nicholson 66**
Doulton Pottery Works, Lambeth, London,
1876–77 (with R Stark Wilkinson) **66**

Waterhouse, **Alfred** (1830–1905) **31, 32, 35, 67,
76, 81, 85, 86, 89, 94, 100–102, 107**
He was born in Liverpool, the eldest of eight
children of an eminent Quaker, and articled to
Richard Lane, 1848–53. He travelled widely
throughout Britain, France, Italy, Switzerland
and Turkey before setting up in practice in
Manchester in 1854, first alone, then from 1891
in partnership with his son, Paul Waterhouse
(1861–1924). He was awarded the RIBA Gold
Medal in 1878 and was RIBA President,
1888–91, when he retired from active practice.
Fryer and Binyon Warehouse, Manchester, 1856
(demolished) **67**
Hinderton House, Neston, Cheshire, 1856
Barcombe College, Fallowfield, Manchester,
1858 (demolished)
Assize Courts, Manchester, 1859 (demolished) **81**
Royal Insurance offices, King Street,
Manchester, 1861 (demolished)
Market, public offices and Barclays Bank,
Darlington, 1864
Foxhill, Whiteknights Park, Reading, Berkshire,
1866
Strangeways Gaol, Manchester, 1866–68
Allerton Priory, Allerton Road, Liverpool,
1867–70 (house)
Balliol College, Oxford, 1867–77 (south front) **86**
Gonville and Caius College, Cambridge, 1868 **86**
Lime Street Station Hotel, Liverpool, 1868–71
Town Hall, Manchester, 1868–77 **76, 76, 81**
Owen's College (*now* University), Manchester,
1869 **86**
Blackmoor House, Hampshire, 1870–73
Eaton Hall, Cheshire, 1870–83 (partly
demolished) **31, 32, 35**
Market Hall and Town Hall, Knutsford,
Cheshire, 1871
17–18 Lincoln's Inn Fields, London, 1871–72
Pembroke College, Cambridge, 1871–74
(additions) **86**
Girton College, Cambridge, 1872 **85**
Town Hall, Reading, Berkshire, 1872–75
Natural History Museum, Cromwell Road,
London, 1873–80 **94, 94**
College of Science (*now* University), Leeds,
Yorkshire, 1877–1908 **86**
Iwerne Minster House (*now* Claremore School),
Dorset, 1878
Assize Courts, Bedford, 1878
Yattendon Court, Berkshire, 1878 (own house;
demolished)
Prudential Insurance offices, High Holborn,
London, 1878–1906 *below*

1 Old Bond Street, London, 1880
Turner Memorial Home, Toxteth, Liverpool,
1881–83
St Paul's School, Hammersmith, London,
1881–84 (partly demolished; Master's House
survives)
St Elizabeth's Church, Reddish, Lancashire,
1882–83
Congregational Church, Lyndhurst Road,
London, 1883
Prudential Assurance offices, Queen Street,
Nottingham, 1885
National Liberal Club, Victoria Embankment,
London, 1885–87 **100, 100**
Prudential Assurance offices, Dale Street,
Liverpool, 1886
Royal Infirmary, Liverpool, 1886
Hotel Metropole, Brighton, 1888 **102**
Liverpool College (*now* Victoria Building of
Liverpool University), begun in 1889 **86**
King's Weigh House Chapel, Duke Street,
London, 1889–91
Lloyds Bank, Cambridge, 1891
Prudential Assurance offices, Edinburgh, 1895
University College Hospital, Gower Street,
London, 1897–1906 **89**
Manchester Refuge Assurance offices, Oxford
Street, Manchester, 1893–1913 (with Paul
Waterhouse)

Watson, **Thomas Lennox** (1850–1920)
A pupil of **Alfred Waterhouse**.
Wellington Church, University Avenue,
Glasgow, 1883
Clyde Yacht Club, Hunter's Quay, 1886–88
24 St Vincent Place, Glasgow, 1889

Watt, **Richard Harding** (1842–1913)
Ruskin Rooms, Knutsford, Cheshire, 1899–1902
High Morland House, Leigh Road, Knutsford,
Cheshire, 1905
Gaskell Memorial Tower and King's Coffee
House, Knutsford, Cheshire, 1907

Webb, **Sir Aston** (1849–1930) **82, 94**
The son of Edward Webb, an engraver and
watercolour artist; he attended school at
Brighton and was articled to R R Banks and
Charles Barry Jnr. In his time Aston Webb
had the largest practice in the UK, concerned
principally with the design of public buildings;
he was a partner to Edward Ingress Bell,
became President of RIBA, 1902–04, was
knighted in 1904 and awarded the RIBA Gold
Medal in 1905.
St Bartholomew the Great church, Smithfield,
London, 1885–97 (restoration)
Assize Courts, Birmingham, 1886–95 **82, 82**
Royal United Services Institution, Whitehall,
London, 1893–95
Christ's Hospital, Horsham, Sussex, 1893–1904
Victoria and Albert Museum, London, 1899–
1909 (Cromwell Road front; designed in 1893)
93, 93, 94
Royal Naval College, Dartmouth, 1899–1905

Webb, **Philip Speakman** (1831–1915) **8, 9, 19,
37, 41**
The son of a doctor, he was articled to John
Billing of Reading and worked for **George
Edmund Street** in Oxford, where he rose to
become his chief assistant. He set up in practice
in London in 1856, in 1861 joining the firm of
William Morris and founding the Society for
the Protection of Ancient Buildings.
Red House, Red House Lane, Bexleyheath,
Kent, 1859–60 (for Morris) **9, 37, 37**
Sandroyd (*now* Benfleet Hall School), Fairmile,
near Cobham, Surrey, 1860
91–101 Worship Street, London, 1861–62
Arisaig House, Inverness, 1863
1 Holland Park Road, London, 1864–66
35 Glebe Place, London, 1868–69
1 Palace Green, Kensington Palace Gardens,
London, 1868–70 **19, 19**

19 Lincoln's Inn Fields, London, 1868–70
Rounton Grange, Yorks, 1872–76 (demolished)
St Martin's Church, Brampton, Cumbria,
1874–78
Four Gables, Brampton, Cumbria, 1876–78
Smeaton Manor, Yorkshire, 1877–79
Clouds, East Knoyle, Wiltshire, 1879–91
(altered)
Bell Bros Offices, Zetland Road, Middlesbrough,
Yorkshire, 1889–90
Standen, near East Grinstead, Sussex, 1892–94

Webster, **George** (1797–1864)
Town Hall, Market Square, Settle, Yorkshire,
1832
Downham Hall, Clitheroe, Lancashire, 1834–35
Holy Trinity R C church, Kendal, Cumbria,
1835–37
St George's Church, Castle Street, Kendal,
Cumbria, 1839–41
St Thomas's Church, Stricklandgate, Kendal,
Cumbria, date unknown

Weightman and **Hadfield 45, 89**
Weightman, **John Grey** (1801–72) in
partnership 1838–58, with **Matthew Ellison
Hadfield** (1812–85). Weightman had been an
assistant of **Sir Charles Barry** and of **Charles
Robert Cockerell**.
From 1858 the firm became Matthew Ellison
Hadfield, and in 1864 Charles Hadfield, the
son of Matthew Ellison Hadfield, became a
partner; *see also* **Robson**, **Edward Robert**.
Town Hall, Glossop, 1838
St Bede's R C church, Rotherham, Yorkshire,
1843
Salford R C cathedral, 1844–48 **45**
St Mary's R C church, Little Crosby,
Lancashire, 1845
St Marie's R C church, Sheffield, 1846
St Mary's R C church, Burnley, Lancashire,
1846
St Mary's R C church, Mulberry Street,
Manchester, 1848
Walton Gaol, Liverpool, 1848–55 **89**
Westwood Hall (*now* a High School), Leek,
Staffordshire, 1850
Victoria Station, Sheffield, 1851 (demolished)
Victoria Station Hotel, Sheffield, 1861
St Mary's R C church, Grimsby, Lincolnshire,
1879

Welch, **Edward** *see* **Hansom**, **Joseph Aloysius**

Wheeler, **Frederick 51**
Mount Vernon Hospital chapel, Northwood,
Middlesex **51**

Whichcord, **John** (Snr, 1790–1860)
Oakwood Hospital, St Andrew's Road,
Maidstone, Kent, 1830

Whichcord, **John** (Jnr, 1823–85) **102, 103**
Educated at King's College and the Royal
Academy Schools, he entered into partnership
with **Arthur Ashpitel**, 1850–58, before being
independent. He was elected RIBA President,
1879–81.
Grand Hotel, Brighton, 1862–64 **102, 103**
Clarence Hotel, Dover, 1863

White, **William** (1825–1900) **36, 37, 50, 83, 85**
The great-nephew of Gilbert White, he worked
in the offices of **Sir George Gilbert Scott**
before setting up in practice in Truro in 1847.
Parish School, Probus, Cornwall, 1849 **85**
Old Rectory, St Columb Major, Cornwall,
1849–50
All Saints' Church, Talbot Road, London,
1852–55
Church, St Hilary, Cornwall, 1853
Chaplain's cottage, Arley Hall, Cheshire, 1854
Shops, Audley, Staffordshire, 1855
St Michael's Home, Wantage, Berkshire, 1855
Church and school, Hooe, Devon, 1855

Penmellyn, St Columb Major, Cornwall, 1855 (house) **37**
Christ Church, Smannell, Hampshire, 1856
St Mary's Church, Hawridge, Buckinghamshire, 1856
Bank, St Columb Major, Cornwall, 1857
Vicarage, Little Baddow, Essex, 1858
St Michael's Church, Lyndhurst, Hampshire, 1858–69 **50**
Bishop's Court, Sowton, Devon, 1860–64
St Saviour's Church, Aberdeen Park, London, 1865–66 **50**
Humewood, Co Wicklow, Ireland, 1866–70
St Mark's Church, Battersea Rise, London, 1873–74
St Peter's Church, Plough Road, London, 1875–76
St Mary-le-Park Church, Albert Bridge Road, London, 1881
St Stephen's Church, Battersea Park Road, London, 1886–87

Wightwick, George (1802–72)
An assistant to Sir John Soane (1753–1837), he continued John Foulston's (1772–1842) practice in Plymouth from 1829.
Sussex Place, Plymouth, Devon, 1832–36
Town Hall, Plymouth, 1839
Christ Church, Plymouth, 1846
Public and Cottonian Libraries, Plymouth, 1850 (new fronts)

Wild, James William (1814–92) **84**
The son of the artist Charles Wild, he was a pupil of **George Basevi**, visited Egypt in 1842 and continued to travel abroad until 1848. He was decorative architect to the Great Exhibition and later became the curator of the Soane Museum, London 1878–92.
All Saints' Church, Botley, Hampshire, 1836
Holy Trinity Church, Blackheath Hill, London, 1838–39
St Paul's Church, Valletta, Malta, 1839
St Lawrence's Church, Southampton, 1839–42 (demolished)
Christ Church, Christchurch Road, London, 1840–41
St Paul's Church, Newport, Isle of Wight, 1844
St Martin-in-the-Fields Northern District School, Shelton Street, London, 1849–50 (demolished) **84**
Dock Tower, Grimsby, Lincolnshire, 1852
Bethnal Green Museum, London, 1872 (façade)
with Henry Young Darracott Scott
Work on South Kensington Museum, 1867–71

Wilds, Amon Henry
The son of Amon Wilds Snr (*c.* 1762–1833).
Chestham Park, near Henfield, West Sussex *c.* 1830 (thought to be by)
Milton Park Estate, Gravesend, Kent *c.* 1830 (including Berkeley Crescent)
Town Hall, High Street, Gravesend, Kent, 1836 (refronting)
Cemetery, Old Road West, Gravesend, Kent, 1838–41

Wilkins, William the Younger (1778–1839)
Born in Norwich, he gained his BA from Caius College, Cambridge, in 1800. His buildings are a central part of the achievement of the early nineteenth-century Greek revival in northern Europe, for he was the pre-eminent English exponent of that style. In Cambridge, where he built more than anyone else, he also designed in the Gothic and Tudor styles.
National Gallery, Trafalgar Square, London, 1833–38 *right*

Wilkinson, R Stark (1844–1936) *see* **Waring** and **Nicholson**

Wilkinson, William (1819–1901)
Norham Manor Estate, Oxford (1 Norham Gardens, 1864, 11 Norham Gardens, 1866, 13 Norham Gardens, 1868), 1860

Randolph Hotel, Oxford, 1864
60 Banbury Road, Oxford, 1865
Parsonage, Upper Heyford, Oxfordshire, 1869
Brashfield House, Caversfield, Oxfordshire, 1871–73

Williams, Arthur Y and **George 27**
Athenaeum, Lowther Street, Carlisle, Cumbria, 1840 (later Savings Bank)
Brunswick Buildings, Liverpool, 1841 **27**

Wilson, Charles (1810–63)
Worked for **David** and **James Hamilton** 1827–37.
Hospital, Gartnavel Road, Glasgow, 1841
Kirklee Terrace, Glasgow, 1845
Glasgow Academy, 1846 (later High School)
Neilson Institution, Paisley, 1849
Faculty of Procurators, St George's Place, Glasgow, 1854
Quadrant and Terrace, Park Circus, Glasgow, 1855
Free Church (Trinity) College, Glasgow, 1856
Queen's Rooms, La Belle Place, Glasgow, 1857

Wilson, Henry (1864–1934) **51**
Wilson was born in Liverpool, and went to Kidderminster Art School, after which he served his articles in Maidenhead, Berkshire. He was also a noted sculptor, metalworker and silversmith, and worked for **John Oldrid Scott** and **John Belcher** Jnr. Later on he became the chief assistant to **John Dando Sedding** before taking over his practice when the latter died, in 1891.
Public Library, Ladbroke Grove, London, 1891
St Clement's Church, Boscombe, Bournemouth, Hampshire, 1893 (tower)
St Bartholomew's Church, Brighton, Hampshire, 1897–1908 (furnishings)

Wilson, James (1816–1900)
St Stephen's Church, Lansdown Road, Bath, 1840–45 (chancel was of later date)
Cheltenham College, Cheltenham, 1841–43 (with later additions)
Westminster College, Horseferry Road, London, 1849–51 (chapel 1872)
Kingwood School, Lansdown, Somerset, 1851

Wimperis, John Thomas (1829–1904)
A partner of East, 1889.
Invercauld Castle, Braemar, Aberdeenshire, 1870–75
27 Grosvenor Square, London, 1889
8 Grafton Street, London, 1891

Withers, Robert Jewell (1823–94) **65**
School, Poyntington, Dorset, 1848
St Mary's Church, Llanfair Nantgwyn, Pembroke, 1855
Municipal buildings, Cardigan, 1859

Lavers and Barraud's Stained Glass Works, 22 Endell Street, London, 1859–60
Anglican Church of the Resurrection, Brussels, Belgium, 1862–65
St Mary's Church, Bourne Street, London, 1873–74

Wolfe-Barry, Sir John (1836–1918) **54**
A civil engineer whose work includes extensions to the London District and Underground railways.
Tower Bridge, London, 1886–94 **54**

Wood, Edgar (1860–1935) **41**
Having served articles with **Mills** and **Murgatroyd** in Manchester, he opened his own practice, and left a considerable legacy of houses, churches and schools; some of his designs anticipating the Art Deco style.
Long Street Wesleyan church and schools, Middleton, Lancashire, 1899–1901
First Church of Christ Scientist (*now* the Edgar Wood Centre), Daisybank, Manchester, 1903
Holly Cottage, Bramhall, Stockport, 1905
Upmeads, Newport Road, Strafford, Staffordshire, 1908

Wood, Henry Moses (*d.* 1867)
Judge's Lodgings (*now* record office), High Street, Nottingham, 1833

Wood, Sancton (1816–86)
A pupil of **Sydney Smirke**.
Kingsbridge (*now* Heuston) Station, Dublin, 1845
Queen's Assurance offices, 42 Gresham Street, London, 1850–52 (demolished)
Lancaster Gate House, Bayswater, London, 1857

Woodhouse, George (1827–83) **66**
Messrs Rylands & Sons' Gidlow Works, Wigan, Lancashire, 1865 **66**

Woodward, Benjamin *see* **Deane, Sir Thomas**

Woodyer, Henry (1816–96)
Worked with **William Butterfield**, 1844.
St Mark's Church, Wyke, Surrey, 1845–47
Holy Innocents' school, vicarage and lodge, Highnam, Gloucestershire, 1847–52
House of Mercy (*now* Convent of St John the Baptist), Clewer, Windsor, Berkshire, 1853–96
St Michael's Church and College, Tenbury, Worcestershire, 1854–56
School, Lower Whitley, Reading, Berkshire, 1860
St Mary's Church, Buckland, Surrey, 1860
Christ Church, Whitley, Reading, Berkshire, 1861–65
St Martin's Church, Dorking, Surrey, 1866–77

Worley, Charles H 17
42 Harley Street, London, 1892 *17*
Wimpole House, 28–29 Wimpole Street,
London, 1893 *17*
London Pavilion, Piccadilly Circus, London,
1885 (with Saunders) 97

Worth, Samuel (1779–1870)
see also **Taylor, Benjamin Broomhead**.
General Cemetery, Cemetery Road, Sheffield,
South Yorkshire, 1836 (chapel and offices)

Worthington, Thomas (1826–1909) **81**
A pupil of **Henry Bowman** and **Joseph Stretch
Crowther**.
Overseers' and Churchwardens' Offices,
Fountain Street, Manchester, 1852
Botanical Society Building, Manchester, 1854
(demolished)
Mayfield Baths, Ardwick, Manchester, 1857
Albert Memorial, Manchester, 1862–67
Memorial Hall, Manchester, 1864
Prestwich Union Workhouse (*now* Withington
Hospital), Manchester, 1866
The Towers (*now* Shirley Institute), Didsbury,
Manchester, 1868
Police Court, Manchester, 1868–71 **81**
Brookfield Unitarian Church, Hyde Road,
Manchester, 1869–71
Greengate Artisans' Dwellings, Salford, 1870
(demolished)
Nicholls Hospital, Hyde Road, Manchester, 1879
Sefton Park Unitarian Church, Liverpool,
1896–99 (with Percy Scott Worthington)

Wright, Frank Lloyd (1867–59) **106**
Educated at the University of Wisconsin,
Madison, where he studied engineering
between 1885–87. He worked briefly in the
offices of Dankmar Adler and **Louis Sullivan**
before working from his own studio in Oak
Park, Chicago, in 1889. He then went into
partnership with Cecil Corwin before
establishing his own practice in 1896. His work
was exhibited in Berlin in 1909 and the
following year he published *The Wasmuth
Portfolio*. During the years of the Depression,
Wright developed a new type of economical
detached residence known as the Usonian
House, and in 1945 he published *When
Democracy Builds*. Later publications included
The Future of Architecture in 1953 and *The Living
City* in 1958.
Winslow house, River Forest, Illinois, 1894
Willitts house, Highland Park, Illinois, 1901–02
Martin house, Buffalo, 1904
Unity Temple, Oak Park, Illinois, 1904
Larkin Building offices, Buffalo, 1904–05
Robie house, Chicago, 1906–10 **106**, *106*
Coonley house, Riverside, Illinois, 1907–08
Taliesin, Spring Green, Wisconsin; own house
1911 (twice rebuilt)
Barnsdall house, Los Angeles, 1917–20
Imperial Hotel, Tokyo (with Antonin Raymond)

Wyatt, Thomas Henry and **Brandon, David**
Shire Hall (*now* Brecknock Museum),
Glamorgan Street, Brecon, Powys, 1839–43

Wyatt, Benjamin Dean (1775– *c.* 1855)
Duke of York's Column, Carlton Gardens,
London, 1831–34

Wyatt, Lewis William (1777–1853)
Hawkstone Park, Shropshire, 1832–34
(restoration and extensions)

Wyatt, Sir Matthew (1805–86)
Victoria Square, Pimlico, London, 1837

Wyatt, Sir Matthew Digby, (1820–77) **11, 59**
The younger brother and a pupil of **Thomas
Henry Wyatt**, he published *Geometric Mosaics of
the Middle Ages*, 1848. He was the Secretary to
the executive committee of the Great

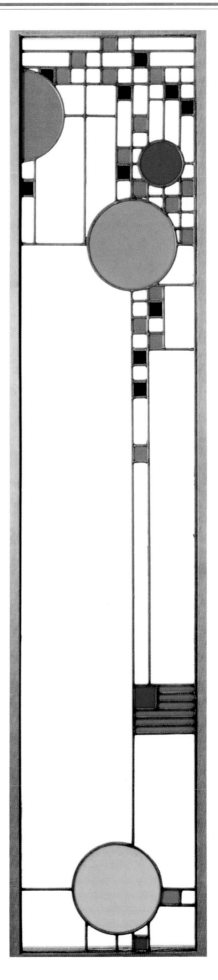

Exhibition of 1851, and surveyor to the East
India Company, 1855, the same year in which
he was knighted and made honorary secretary
of RIBA. He received the RIBA Gold Medal in
1866 and was the first Slade Professor of Fine
Arts at Cambridge, 1869.
Paddington Station, Praed Street, London,
1851–54 (detailing work for Isambard
Kingdom Brunel) *11*, 58, *58*
Garrison Chapel, Little Warley, Essex, 1857
Addenbrooke's Hospital, Cambridge, 1864–65
Durbar Court (of the former India Office, *now*
the Foreign and Commonwealth Office),
Whitehall, London, 1864–67
Temple Meads Station, Bristol, 1865–78 (main
entrance and shed)
Possington Manor, Sussex, 1866
Alford House, Princes Gate, London, 1872
(demolished)

Wyatt, Philip William (*d.* 1835)
Conishead Priory, Cumbria, 1821–36
Wynyard Park, Co Durham, 1822–30

Wyatt, Thomas Henry (1807–80) **81, 89, 96, 97**
The elder brother of **Sir Matthew Digby
Wyatt**, he was articled to **Philip Hardwick**
before setting up in practice in 1838 with
David Brandon, his partner until 1850. He
was the district surveyor of Hackney, 1832–61,
President of RIBA 1870–73, and awarded the
RIBA Gold Medal in 1873.
Llantarnam Abbey, Torfaen, 1834 (remodelling)
Assize Court, Northgate Street, Devizes,
Wiltshire, 1835
Llangattock Park House, Llangattock, Powys,
c. 1839
Orchardleigh Park, Somerset, 1855–58
Adelphi Theatre (*now* Theatre Royal, Adelphi),
Strand, London, 1858 96, 97
St Katherine's Church, Savernake Forest,
Wiltshire, 1861
Liverpool Exchange, 1865 **81**
Holy Trinity Church, Fonthill, Gifford,
Wiltshire, 1866
Knightsbridge Barracks, London, 1875–79
(demolished)
Manor House (*now* a school), North Perrott,
Somerset, 1878
Norfolk and Norwich Hospital, Norwich 1879
(with E Boardman) **89**
with David Brandon
St Andrew's Church, Bethnal Green, London, 1841

Wyatville, Sir Jeffry (1766–1840)
Chatsworth House, Derbyshire, 1820–41 (north
wing extension)
Windsor Castle, Windsor, Berkshire, 1824–40
(remodelling)
Lilleshall Hall, near Newport, Shropshire, 1826–33
Golden Grove, Pembroke, Dyfed, 1826–37
Fort Belvedere, Great Park, Windsor, Berkshire,
1827–30 (extensions)

Young, William (1843–1900) **77**
A Scottish architect who was articled to James
Lamb at Paisley, and worked in Glasgow before
moving to London, entering the office of the
Surrey County Surveyor.
Holme Wood House, Cambridgeshire, 1873–74
Oxhey Grange, Hertfordshire, 1876
23 Oakhill Road, East Putney, London, 1879
Gosford House, East Lothian, 1880–90
(remodelling)
City Chambers, Glasgow, 1883–88 **77**
Elvedon Hall, Suffolk, 1893 (large additions)
War Office, Whitehall, London, 1898

Left: *window, designed by Frank
Lloyd Wright, for the country
house of Avery Coonley, Riverside,
Illinois, USA, 1912*